Breathing Space

Breathing Space

The Architecture of Pneumatic Beings

Tim Altenhof

ZONE BOOKS · NEW YORK

2026

ZONE BOOKS
633 Vanderbilt Street
Brooklyn, NY 11218

Printed in the United States of America
Distributed by Princeton University Press,
Princeton, New Jersey, and Woodstock, United Kingdom

Library of Congress Control Number 2025035021

In memory of Kurt and Tony

Contents

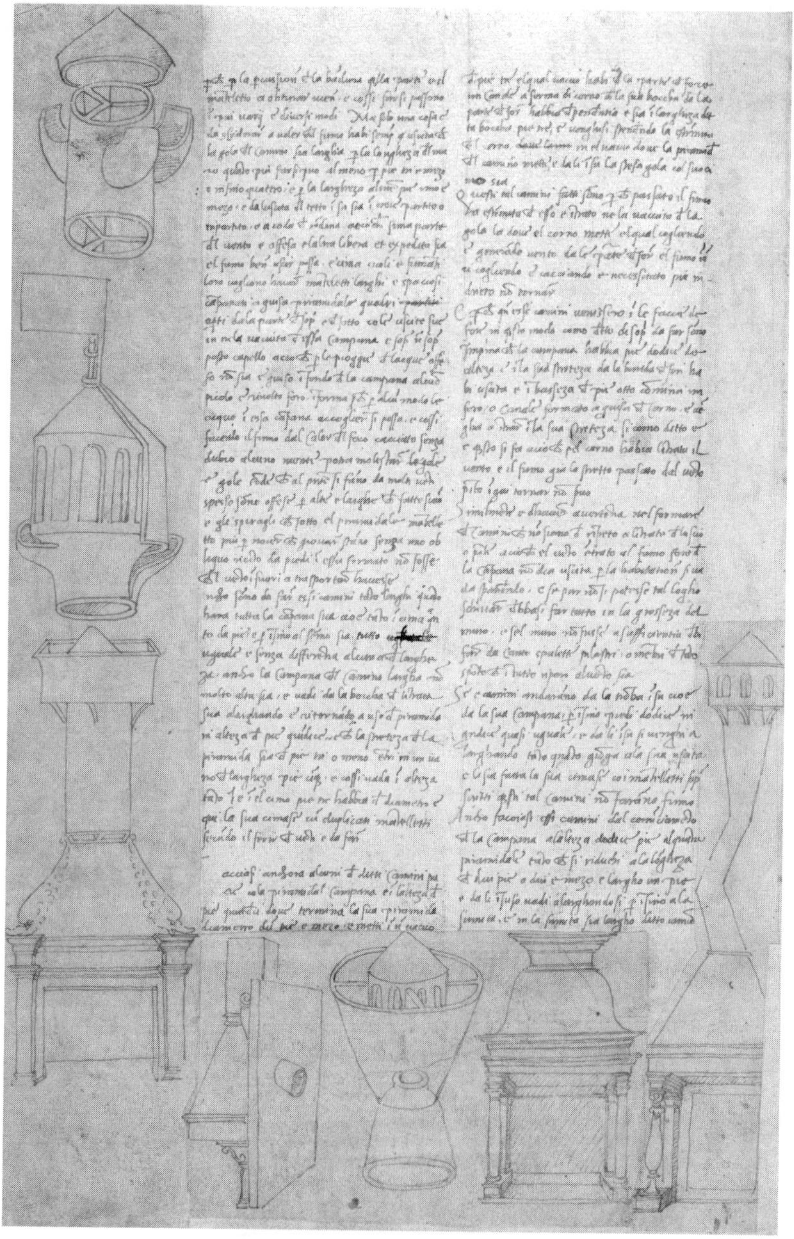

Figure 1.1. Chimney variations by Francesco di Giorgio Martini. From Francesco di Giorgio, *Trattati di architettura ingegneria e arte militare* (between 1500 and 1515). Manuscript on paper of what is probably the first version of the treatise, finished ca. 1476–1477. Beinecke Rare Book and Manuscript Library, Yale University, https://collections.library.yale.edu/catalog/2047311, image 50.

CHAPTER ONE

Exhaling Chimneys

A chimney is a component of a heat source in a room, but it is also much more than that. A chimney is a passage for all kinds of particles, exhalations, and supernatural creatures, a loophole into and out of the world of mysteries and that of the dwelling house. It conflates folklore and domestic technology. Analogous to a windpipe, an air passage connecting the throat with the lungs, a chimney usually runs vertically, extracting exhaust fumes in a confined space from the emitting source to the open air. The term derives from the Old French *cheminee*, which means "fireplace" or "room with a fireplace," its etymology carrying notions of flames and spatial magnitude from the onset.[1] In its early meaning, the term thus designated something to which it later became attached.

If placed in the center of a room, in a house whose exterior walls are free from fireplaces, a chimney can become the dominating element — or one's "superior," as in Herman Melville's short story "I and My Chimney."[2] Reminiscent of the pyramid of Cheops, his chimney is not only big and solid, but also strong in personality, more a personage than merely masonry.[3] Indeed, Melville and his chimney cohabit (in fact, they philosophize together), but they do so unlike common roommates, for his chimney is "the king of the house."[4] Just as a king holds the preeminent position in a monarchy, Melville's chimney occupies the dominant symbolic and geometrical center of his house, a position to which everything else is subordinate. It is the backbone of the house and will outlive every other part.[5] The impression it makes on others is profound, if not awe-inspiring. A token for domestic life, his puffing chimney even protects it from burglary, preventing home invasion by releasing fleeting signs of human activity into the surrounding air. Communicating with the atmosphere, it signals presence and alertness and in so doing, it also ties the interior to the exterior.

But tying the interior to the exterior opens the interior to threats from the outside.[6] Throughout the fifteenth century, witches were held to fly through the air riding on brooms. Yet even if some ascribed magical powers to them, witches still had to fulfil ordinary needs in the eyes of many, among them eating and drinking, and adequate nutrition could easily be found in people's houses. But how to get in? While some thought witches penetrated solid doors, and others believed they simply opened and closed them imperceptibly fast, slipping through the gap without being perceived by residents, many assumed they slipped down the chimney in a fashion not unlike Santa Claus.[7] Indeed, the fireplace seems especially prone to attract intruders. In Alfred Hitchcock's horror-thriller *The Birds*, a host of sparrows shoot down the chimney to invade the house. Someone tilts over the wooden coffee table to block the open fireplace, but the whole living room already has been invaded.

Chimneys also serve as important components of social spaces. Historically, the fireplace was the focus of the daily life of a building's inhabitants. It invites small gatherings and is a place where the inhabitants literally conspire — that is, breathe together. Indeed, at the hearth, the inhabitants and the building itself breathe together, both the fire and their breath consuming oxygen and producing carbon dioxide, a circumstance often repeated by naturalists such as Jean-Henri Fabre (1823–1915), who, in his short text *L'air, nécessaire à la vie*, noted in the late 1850s that an "animal requires air to live, and the candle requires air to burn."[8]

The chimney thus plays an important role in the inhabitants' biological life, as well as their social life, and beyond that, in their environment. It is a vertical structure built to discharge the products of combustion — pollutants, impurities, and carbonic molecules — by a draft of warm air, whose decreased density naturally propels them upward (fig. 1.1). Like a smoker puffing on a cigarette, the flue draws the byproducts of domestic combustion into the atmosphere, and it is because of these exhalations that chimneys, for a long time, have also been a symbol of air pollution, especially in their industrial form as smokestacks.

The chimney can thus signify various things: a mediator in post-medieval superstition, the existence of a cozy family space, technological progress, but also industrialization and with it, complicity in environmental pollution. Most often, it is simply a means to an end, a practical contrivance to evacuate smoke and to keep the fireplace running. Yet the chimney also symbolizes breathing.

Throughout architectural history, the house, like its inhabitants, has been said to "breathe." For example, Leon Battista Alberti ascribed parts of the human body to parts of the hearth, instructing his architect readers that the mouth at the bottom of a fireplace ought not to be too prominent. His descriptions are technical and scientific, but also highly metaphorical. When he suggests that "the throat should be deep," he refers to the chimney's height, which should rise well above the roof ridge.[9] The throat, for Alberti, is what traps and channels smoke, while the burning flames in turn help eject it "in the same manner as sound is [expelled] from a trumpet."[10] The chimney exhales. Different ways of exhaling the air can bring about differences in air temperature: exhaling with an open mouth produces warmer air compared with doing it with pursed lips, because the former slows down the force of breath, while the latter sets it in motion, and "so also in a building," Alberti asserts.[11]

As we'll see in what follows, the physiological process of breathing in living beings long has its correlate in a parallel process of ventilation in architecture. The chimney has had both physiological and architectural implications, articulated in terms of an analogy to human respiration in its role of inducing airflow through the lungs and blurring the boundaries between the organism and its surrounding atmosphere, between inside and outside. As a result, in this book, the terms "breathing" and "ventilation" frequently overlap and oscillate in meaning. "Ventilation" privileges the replacement of stale air with fresh air by virtue of mechanical or natural means, while breathing involves the intake of oxygen and the expulsion of carbon dioxide, a process that rests on the respiratory system, primarily in the lungs. In different contexts, the comparison rests on different emphases on the mechanical or organic elements of the comparison of the parts of the house to the parts of the human body. One of the goals of this book is to illuminate the centrality of the notion of breathing within the context of modernist architecture, embracing the heterogeneous implications it holds for living organisms.

Here, like witches or Santa Claus, we enter that topic through the chimney as a special kind of portal. Once inside, the book charts architecture's embeddedness within a culture of pneumatic beings that I am calling "respiratory modernism." In contrast to modernity and modernization—terms that refer to a specific historical period and the transformation of material culture—I understand modernism with Detlef Mertins "as the cultural response that aspires to the status of a new norm."[12] Breathing played a major role in this cultural response, shaping the zones and areas it produced, as well as the accompanying discourse, which I refer to as "breathing space." There are many metaphors and characteristic themes related to this activity, one of which has to do with the idea of the house as chimney.

The House as Chimney

Chimneys always had let smoke spill into the rooms they heated, and in the eighteenth century, a number of inventors set out to do something about it. How they accounted for the fact that smoke ascends was based on the so-called caloric theory, which understood both heat and combustion in terms of an imaginary fluid, the caloric, and not in terms of energy transmission—the caloric, a material substance of heat, was assumed to be what carries smoke along its trajectory from warmer to colder areas.

Scientists such as the British Count Rumford (1753–1814), as well as Benjamin Franklin (1706–1790), set out to enhance the way chimneys draw, as well as to improve their use of fuel and reduce their loss of heat. A title such as Franklin's 1787 *Observations on Smoky Chimneys* testifies to the attention paid to this widespread problem.[13] Franklin's eponymous Franklin stove was a fireplace equipped with a U-shaped duct at its bottom, turning the flue into an inverted siphon. This feature drew smoke downward before directing it up the chimney, effectively preventing it from entering the room. Likewise, Count Rumford's invention, the Rumford fireplace, optimized the updraft of air by reconfiguring the hearth with angled side walls, restraining the chimney's opening, and streamlining its flue.

The reasons for a chimney not to draw where so numerous that one could fine-tune a whole range of parameters: the proportions of the chimney openings; the length of the funnel; two chimneys getting in each other's way; interferences caused by surrounding houses and topographical peculiarities at the level of chimney pots; but also a door's position and its degree of openness in relation to the chimney. Whether understood in terms of caloric theory or in terms of modern thermodynamics, however, the most important aspect of the drawing chimney is that a supply of fresh air must be provided at all times during combustion. Not unlike a breathing animal, it can exhale smoke only for as long as it inhales fresh air through the apertures and crevices of its surrounding room. This incoming air then takes the place of the warm air and smoke, which, in a continuous outward current, leave the interior as long as the process remains active. But while the presence of small carbon particles emitted from a fire render the outflowing air visible, the inflow of fresh air remains invisible. In order to stress this imbalance and to draw attention to the necessary inflow, Franklin succinctly noted that "the chimney wants air."[14]

As a device that, in tandem with a fireplace, could draw fresh air into the house and also extract pollutants from the indoor environment, the role played by the chimney formed a major theme in nineteenth-century discussions on ventilation and hygiene. In this line of thought, a chimney appears Janus-faced, serving the ventilation of interior spaces while also affecting the general atmosphere. The architecture critic Reyner Banham (1922–1988) was perhaps the first to draw attention to awareness of this problem in his seminal 1969 book *The Architecture of the Well-Tempered Environment*.[15] In his chapter on the "satanic" nineteenth century, Banham rightly observed the parallel rise of air pollution and the contamination of interior spaces "by human respiration and the inefficient combustion of illuminants."[16]

However, Banham's focus on the mechanisms and tools for environmental engineering overlooked the particular breathing culture in which they developed, the culture that I call respiratory modernism and that I seek to uncover in this book. My focus will be less on the mechanisms or technical media that create specific spatial environments. Instead, I will explore the analogical patterns between the house and the breathing body in discourses ranging from domestic hygiene to architecture in the modern period from the mid-nineteenth century to the early twentieth, beginning here with the concept of the house as chimney.

Industrial Chimneys

It is rare for chimneys to become fully absorbed into the house as a whole; they typically stand alone as separate, iconic structures. One industrial example, which I will mention only as a foil for the house as chimney, is the first German chimney made of reinforced concrete, masked as a Doric column (fig. 1.2). It dates from the winter of 1906–1907 and served the power station of the Henriettenhütte ironworks at Primkenau (today Przemków), in Lower Silesia. The flue, some 5 feet (1.5 meters) in diameter and 155 feet (47

Figure 1.2. Doric smokestack, Primkenau, reproduced in Ludwig Hilberseimer, "Bauten in Eisenbeton und ihre architektonische Gestaltung," in Julius Vischer and Ludwig Hilberseimer, *Beton als Gestalter: Bauten in Eisenbeton und ihre architektonische Gestaltung, Ausgeführte Eisenbetonbauten* (Stuttgart: J. Hoffmann, 1928), p. 15.

meters) high, was tapered toward the top and concealed from the outside. It was wrapped in a cubic pedestal, an unfluted shaft, and a capital — staples of the Doric order. As a historicizing structure, it is reminiscent of the Monument to the Great Fire of London from 1677, and in retrospect, it also evokes Adolf Loos's contribution to the Chicago Tribune Tower competition from 1922. Apart from their common exterior, a riff on the Roman Doric column, all three of these structures share a striking inversion: usually solid and load bearing, they are hollow inside and free-standing in space.

Built to commemorate the Great Fire of 1666, the monument's fluted column in London houses a spiral staircase to climb to the viewing platform atop the capital. A pun on the newspaper "column" of the Chicago Tribune, the shaft of Loos's scheme, which was never realized, features a radial array of office spaces around a central core of elevators. A rare case in architectural history, the Doric column at Henriettenhütte might well be the only one ever able to puff.

Above the capital, black smoke quickly dissipated into the atmosphere. Where a gilded urn of fire marks the Monument in London, the German column released a sooty substance that could have only derived from the process of combustion. The rising smoke as an indexical sign for fire is a common trope in semiotics, and in this instance, it also betrayed what was otherwise a suppressed expression of use. Thus animated by smoke, the Doric chimney appears equally cartoonish and comical, as does Loos's scheme for Chicago, but unlike the latter, which was always meant to be a provocation, the former was dead serious. In a 1928 review on ferroconcrete, the German-born architect and city planner Ludwig Hilberseimer mocked this chimney precisely on the grounds of its ostensible falsehood, portraying it as "a smoking triumphal column, standing right next to a faux farmhouse, a dummy arrangement that could not be more perfectly imagined."[17]

Yet even if the ordinary chimney dispenses with such antiquated jackets, not every architect takes pleasure in their soaring elegance. For Emil Fader, a German teacher of architecture, they were a nuisance of the first order, disturbing the design of industrial buildings in the modern period. In 1927, he lamented the unavoidable disorder they would cause in the spatial composition of a plant whose harmony could only suffer under the presence of such purely functional elements. "No matter how high the architectural achievement in the individual building," Fader explained, "it is somehow always disturbed by a chimney, the appearance of which is determined solely by its purpose."[18] With its appearance determined by everything but its purpose, Fader clearly left this Doric chimney out of account. Perhaps it is too special a case, with its historicist jacket, but free-standing as it was, it clearly reflected his aversion. As a discrete element, the smokestack often disrupts formal unity, and Fader, recognizing the complicated nature of industrial buildings, saw full harmony to be forever out of reach.

Only two years earlier, in August 1925, Russian representatives of the Leningrad textile trust ventured to Germany to look at contemporary architecture abroad; in fact, they came to expose themselves to industrial buildings. Earlier in the spring, the newly founded commission for the construction of textile factories had objected to a proposal for the extension of the Red Banner factory in Leningrad, the so-called Krasnoye Znamya. In Berlin, the Russian delegation was soon introduced to Erich Mendelsohn (1887–1953), no doubt the city's most prolific architect at the time. What evoked their curiosity was precisely what Fader would later consider impossible in the context of industrial designs: the house as chimney. As part of the famous hat factory Steinberg, Herrmann & Co., it stands as a classical modernist masterpiece in the small town of Luckenwalde, some forty miles south of Berlin, and was designed and built by Mendelsohn in 1921 (fig. 1.3).

Luckenwalde's Hat Factory

Luckenwalde had long become the cradle of German hat fashion; the town witnessed an increase in textile and metal factories from the mid-nineteenth century onward, and in 1871, the first company adapted its production from textiles to hats.[19] For a long time, the German hat producer Friedrich Steinberg vied with Gustav Herrmann for the best fashion designs, but after merging their companies, they commissioned Mendelsohn to devise a new manufacturing plant on an empty lot on the outskirts of town. It became one of the paradigmatic expressions for an industry of the future, with critics such as Adolf Behne (1885–1948) pointing out the functional layout and its compelling translation into a tight spatial form.[20] The factory's dye house, with its shaftlike hood, recreated the outline of

Figure 1.3. Close-up of the dye works, with trapezoidal roof and operable louvers at the ridge. Thomas Drachenberg, *Die Baugeschichte der Stadt Luckenwalde von 1918–1933: Siedlungen, Industriebau, Verwaltungs-, Wohlfahrts- und Privatbauten (Beiträge zur Denkmalpflege im Land Brandenburg)* (Worms: Wernersche, 1999), p. 85.

a hat while at the same time funneling through the roof the toxic fumes building up inside. The whole structure, in other words, acted as a chimney, whose soaring form evinced the upflow of hostile steam inside.

It was this feature, in particular, that aroused a great deal of Russian interest. On a warm Sunday in August 1925, two days after receiving a first phone call from the Russian trade mission declaring their interest in the hat factory, Mendelsohn made a day trip to Luckenwalde, mainly to prepare for the upcoming meeting the following day, but also to go swimming in the morning. The Russian delegation had already been to Luckenwalde to examine the structure independently. Over the course of a sweltering summer day with temperatures well above 96 degrees Fahrenheit, the first gathering in his office took place on Monday, August 10, 1925. Mendelsohn's involvement seemed limited to a consultant's role, but with inchoate longings to develop the Leningrad scheme, he was eager to seize upon "the whole affair."[21] Shortly afterward, he succeeded in decoying the Russian committee back to Luckenwalde, where Gustav Herrmann, the industrialist and patron of Mendelsohn, gave a personal tour of his own company, the hat factory Steinberg, Herrmann & Co. "Quite excited and with what seems to be the best success," as Erich wrote to his wife Luise Mendelsohn.[22]

After a long haul and tenacious negotiations, during which the architect's expectations seemed moderate until the very end, Mendelsohn was finally commissioned to build the Russian Red Banner factory. In October 1925, at the invitation of the textile trust, Erich and Luise travelled to Moscow and Leningrad, and with plenty of opportunity for sightseeing, both went to visit all the monuments. The country, imbued with revolutionary spirit, unalloyed energies, and a great deal of optimism, deeply wowed Luise, but the many privations she encountered abroad also left her baffled upon returning to Berlin, where life was comparatively spoiled. With luscious meals, stimulating conversations, and shows by the Russian ballet, she found the stay in Leningrad particularly "exhilarating." For lunch, she often relished caviar and vodka.[23] Her vivid memoirs recall the circumstances that led to the contract in Leningrad, a passage worth quoting at length:

> Among the most fascinating people who came to his office were a group of Russians. Their purpose was to receive information about the dye works which were a part of the Luckenwalde hat factory built in 1921. When Eric [sic] received the commission to build the hat factory he carefully studied the manufacturing process and became appalled by the working conditions of the laborers. The steam of the dye vats permeated the whole shed, in spite of large exhaust fans, which only caused a strong draft and afflicted a large number of workmen with pneumonia. Eric found an excellent solution to this problem, which became widely published in industrial magazines and must have come to the attention of the Russians who planned to build a large textile factory. The principle on which Eric solved the problem of achieving a dry vat shed was a very simple one. He constructed a chimney-like hood over the dye vats and upper arches into which the steam was exhausted. This created a chimney over the whole length of the building and effected constant and uniform air exchange. Eric led the Russians through the entire factory, and they were sufficiently impressed to offer him the commission to build a textile factory with three dye vats close to Leningrad in 1925. Planning a large complex of building for Russia, a rather enigmatic country and unknown to most Europeans, excited not only Eric, but the whole office. A day was set for bringing the plans to Leningrad. and the work in the office extended into the midnight hour. Bach records were played, inexhaustible quantities of coffee were provided—the atmosphere was pregnant with creation. We left for Leningrad in the fall of 1925, one year after Lenin's death. The textile factory was going to be built outside of Leningrad and combined a power station, three dye works, an administration building, and the actual factory—in other words it was a tremendous commission.[24]

Though it is tempting to interpret this anecdote in terms of its optimism, the Russian factory was an endeavor more frustrating and wearisome than Erich Mendelsohn foresaw. In mid-July of 1926, he received a distress signal in the form of a telegram and informed

Luise that he had to leave for Leningrad, working on site for eight days.[25] From there, he avowed on July 31, 1926: "Construction started and—blighted. I try everything possible to repair."[26] But the episode above is also revelatory, because so often when large architectural projects come to fruition, the exact circumstances leading to their formation remain obscure.

The trust commissioned Mendelsohn because of the extraction system embedded in the dye house at Luckenwalde. Luise's record not only brings out her husband's eager resolve to engage in issues of health and industrial safety, but also his vision of space, which, in this case, centered on well-being and formal harmony. Contrary to common industrial plants at the time, the chimney here formed an integral part of the design, a simple solution with the objective to prevent the workers from developing inflammatory lung conditions such as pneumonia. The architect took issues of breathing to heart.

The Luckenwalde factory's geometry was well conceived: the plan, striking and rigid in its symmetry, led to a structure firmly rooted to its site. The photographs authorized for publication, however, countered this assumed state of repose. Presenting the multifaceted geometries of several roofs in diagonal views with often dramatic framings, the factory exuded a dynamism that was further accelerated by the strong black-and-white contrast (fig. 1.4). In fact, the dye house roof became so prominent that several publications, such as Mendelsohn's 1924 issue of the architecture and urban-planning journal *Wasmuths Monatshefte für Baukunst und Städtebau* (Wasmuth's monthly journal for architecture and urban planning), as well as Adolf Behne's *Der moderne Zweckbau* (The modern functional building, 1926) tended to foreground a photograph taken from underneath the gatehouse's roof.[27] With its idiosyncratic clipping, it led the uninformed reader easily to believe that the dye house was the entire factory. But the actual production sheds and the power station were no marginal elements; instead, they formed crucial parts of the organism. Furnished with skylights, the sheds in fact form the centerpiece of the entire complex, bookended by the higher, cubic

Figure 1.4. View of the dye works from underneath the gate house, which no longer exists. Thomas Drachenberg, *Die Baugeschichte der Stadt Luckenwalde von 1918–1933: Siedlungen, Industriebau, Verwaltungs-, Wohlfahrts- und Privatbauten (Beiträge zur Denkmalpflege im Land Brandenburg)* (Worms: Wernersche, 1999), p. 87.

power station and the popular dye works on both ends of the shorter axis. The height of the manufacturing sheds was echoed in the height of the gatehouse.

A continuous grid governs much of the overall plan and combines the manufacturing sheds with the dye works. Reinforced concrete girders arrayed in the longitudinal direction with an interval of 16.4 feet (5 meters) form the primary structure inside the dye house. Invisible from the outside, they are tapered toward the top and the bottom, resemble pointed arches, and rise up to a height of 33 feet (10 meters). Kinked twice, the girders' geometry in the dye works differs from that of the sheds, but they are also significantly higher. Right above the frames' tip is an extension to the primary construction—part of the reason why it seems reasonable to call it a hood—in the shape of an isosceles trapezoid. Both parts together add up to a considerable height of 58 feet (17.75 meters). Above these trapezoidal frames sits another cap that continues the roof's outline in cross section, and it is here that the sides are louvered, while the top is covered with wooden planks (fig. 1.5). In this way, Mendelsohn could completely close off the hood against the atmospheric environment and the fabrication spaces underneath and vice versa. Opening the upper and lower louvers initiated the natural exhaustion of the steam that accumulated in the dye house without causing much draft. In the crawl space at the top, the felt required for the production of hats was dried and aired.[28]

"Chimney Structure"

Ventilation concerns went beyond the dye works and also informed the design of the production sheds, but here, they were less pronounced. A pitched roof following the outline of the three-hinged frames below incorporated skylights and ventilation openings individually adjustable by pulling cables from below. On either side of every second girder, Mendelsohn had steel bushings built into the timber sidewalls in order to guide the louvers, which, opening outward, helped to create a constant flow of air.[29] In the *Wasmuth*

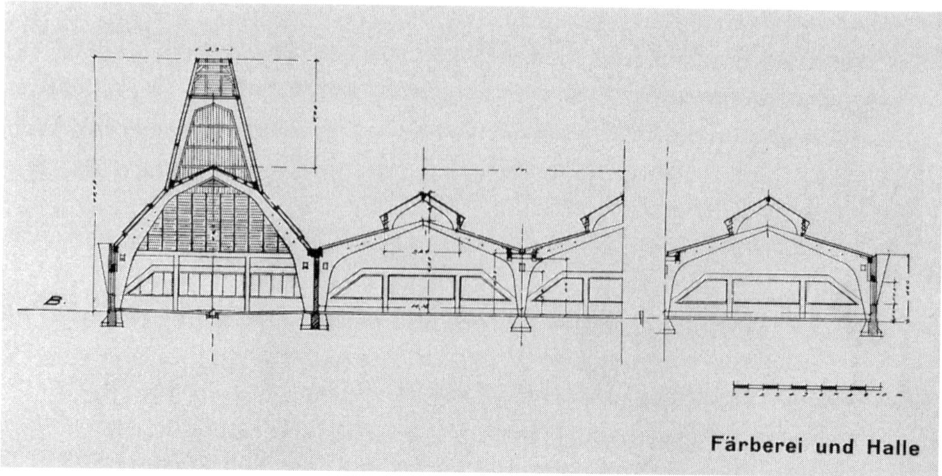

Figure 1.5. Cross section through the dye works and manufacturing sheds. Erich Mendelsohn, *Das Gesamtschaffen des Architekten: Skizzen, Entwürfe, Bauten* (Berlin, R. Mosse, 1930), p. 65.

journal, Mendelsohn also included one interior photograph of the production sheds, but the dye house, both the elegance of its outer appearance, and the performance of its embedded ventilation system, is what received the most attention.

Mendelsohn needed to solve a problem that sooner or later afflicted nearly every worker in the dye vats. Not only did the poisonous fumes cause high humidity levels inside, a situation that negatively affected the workers' lungs as well as the materials required for the production process, it also impeded interior visibility, further complicating the work process. While several methods had been previously tested to solve the steam issue—either smokestacks or fans had been used in order to attenuate the fog's emergence—they all resulted in hitherto unseen problems, including unpleasant side effects such as drafts and an excessive temperature rise. Whereas stacks alone were too exposed to the fluctuation of outside temperatures and thus simply furthered the condensation of steam, fans were either too weak or produced too much turbulence inside.

Mechanical ventilation had been of no avail, and Mendelsohn's hat factory was the first dye works that passed muster. The answer came in the form of negative air pressure, something he had gleaned from a small, still-operating dye factory. According to John Berlowitz, a Berlin-based engineer and contemporary of the German architect, this existing plant reasonably managed to defog the interior by employing an "accidentally abandoned" smokestack. This discovery and years of research on "primitive" structures excited Mendelsohn to graft a chimney onto the dye house.[30] It was, in other words, a conjunction of mastermind and haphazard events, a serendipitous discovery, that led Mendelsohn to envision the dye works' interior space as a flue and its structure as a chimney.

The result is what Berlowitz called "chimney structure" (*Schlotbau*). While the side effects of previous solutions, such as increased draft and an enormous rise of temperature, further damaged the workers' lungs already under threat of the ubiquitous fog, here, the interior was completely free of waste steam, even when operating at full capacity with twenty-four dye tubs. For Berlowitz, it was the architectural problem-solving design that fixed the issue for the first time, primarily through the spatial form itself rather than by auxiliary technologies:

> As far as we know, it is the Berlin-based architect Erich Mendelsohn who managed for the very first time to build a dye works, that, despite its large dimensions, has completely resolved the problem of defogging. Only the insight that the building itself, i.e. its cross section, the arrangement of windows and ventilation ducts, would have to enhance the natural buoyancy of the steam from the outset, brought about radical progress here.[31]

The passage brings out the direct and interdependent relationships between architectural form and individual elements and their effect on thermodynamics. Pressurized outlets for heated air at a height of 7 feet (2.2 meters), just above the factory workers' heads, enhanced the buoyancy force acting upon the dye house, making for a total air exchange in as little as one hour. It proved a most effective way to initiate the stack effect, which is able to move large volumes of air through space, above all work-related events, that is, above the workers' comfort zone, so as not to compromise work sequences. Adjusting the air flow allowed the dye house to respond to seasonal changes and alternating climate conditions; it appeared to operate equally well "during clear, frosty weather or misty rain, during a calm or a strong breeze."[32] In colder weather, warm air from the vents blew toward the factory's bottom in order to heat up lower areas, while the opening direction was flipped during warmer periods to expedite the stack effect.[33]

Most accounts on Mendelsohn's factory refer to the dye house as a kind of *invention*.[34] But the factory was neither a forerunner of modern ventilation systems nor a real innovation. What made the dye works revolutionary in a characteristically modern way was solving a physical problem by translating age-old technology into modern contexts. Mendelsohn's dye house roof, with its skylights and ventilation openings is a simple chimney. He just discovered how to apply its principles to the dye house at the hat factory in Luckenwalde. As we will see, it is the context of respiratory modernism that makes Mendelsohn's adoption of the concept of the house as chimney significant.

The history of architecture is full of lanterns and femerells (from Old French *fumeraille*, derived from the Latin *fumus*, meaning "smoke"), small, open structures placed in the ridge for the purpose of lighting and ventilation. Provided with slatted apertures, such roof lanterns, or louvers, were to dissipate smoke and vitiated air emerging in the interior of medieval buildings.[35] Even the production sheds' structural system is called *Laternenshed* in German, an obvious reference to the lanterns running along the roof's gable. An alternative to the sawtooth roof, it was commonly used throughout

Europe, and not only for industrial buildings.[36] Glassed lanterns span the intervals between each concrete frame, and in combination with pitched roofs, the structural frames yield higher interior spaces with enhanced ventilation.[37]

Even if Mendelsohn stayed aloof from inspirations common at the time, the copious precedents he resorted to were diverse to an extent that they finally ended in smoke, as architect and historian Bruno Zevi remarked.[38] One precedent he doesn't mention can be seen in a cutaway section reminiscent of the dye works, not least because it is rendered in brick, but also on the grounds of its outline and general proportion. It is included in Philibert de L'Orme's architectural treatise *Le premier tome de l'architecture*, published in 1567.[39] A French architect and writer, de L'Orme (1514–1570) put together one of the great treatises on architecture and instructed the master builders of the French Renaissance in the general layout of schemes as much as in the different ways of assembling them. In this manual—the first and only volume of what was intended to be a two-volume treatise—a woodcut shows an abstract kitchen whose brick walls, 10 to 12 feet (3 to 3.6 meters) high, are punctured by doors and windows on the ground level (fig. 1.6). After a horizontal kink far above door height, the exterior walls bend inside, two converging lines in section that eventually lead to something that vaguely looks like a baroque lantern, except that it is not cylindrical. The kitchen is defined by four walls, and in de L'Orme's own words, by what is called "the lantern or chimney pipe" (*la laterne ou tuyau de cheminée*). This cap is four times narrower than the kitchen and opens itself to the outside by virtue of three narrow vents in each wall, so that the smoke quickly disappears. Embellished by a cornice, a small, circumferential wall is built on brackets (or mutules) around the lantern, shielding the vents against the wind while at the same time maintaining the upflow of smoke. Like the cap, the small cupola above features a double-layered shell of which the inner one is perforated "in order to release the smoke" (*pour donner issue à la fumée*) at the top. The release system remains

Figure 1.6. The house as chimney: cross section through a kitchen. Philibert de L'Orme, *Le premier tome de l'architecture* (Paris: Federic Morel, 1567), p. 276.

invisible from the outside. This illustration reveals the blueprint for Luckenwalde, even if structurally, it was altogether different. If the house as chimney was a thing in architectural history, this kitchen could be the genre's apotheosis.

Respiratory Modernism

What makes Mendelsohn's use of the chimney to solve the problem of ventilation in the Luckenwalde dye works significant is the place it occupies in the culture of respiratory modernism that had been developing since the mid-nineteenth century in Germany and beyond. The articulation of the concept of the house as chimney as an element of respiratory modernism is a product of the growing cultural awareness of breathing during that period and a broader understanding of the essential need for fresh air.

While concerns about air have long permeated architectural treatises since Vitruvius, there was a particular confluence of physiological knowledge and a heightened awareness of breathing and the functioning of the human lungs is a phenomenon specific to Anglo-European culture beginning around the end of the nineteenth century.[40] Among social and health reformers, educators, and engineers, experimental hygienists and physiologists, chimneys, fireplaces, and furnaces flared up in debates about ventilation. Chimneys offered a simple solution for obtaining a change of air in a room. A number of publications repeated a central admonition, dire and relentlessly didactic: a constant supply of fresh air is vitally important for living organisms. Voices demanding breathable air abounded. The works of hygienists in particular raised awareness about the consequences of encasing breathing subjects, and they took concerns with ventilation increasingly seriously. Yet no one conveyed the sense of urgency with more sensational effect than the American ventilation expert Lewis W. Leeds, who in 1869 warned his readers that without a continuous supply of fresh air they "will surely die."[41] It was absolutely critical, however, he argued that this current of air be as imperceptible as possible—a claim we will revisit later in this book.

Throughout the nineteenth century, people were said to consume atmospheric energy in the form of oxygen much like a burning fireplace. In their book on domestic science, *The American Woman's Home* (1869), Catherine Beecher (1800–1878) and Harriet Beecher Stowe (1811–1896) observed that analogous to the workings of a chimney, drawing in air and thus keeping the flames burning, the human organism requires oxygen to combust the fuel absorbed as part of the daily diet: there are "two modes of nourishing the body, one is by food and the other by air."[42] And much like the fire's exhaust and its concomitant soot, human respiration produces air-polluting substances through metabolic processes. Scientific advances had shown that human air pollution by respiration depletes the amount of oxygen inside an apartment, which therefore required replacement by ventilation.

The dominant debates on the theory of ventilation throughout the second half of the nineteenth century thus were anthropocentric, considering breathing human beings as the most significant part of the equation, the chief reason for air exchange. To a large extent, these writers remained within the discourses of health and hygiene about domestic ventilation and at the periphery of architectural discourse.[43] However, conceptually, these debates stressed the fact that space is not empty, but rather filled with air.[44] Air thus was to become a real substance for architecture.

The discourse on ventilation in the nineteenth century usually attributed notions of wholesomeness and naturalness to fireplaces, because they outmatched stoves to a considerable extent in their ability to draw off deteriorated air.[45] Stoves were chiefly too weak. The theory of ventilation thus can hardly be separated from the concomitant question of warming the air in a room, especially since many ventilation systems relied on differences in temperature and air pressure between indoors and outdoors. Heating the air was the single most important way to propel it inside a flue, which, like no other architectural element, lent itself to consummating air's renewal in a house.[46] However, while a fire's drawing power is an ingenious means to force air along a predetermined passage (as well as through chinks and cracks entirely unpremeditated), it is also prone to fail because of its dependence on atmospheric fluctuations.[47] If there are none, the system collapses. The flue itself has no power to draw, nor is air able to move independently. At the same time, because of solar radiation and the ensuing differences in temperature, air is never really at rest. The question was how to deal with this movement, especially during different seasons. In the summer, when the inside and outside temperatures begin to correlate, the effects of fire on ventilation tend to break down.

If a flue is not already part of the house, disgorging its interior vapors outward, "wooden troughs or channels may be made to answer the purpose," the American physician and sanitarian John Griscom, suggested in 1854. He wanted them jutting into the sky, "somewhat in the manner of a chimney," running vertically toward the attic, where they should end in flues made of iron or brick.[48] Griscom highlighted the continuous flow of vapors, particles, and gases through which the outside atmosphere, the inside atmosphere, and the resident are inextricably tied together. Among the different methods of ventilation, he found chimneys to be the best for warming and oxygenating a house, because a flue slightly warmer than its surroundings resonates naturally with human respiration, removing the impure air that breathing produces while drawing the same quantity of fresh air into the house.

It was this feature, in particular — the natural ability of the chimney to provide a healthy atmosphere within the house — that created mounting excitement among health promoters around the middle of the nineteenth century. The British inventor and godfather of systematic ventilation, David Boswell Reid (1805–1863), offered one of the foundational texts on the subject in 1844. For some, he is a modernist *avant la lettre*, because he defined architecture in terms of space, as a material shell that merely supports an interior atmosphere.[49] Thus wrapped in architecture, this artificial atmosphere is "in reality, to every building what the breath of life is to the human frame — the vivifying principle, without which they would be tenantless and uninhabitable."[50] By analogy, ventilation is to architecture what breathing is for living organisms (fig. 1.7). In his treatise, he offers a variety of cases related to the convergence of body and space, the proximity between structure and creature. Ideally, the provision of fresh air and the removal of vitiated air would employ two independent apertures administering the inflow and outflow of air inside a closed space. In rare cases, however, Reid allowed a single aperture, "as in the case of ordinary respiration, where the mouth and nostrils serve as a passage for air," with alternating patterns of intake and removal.[51] If human breathing was ordinary, he seems to suggest, in architecture it was still something special, which is why he demanded that ventilation concerns be accommodated from the outset.

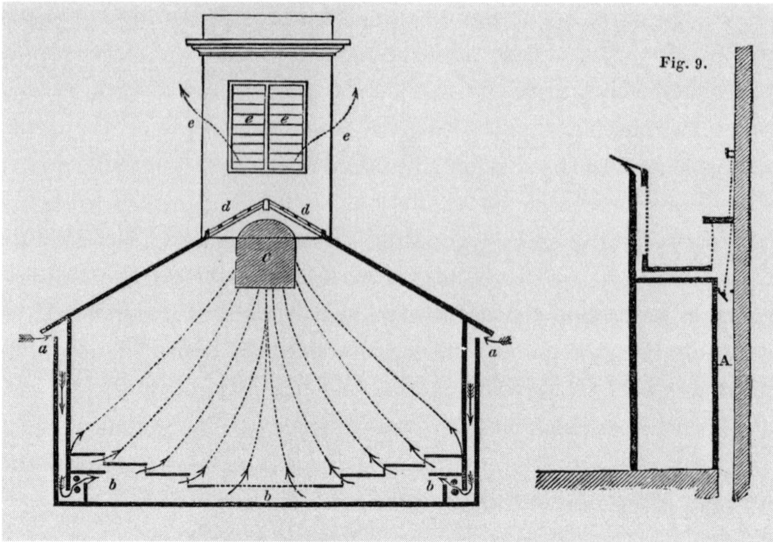

Figure 1.7. Illustration of the house as chimney in the form of a Scotch church. David Boswell Reid, *Illustrations of the Theory and Practice of Ventilation: With Remarks on Warming, Exclusive Lighting, and the Communication of Sound* (London: Longman, Brown, Green & Longmans, 1844), p. 47.

As a passionate advocate of integrated designs, Reid focused on the economic, but issues of health were of equal value. And health was at risk. For Reid, one of the greatest evils of his time originated from truncating the chimney, one of the prevailing alterations in the dwelling house. The resulting reduction in height, together with the helter-skelter arrangement of fireplaces in the interior, left "the zone of respiration" (by which he meant the space from which the air is received when inspired) mainly impure.[52] In 1844, flames and chimneys made an able conjunction as long as they were high enough. All it took was an adroit expert to achieve this.

In France the same year, for the same reasons — the relation of architecture to ventilation and hence to human respiration and health via the provision of fresh air and the removal of vitiated air — architect César Denis Daly (1811–1894) found fault with the Beaux-Arts tradition to impart beauty on forms while at the same time ignoring issues of heating and ventilation. Although his profession knew all too well how to study and mimic nature, he argued, it knew little about the inner workings of the body. If one took nature seriously, one would realize that "animated beings are organized in a way that the sheer fact of respiration is enough to provoke in them a phenomenon of combustion, which maintains the heat in their entire body, and to discharge the deleterious gases from the lungs which so much require this removal."[53] Nature, in other words, had more to offer architects than just the laws of proportion and harmony; Daly called upon his fellow architects to embrace it radically, to learn from it, rather than merely to observe it. The physiological function of the human body was just as important for architecture as was the notion of harmony. Respiration naturally entailed ventilation.

Bad Air

But respiration entailed ventilation because respiration produced bad air. With various competing systems emerging in regard to heating and ventilation, for there to be natural air exchange, almost everyone agreed on the need for open doors and windows during the summer and some sort of chimney discharging the waste products of respiration during the winter. The interior came to be seen as toxic due to anthropogenic pollution, but not in the way as we understand it today, as emissions of human-produced substances such as greenhouse gases and other industrial pollutants. Rather, the human breath itself was seen to produce harmful interior environments simply by discharging carbon dioxide.[54]

In the United States, for instance, Lewis W. Leeds published a series of lectures he had delivered at the Franklin Institute in Philadelphia in the winter of 1866–1867. *Lectures on Ventilation*

(1869), covers a topic that chimes with an opinion shared among experimental hygienists: "Our own breath is our greatest enemy."[55] Ventilation was not simply imperative because humans *inhale* air, Leeds noted, but precisely because they *exhale* it. Breathing inside he deemed noxious and declared, "it is not in the external atmosphere that we must look for the greatest impurities, but it is in our own houses that the blighting, withering curse of foul air is to be found."[56]

Leeds gave weight to his claims with a series of compelling illustrations that visualized airflow using gradients of colored point clouds, rather than traditional arrows and vectors (fig. 1.8). By contrast, a cross section of a hospital ward relies on arrows to indicate the direction of airflow within the interior and its expulsion through chimney pipes and lanterns—a principle that parallels the ventilation strategy later employed at Luckenwalde (fig. 1.9). In the case of this ward, wind currents support ridge ventilation by flowing over angled roof boards that deflect the air without allowing it to enter the interior. This deflection creates a partial vacuum that draws air out of the building. Such illustrations raise important questions about the ways in which to represent a medium that is typically invisible—except when revealed by the presence of recognizable pollutant particles.

Leeds doesn't mention carbon dioxide as the pollutant—he sticks to "air" throughout—but an important study that focused attention on CO_2 already had been carried out by the German chemist and experimental hygienist Max von Pettenkofer (1818–1901).[57] Early in March 1857, he began to accumulate empirical data to determine the threshold when air stopped being pure. He took air samples in various rooms in Munich throughout the year: in his office at the physiological institute, in a lecture hall of Justus von Liebig's laboratory, in a beer tavern, as well as in a classroom. Soon attuned to every nuance of the interior atmosphere, he reasoned that air begins to cause discomfort once the concentration of carbon dioxide exceeds one part per thousand.[58]

Figure 1.8. Illustration of fresh warm air entering the room. Lewis W. Leeds, *Lectures on Ventilation* (New York: John Wiley & Son, 1869), p. 29.

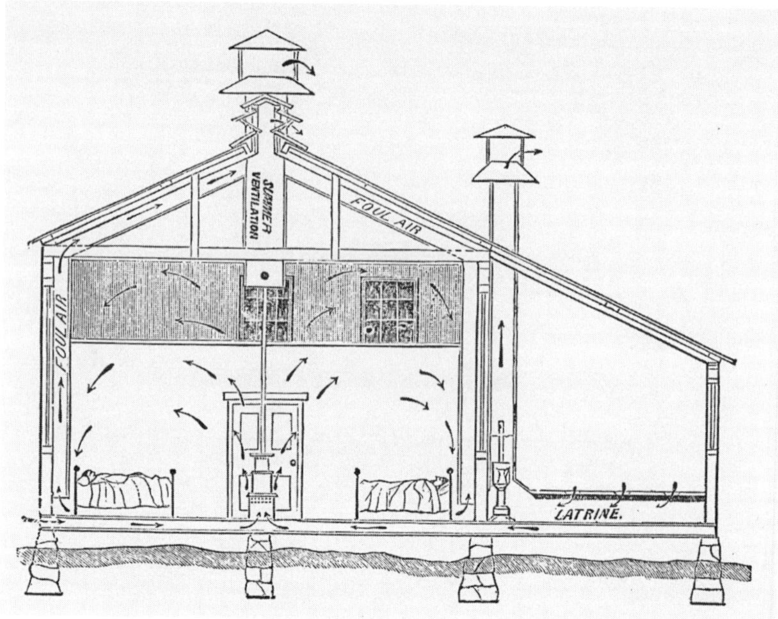

Figure 1.9. Illustration of the so-called ridge ventilation. Lewis W. Leeds, *Lectures on Ventilation* (New York: John Wiley & Son, 1869), p. 53.

Carbon dioxide is not in and of itself responsible for increasing discomfort, but Pettenkofer, like fellow scientists of his time, took it as a standard for the various impurities that saturate the air. Once organic sources of effluvia—rotting garbage, human and animal excreta—were diligently eliminated, what was left as the cause of bad air were respiration and perspiration. Where domestic cleanliness reached its limits, Pettenkofer considered ventilation crucial to restore what human respiration rendered impure.

But exactly how much ventilation was necessary to meet the desired change of air? In order to answer that question conclusively,

Pettenkofer needed to determine the extent of natural air change in a scientific fashion. If one could add the amount of carbon dioxide a human being discharged per hour to the standard portion contained in the air, one could then project a concentration and compare it subsequently with a sample. If both numbers did not match, the discrepancy must be owing to a certain amount of natural ventilation, induced, for instance, through differences in temperature between the inside and the outside. This is exactly what Pettenkofer did. Most of the findings undergirding his experiments thus stemmed from the world of physiology. They postulated, for instance, the need for an hourly influx of 2,100 cubic feet (60 cubic meters) of fresh air per person.[59]

Some four years later, his curiosity gave rise to a wacky contraption that in 1863 he introduced to the readership of a Bavarian specialist journal.[60] The objective of this so-called "respiration apparatus" (*Respirations-Apparat*) was to monitor over a period of at least twenty-four hours the precise amount of carbonic acid excreted through the skin and lungs of larger animals and humans while simultaneously accounting for the physiological processes (such as food intake) occurring during that time.[61] By inspecting the air that entered and left a cubic volume, which he imagined to resemble a living room, Pettenkofer sought to quantify the extent to which carbon acid and water in the air at the outlet is increased by a person staying inside.[62] Made of sheet iron and glass, it measured 8 feet (2.4 meters) on both sides, provided a volume of 512 cubic feet (12.7 cubic meters), and was conceived as a kind of domestic air passage in which a living organism could reside as naturally as possible (fig. 1.10). The cell was almost airtight, sealed with wax, and featured apertures, three circular holes in the door, where the air, drawn out by a pump with two alternating cylinders, was automatically replaced.

Because of these apertures, and gaps around the joints, Pettenkofer saw his respiration space as being able to "communicate freely with the atmosphere," and it was this property, atmospheric communication, he ascribed to the ideal dwelling house more broadly.[63]

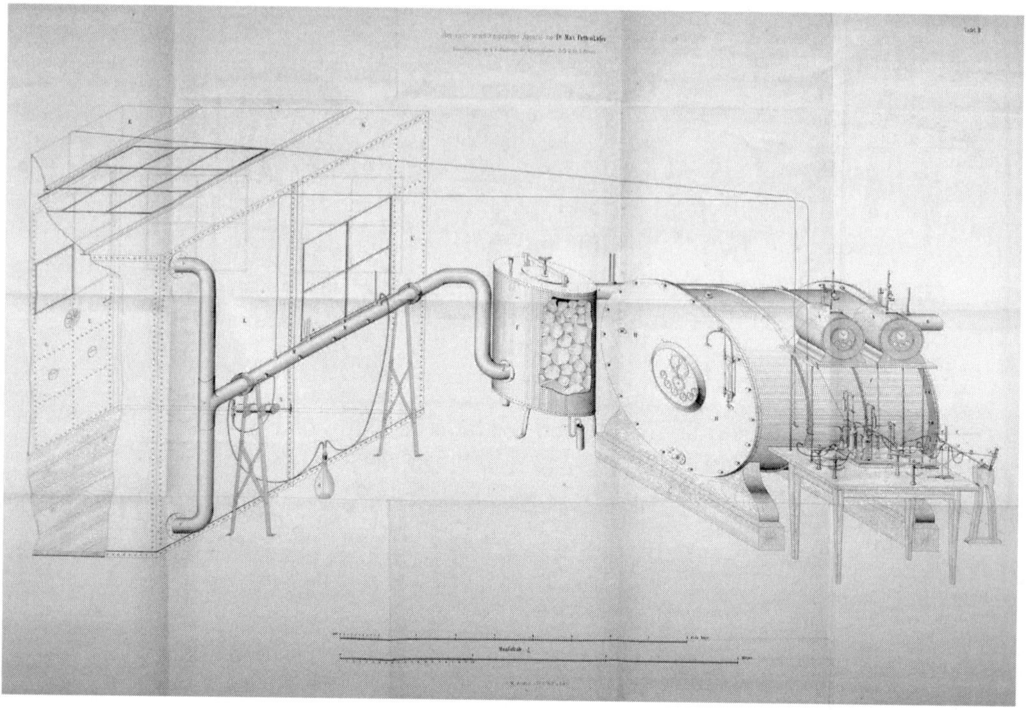

Figure 1.10. Respiration apparatus to measure the amount of oxygen needed by a pneumatic being. Max von Pettenkofer, "Über einen neuen Respirations-Apparat," *Abhandlungen der Mathemat.-Physikalischen Classe der Königlich Bayerischen Akademie der Wissenschaften* 9.2 (1862), foldout table 2.

His research sought to transform air from something culturally taken for granted, unquestioned, and imperceptible into a discursive object in the domain of concerns about health and hygiene. In the end, his thinking put a positive value on air intrusion, for he believed it ameliorated the ramifications of dwelling in closed spaces. Indeed, interior spaces of the nineteenth century were seen to be imbued with vitiated air. This, however, was not the conclusion Pettenkofer drew from his research. An ideal house would be a regulating mechanism, metering the intrusion of air from the outside.

For a series of lectures published in 1872, Pettenkofer further refined many of his claims, prepared for a general audience. There, as others had noted before him, he asserts that houses "act just like large chimneys," and Pettenkofer thus demands that "no more than our clothing ought the house to be a contrivance for excluding us from the air outside."[64] Just as clothing had to regulate the exchange between skin and air, the house had to mediate between organism and atmosphere.[65] "No house can have an atmosphere of its own," he remarks, because "it has that by which it is surrounded, which travels and flows through it slower and quicker, while the house, and whatever exists and goes on in it, have no other power than to render this air more or less impure."[66]

The trick was to keep the supply with fresh air imperceptible. Although drafts, unregulated currents of air in closed-in spaces, were related to ventilation, their presence was felt by their detrimental effects, and the drafty house was the opposite of the ideal house as Pettenkofer envisioned it. He mapped out a combination of factors amenable to ensure a minimum indoor air quality that a dweller could count on, factors that included not only the prevention of overcrowded housing, but also the use of thoroughly dried walls for construction, as well as the periodic opening of doors and windows. The consequence of attempts such as Pettenkofer's to bring the issue of air quality into the discourse of health and hygiene as an explicit technical topic for research was thus that while the modern subject was still to take the presence of air taken for granted, an unquestioned, ubiquitous presence, it nevertheless was one whose presence had been engineered.

Pettenkofer's seminal method set new standards, as evidenced by the Basel-born physician Carl Breiting, who in 1870 published his studies on the quality of air in classrooms. Breiting recognized the need for a method that was both "simple and handy" to measure carbon dioxide levels accurately during class—Pettenkofer's method of measuring the amount of carbon dioxide the humans in the room discharged had long been validated for this purpose. Breiting was also aware of other potentially harmful factors beyond the effect of carbon dioxide buildup, including the air temperature, water vapor density, and "effluvia stemming from decaying organic matter."[67] At different times during class, he collected air samples from the classroom, pumped into specially sealed bottles that he stored at a laboratory overnight (fig. 1.11). For his analysis, Breiting employed a suspension of barium sulphate to release small quantities of air, allowing for precise examination.

If such concerns seem distant from our contemporary world, it is worth noting a historic recurrence that prompted the *Berliner Morgenpost* to publish a 2016 article on poor air quality in schools, titled "Wenn Gebäude Atemnot haben" (When buildings have difficulty breathing).[68] The story highlights an unintended consequence of new building codes aimed at reducing energy consumption: the hyperefficient thermal insulation recently installed in several Northern German school buildings led to a significant increase in carbon dioxide levels inside. Additionally, harmful environmental agents—germs, allergens, and pollutants—became concentrated in the interior air. With windows kept closed during class and breaks too short for students to go outside for fresh air, the situation quickly deteriorated. As a result, all classrooms were retrofitted with ventilation systems designed to activate automatically when carbon dioxide levels reached a critical threshold. The irony was that the energy consumed by these ventilation systems likely offset

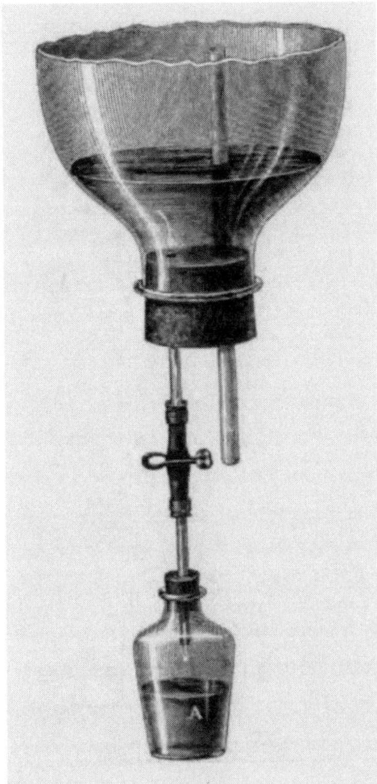

Figure 1.11. Contraption to collect air samples in classrooms. Carl Breiting, "Luft in Schulzimmern," *Deutsche Vierteljahrsschrift für öffentliche Gesundheitspflege* 1.2 (1870), p. 20.

the energy savings initially intended by the insulation measures. A breathing structure, as the article subtly suggests, could break through this vicious cycle.

The Sick House

Like-minded physicians such as the Hungarian Josef von Fodor (1843–1901) followed in Pettenkofer's footsteps. In a series of talks delivered to the Hungarian Scientific Association in Budapest in February and March 1877, Fodor shared his opinions on issues of air quality and health. Published a year later, *Das gesunde Haus und die gesunde Wohnung* (The healthy house and the healthy apartment) examines the effects of vitiated air, or what he aptly calls a "slow, but effective poison," exposure to which causes weakness and paleness.[69] Any evidence of unsanitary air dramatically called for appropriate countermeasures. After all, the whole human body stood to suffer, potential symptoms — loss of appetite, loss of weight, and immune deficiency — were numerous, and good air was the only remedy, a reliable prevention as much as an effective cure.

Fodor transcribed the physiology of the human body directly onto the house. Just as a person could be affected by illness, so the house could fall ill. A sick and untreated house poses a threat to its inhabitants, who, through their very appearance, reflect the condition of their dwelling.[70] By this analogy, the ventilation of dwellings took up the place of human medication, but healthy air flow in the interior remained an unattainable ideal as long as one attempted to prevent annoying drafts. To illustrate this, Fodor included a drawing of a small house in which a burning stove expels the room's air "with great speed," while outside air enters through an opening in the opposite wall "with a strong current" (fig. 1.12).[71] Keeping indoor air clean also presented a Sisyphean challenge, for in terms of pollutants such as carbon dioxide, germs, and "effluvia," the external atmosphere was inevitably purer than the one inside, a factor that startled Fodor. Air pollution, despite its sweeping and extensive presence in many a city around the globe, played only a minor role.[72] Rather, he focused on the breathing subject, the source of all evil inside the four walls. Writing about the house he notes "the first one who pollutes it is the person living inside, constantly spoiling the indoor air through breathing and perspiration."[73] To live inside a house means to render it unhealthy. The Galton chimney offered a means to capitalize on the stove's drawing power while avoiding interior drafts, for it was specifically designed to draw outside air directly into its flue, thereby eliminating the draft depicted in the previous illustration (fig. 1.13). A tube encircling the flue led to an external intake and included an outlet just below the ceiling, which could be opened and closed as needed.

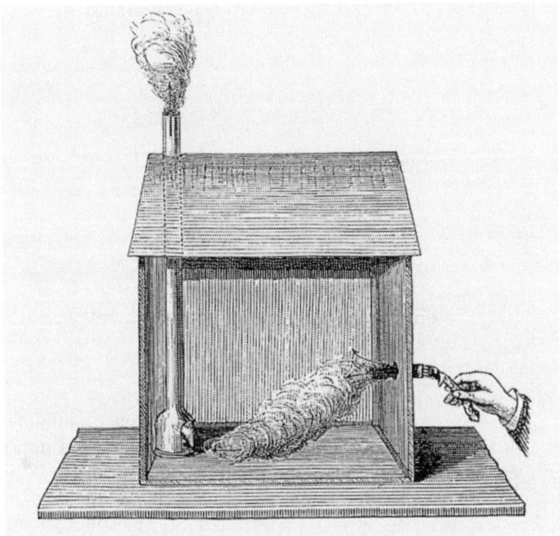

Figure 1.12. Stove-induced ventilation as illustrated in Josef von Fodor, *Das gesunde Haus und die gesunde Wohnung* (Braunschweig: Druck und Verlag von Friedrich Vieweg und Sohn, 1878), p. 71.

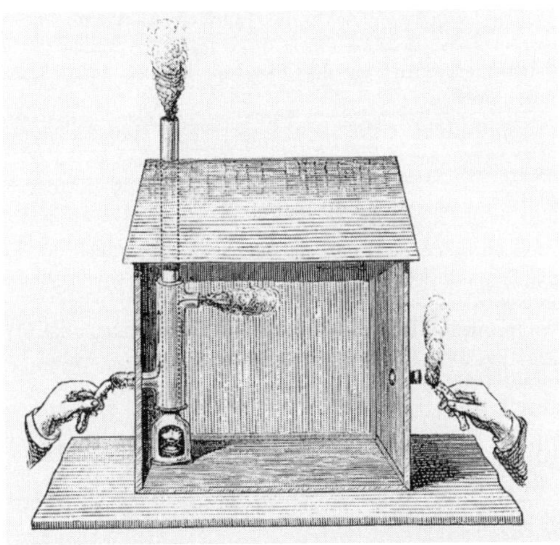

Figure 1.13. Chimney flue after Galton to prevent strong interior drafts as illustrated in Josef von Fodor, *Das gesunde Haus und die gesunde Wohnung* (Braunschweig: Druck und Verlag von Friedrich Vieweg und Sohn, 1878), p. 74.

Fodor's scientific deliberations are in line with Pettenkofer's as they confront a familiar dilemma: the creation of shelter entails its own, at times undesirable atmosphere. And both had realized that it isn't just the surrounding atmosphere that affects the health of the air in a dwelling. The construction of a house usually requires a foundation, and they knew a house can face serious threats not just from its occupants, but also from the ground on which it's built. Understanding of this phenomenon was relatively new, but Pettenkofer already had pointed out the effects of the soil's porosity. Fodor expected that up to half of the earth on which a foundation rested could contain a mix of gases, a belief suggesting a house rests partially on air. He also believed that the decomposition of organic matter in the soil, if cut off from air currents, could taper off and even stop entirely, giving rise to rot and advanced putrefaction. Fodor attempted to give such claims scientifically validity, and while at times they rested on objective facts, often they were based on false assumptions. For example, he still espoused the outdated idea that cholera is transmitted from the environment to the human body through the soil.[74]

Amid a welter of facts and speculation, Fodor warned against soil-born gases because the dwelling house of his times was constructed without an airtight seal at the base. Dangerous as it could be, soil air would not simply rise all by itself; it required the house, with its warmer interior atmosphere, to take it up through constant suction.[75] Just as a fireplace draws in air, Fodor noted, a house imbibes soil air from below. And once this air, foul and infectious, has gained access—a process that only accelerates during the colder seasons, as well as at night—it begins to waft through the rooms, contaminating the breathing occupants.[76] In this respect, like Pettenkofer before him, Fodor saw the house as a chimney.

Pneumatic Beings

In adopting and adapting the concept of the house as chimney for his design for the Luckenwalde dye house, Mendelsohn thus participated in the long history of applying the dynamics of the house as chimney to efforts to preserve and improve the health, well-being, and comfort of those who inhabit built structures. On the one hand, Mendelsohn's ventilation system is basically a refined version of de L'Orme's kitchen and reflects the same concern "that the chimneys are not allowed to give off smoke" into the building, as de L'Orme put it.[77] However, even though both the sixteenth-century kitchen and the twentieth-century dye works responded to immediate problems in architectural terms by engaging the chimney effect, the dye works differs from this antecedent in one crucial aspect: Mendelsohn's awareness of the need to protect the workers' lungs was the product of the culture of respiratory modernism whose nineteenth-century origins we have begun to trace. What made Mendelsohn's space so modern at the time was its place as the culmination of discourses over the preceding decades that had articulated an immediate connection between body and building in terms of health and hygiene and that eventually shaped architecture in the modern period.

The hat factory was the architectural form that recuperated the direct link between breath and buildings. While Luise Mendelsohn's recollections about the pneumonia that afflicted workmen in the dye house draw a direct line between the dye works and human lungs, the connection between architecture and breathing was often more implicit, yet no less revealing. The September 1927 edition of *Der Querschnitt* (The cross section), a German avant-garde art magazine published between 1921 and 1936, features a black-and-white photograph of Mendelsohn's hat factory. In a striking juxtaposition, the same issue includes an essay on breathing by a voice teacher named Wilhelm Flam titled "Wie Du atmest, so lebst Du!" (As you breathe, so do you live!), emphasizing how most people take breathing for granted. Flam notes that because breathing is so self-evident, it is one of the "lesser cultivated" human functions. He argues that "the more humankind has been alienated from nature through technical progress, the less it heeded the fostering of natural breathing [*die Pflege des natürlichen Atems*], which is the beginning of all life and experience."[78] A timid person breathes differently from a successful one, whose inspirations are more profound, rhythmic, and lateral, he claims. Concerned that this vital function was being neglected, Flam seeks to alert his readers to the complexities of breathing, which he considers "the basis of all life."[79]

He points out that the ancients saw this connection more clearly than his contemporaries, expressing it through the ancient Greek concept of *pneuma*—breath as spirit or soul.[80] In classical medicine, it also referred to an invisible fluid essential to life that circulates throughout the body. Today, "pneumatic" commonly refers to something "moved or worked by air pressure," as defined by Merriam Webster, or more broadly, something moved by means of air. Its etymology traces to the Latin word *pneumaticus*, meaning "of the wind, belonging to the air," and the Greek word *pneumatikos*, meaning "of wind or air."

The pre-Socratic philosopher Anaximenes of Miletus (ca. 585–ca. 528 BCE) viewed *pneuma* as the source of all existence, "the breath of life," a blend of air and fire that not only animates the soul, but also holds the universe together.[81] Stoic philosophy further developed this idea, interpreting *pneuma* as a tonic, fluid substance that serves as both the organizing principle of the cosmos and the life force within individual bodies. *Pneuma* was believed to function on both a macro and micro scale, maintaining cosmic integrity and binding the human body together, departing only at the moment of death. In Stoic "cosmo-biology,"[82] the geocentric cosmos was seen as enveloped by a sphere that harmonizes heaven and earth, playing a role similar to what we now refer to as the atmosphere, though the term "atmosphere" is an anachronism and did not exist at the time. In this account, as *pneuma* moves through cycles, it separates into layers: water above the earth, air on top of the water, and increasingly pure *pneuma* reaching the firmament.[83] Philo of Byblos later described *pneuma* as wind in motion, contrasting it with air at rest.

Space itself thus was not seen as empty, but always as filled with air. Ancient theories also claimed that vision requires physical contact between external objects and the observer, and Philo of Byblos emphasized *pneuma*'s role as a "directed energetic movement," crucial in vision and as a mediator between the observer and the observed.[84] *Pneuma* thus played an active role in bridging actual distances in space, serving as a transmitter in conjunction with air.[85] This view reinforced the idea that *pneuma* was not only a vital force of life within the body, as respiration coterminous with life itself, but also as always outside the body, something that could be internalized through breathing. In the Renaissance, for this reason, architects aimed to harness the power of *pneuma* by channeling wind into the interiors of certain houses through subterranean vaults.[86] Thus infused with invigorating breezes drawn in through external ventilation channels, their Italian villas were believed to be energized by a vital, invisible force.[87]

Pneuma thus offers a dynamic and multifaceted concept that connects the human body to the cosmos, blurring the lines between interior and exterior space. As we will see next, modern culture around the turn of the twentieth century was profoundly influenced, if not haunted, by modern versions of this ancient philosophical idea, the vital importance of breath and breathing space. The resultant interplay between the respiratory mentality of modern culture and its architectural realization—both in written and built form, through discourse and buildings—lies at the core of the concept of breathing space. Breathing space was important to modern architects and modern architecture because they viewed humans as pneumatic beings.

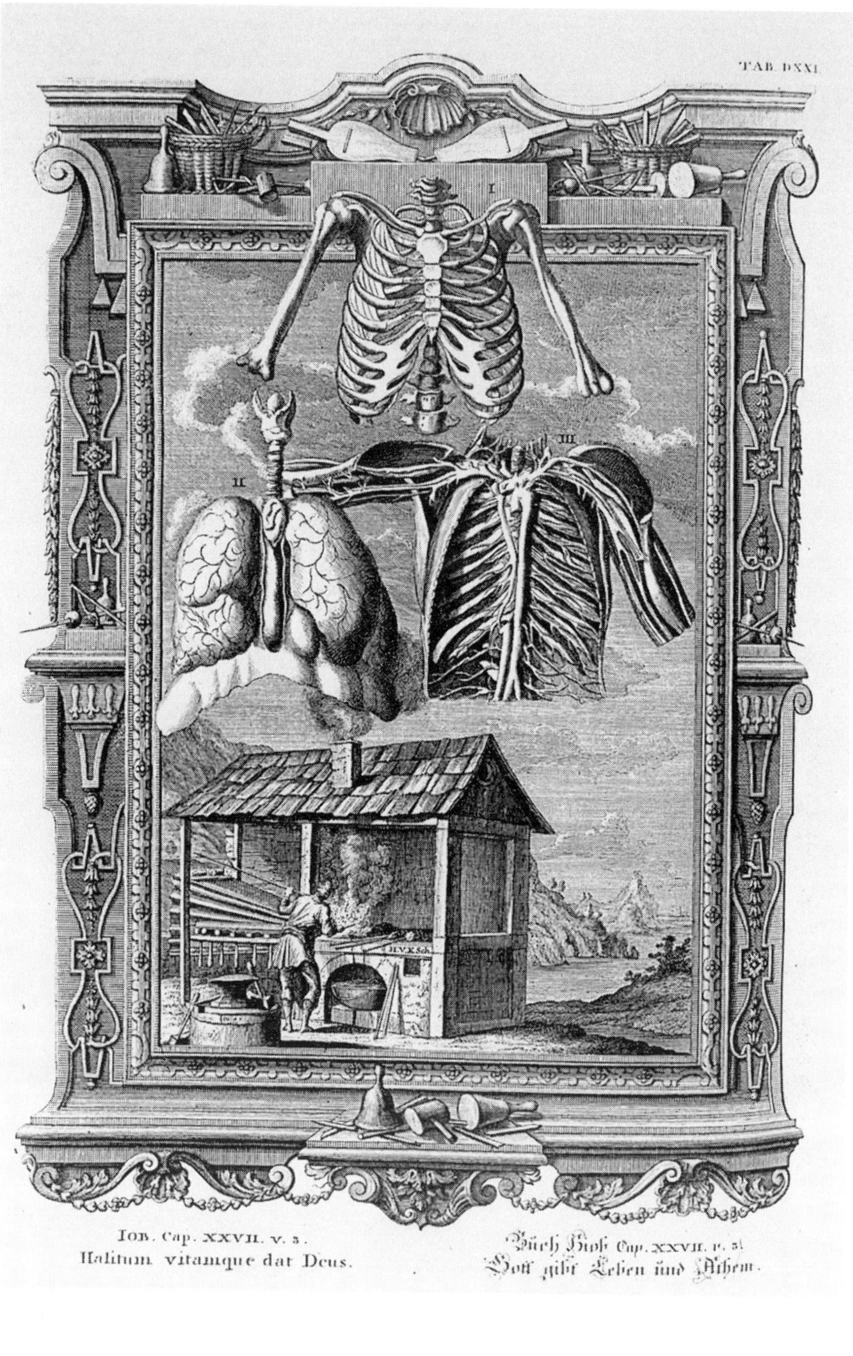

Figure 2.1. Convergence of puffing chimney, lungs, and atmosphere in a plate in Johann Jakob Scheuchzer, *Physica Sacra*, 4 vols. (Augsburg, Ulm: Augustae Vindelicorum & Vlmae, 1731–1735), vol. 3, plate 521.

CHAPTER TWO

Inhaling Lungs

Above a small hut, human lungs hover midair, as if buoyed by the warm air rising from the puffing chimney below (fig. 2.1). The scene is fantastical. Disconnected from other body parts that float separately in the air, these lungs offer a didactic visualization of the human respiratory system. Adjacent to the lungs, we see an opened chest and the skeletal framework of the rib cage above. Just below this triangular arrangement, a blacksmith forges a steel rod in a smithy located beside what appears to be a fjord—a narrow inlet of the sea flanked by steep slopes, with the water receding deep into the background. This print, created by the Nuremberg engraver Jacob Andreas Fridrich (1683–1751), is featured in Johann Jakob Scheuchzer's *Physica Sacra* from 1733. A Swiss physician and natural scientist, Scheuchzer (1672–1733) produced this lavishly illustrated four-volume opus in Latin and German to demonstrate God's existence by dint of the natural sciences, as is evident in the engraving's title, *Gott gibt Leben und Athem* (God gives life and breath). On closer inspection, it becomes evident that the anatomical elements that occupy the foreground exist on a different picture plane from the forge house, with its puffing chimney; in fact, they seem to emerge from the picture frame itself. Although the lungs partially eclipse the smoke, both elements begin to blend at their point of intersection, owing to a similar hatch pattern.

The engraving vividly illustrates the close proximity between architecture and anatomy, particularly the striking analogy between chimneys and lungs. The lungs are depicted frontally, showing individual lobes, the airway and the diaphragm, all informed by eighteenth-century medical knowledge. In this scene, architecture — the forge, with its bellows — serves as the backdrop for the true protagonist: human respiration, facilitated by the lungs, "the bellows through which the breath goes in and out."[1]

In the accompanying pages, Scheuchzer explores the mechanics of breathing, but what stands out is the overall composition of this image: a house with a central fireplace and its adjoining chimney, releasing smoke into the atmosphere made palpable through the presence of dramatic clouds near and far in which lungs hover as the epitome of human vitality. This composition, with its staging of the lungs, powerfully evokes *breathing space*, capturing the analogous, metaphorical, and direct relationships between human respiration, architectural space, and the broader atmosphere. As if portending this confluence of pneumatic phenomena, Scheuchzer's discourse anticipated a culture that began to gain traction in the second half of the nineteenth century.[2] The idea on what follows is not so much to dwell on what is specifically physiological in lungs or technological in architecture as to examine the points of contact between a broader turn-of-the-century breathing culture in Europe and architectural discourse. This approach allows us to understand lungs as fundamentally spatial and to view the inhabitants of modern architecture as consciously breathing, pneumatic beings.

Through breath — *pneuma* — we are inextricably linked to the atmosphere and thrive on air.[3] Lungs like no other organ tie the living body directly to its surroundings, thus posing a topological problem. Engaging in atmospheric transfer, the lungs collapse the division between inside and outside, and despite being an internal organ, they sustain a permanent connection to the external world. This means that the lungs, as an organ, simultaneously belong to the atmosphere and occupy a physical place inside the body, a dual orientation that creates a complex terrain where different mixtures of gases find a point of contact. This interplay is what constitutes the spatial dimension of breathing, an activity that around the turn of the twentieth century, many believed needed to be consciously addressed and mastered, as we will explore in this chapter. The modern human body needed to become proficient at breathing, they claimed, precisely because it had neglected proper technique or execution and because modernization had introduced and exacerbated ailments for which no cures existed. This necessity for proficiency in turn inflected architecture, the encasements, containers, and protective cocoons that provide shelter and serve as an interface between the atmosphere and the consciously breathing body. With this chapter, I wish to accentuate the wide range of ideas that emerged when physiological knowledge about the lungs was translated into spatial thinking and when breathing was turned into a widespread cultural technique. Alongside this transfer from physiology to space, a distinct breathing culture arose in which the ideology of fresh air was paralleled by an ideology of breathing: respiratory modernism.

Breathing as Technique

In his media analysis of breathing, media scholar John Durham Peters differentiates techniques as practices from technologies as material devices, that is, a respiratory practice used in meditation is unlike the breathing masks used during World War I.[4] A variety of technologies emerged from the second half of the nineteenth century onward to aid both inhalation and exhalation, but while the development of breathing technologies contributed to what can be called contemporary breathing culture, breathing aided by material technologies or apparatuses was more limited in scope than the profusion of body techniques from the late nineteenth century onward.[5] This chapter tracks the evolution of these breathing practices around the turn of the twentieth century by reconstructing some of the scholarship that developed during that time while also looking at a number of popular breathing systems designed to teach their followers how to manage air in relation to the body.

Breathing is a multifaceted function that exceeds the mere intake into and expulsion of air out of the lungs. It is a cultural technique, a form of expression, a means of self-improvement, and a way to relate to form. It can be understood in physiological, analogous, metaphorical, and mechanical terms. What kinds of pneumatic bodies were envisioned to inhabit architecture around 1900? In what corporeal ways was breathing considered within the context of space, form, and architecture? To what extent do these individual instances reveal the presence of a breathing culture that formed the foundations for a pneumatic epistemology?

Due to their constant exposure to the elements, the lungs sometimes fall victim to disease. In the late nineteenth and early twentieth centuries, the most worrisome respiratory illness was tuberculosis (commonly known as TB), which was one of the world's deadliest diseases at the beginning of the twentieth century and still holds that grim distinction today. From its management to its attempted prevention, TB haunted breathing culture though it was but one factor of many, albeit an important one.[6] Among the most common responses was the relocation of tubercular patients to sanatoriums in dry climates or fresh mountain air. But while this therapy undoubtedly had a spatial dimension, breathing in and of itself possesses this quality from the outset.

Our own bodies appear to us simultaneously connected to and disconnected from the world, physical entities oscillating between dependence and individuality. In effect, we plug ourselves into the atmosphere with the first breath we take, forming close spatial ties through our respiratory apparatus. As Maurice Merleau-Ponty noted about early child development, a stage during which the extension of the world is defined by the space that can be enclosed within the mouth, "Not only the mouth but the whole respiratory apparatus gives the child a kind of experience of space."[7] If breathing creates a spatial sensation, then space itself can be perceived as a lung. This is why Merleau-Ponty could describe the connection between his own mouth and "some great lung outside myself" as one that "alternately calls forth and forces back my breath."[8] As pneumatic creatures, we breathe as long as we live and are yet barely aware of it.

In moments of crisis however, when lungs fall ill or breathing comes under duress with respiratory diseases from pulmonary TB to COVID-19, from bronchitis to asthma, the activity comes to the fore. In unbreathable environments or during certain activities—yoga, free diving, or aerobic exercise more generally—breathing can take center stage and has to be either cultivated or technically maintained through breath work or respirators. In the words of John Durham Peters, "Breathing morphs into awareness, art and artifice when threat, absence or curiosity rouse it from its slumber." Consciously or not, we breathe collectively, an act that turns us into "co-breathers" and therefore into "con-spirators."[9]

Breathing Idioms

In everyday life, the idioms that metaphorize breath and its concomitant verb, breathing, are copious, though their ubiquity does not automatically increase our awareness of the activity or for its many ramifications: "a breath of fresh air" usually describes a welcome change to an ordinary situation; to "breathe a word" implies a clandestine way of relaying information; if we "breathe fire," we strongly express (or vent, for that matter) our anger; if something "takes our breath away," it fills us with astonishment; "breathing room" provides us with some buffer of time or a relief from pressure; if we "breathe down someone's neck," we watch that person closely; and ultimately, if we "breathe our last breath," we pass away. Breath and life are complementary, in fact codependent. In metaphor, breath is a figure of life itself, just as it is its very foundation in the ancient theory of the *pneuma*.[10] Indeed, the proximity to life itself is so profound that breathing has remained one of the fundamental themes in philosophical and medical debates since Greek antiquity. By 1909, the German physiologist Heinrich Johannes Boruttau (1869–1923) was able to write a full critical history of breathing theories titled "Versuch einer kritischen Geschichte der Atmungstheorien" (Attempt at a critical history of breathing theories).[11]

Swiss-French architect Le Corbusier (1887–1965), too, saw life as breath and respiration as central to the concerns of architecture and according to architectural historian Stanislaus von Moos as something more than just "a physiological phenomenon."[12] In *La ville radieuse*, his book on the radiant city first published in 1933, he included a photograph of a majestic lily.[13] A flower commonly associated with funerals, here, the lily appears dynamic and festive, with its strong contrast and bright, glowing outlines. A glaring caption set in bold letters and all capitals doubly emphasizes the close ties between both activities: "VIVRE! (RESPIRER)"—to live means to breathe.

Le Corbusier found in this eternal verity an apt tool to express his project of the vitalized modern city. In *La ville radieuse*, a remarkable reflection on his urban planning ideas, he also featured a drawing of a lung, alongside which he introduced his own version of an early air-conditioning system (fig. 2.2). The Fondation Le Corbusier in Paris holds a sketch of this page, clearly depicting the outlines of the right and left lobes of the lungs, the trachea, and the bronchi, all penciled by Le Corbusier in black ink and nestled between two paragraphs of handwritten text (fig. 2.3). The sentence directly below his drawing states the obvious: "The lungs are the organs essential to respiration."[14]

This text finally found its way into the printed book. Placed alongside an illustrated lung, it provides a meticulous report of the human respiratory system, asserting that "750 grams of oxygen are retained by the lung every 24 hours; this represents 530 liters."[15] This, however, was not the first time Le Corbusier incorporated imagery of lungs into one of his publications. As early as 1928, his book *Une Maison—Un Palais* included a page featuring a prominent drawing in which the right lung is partially and the left lung

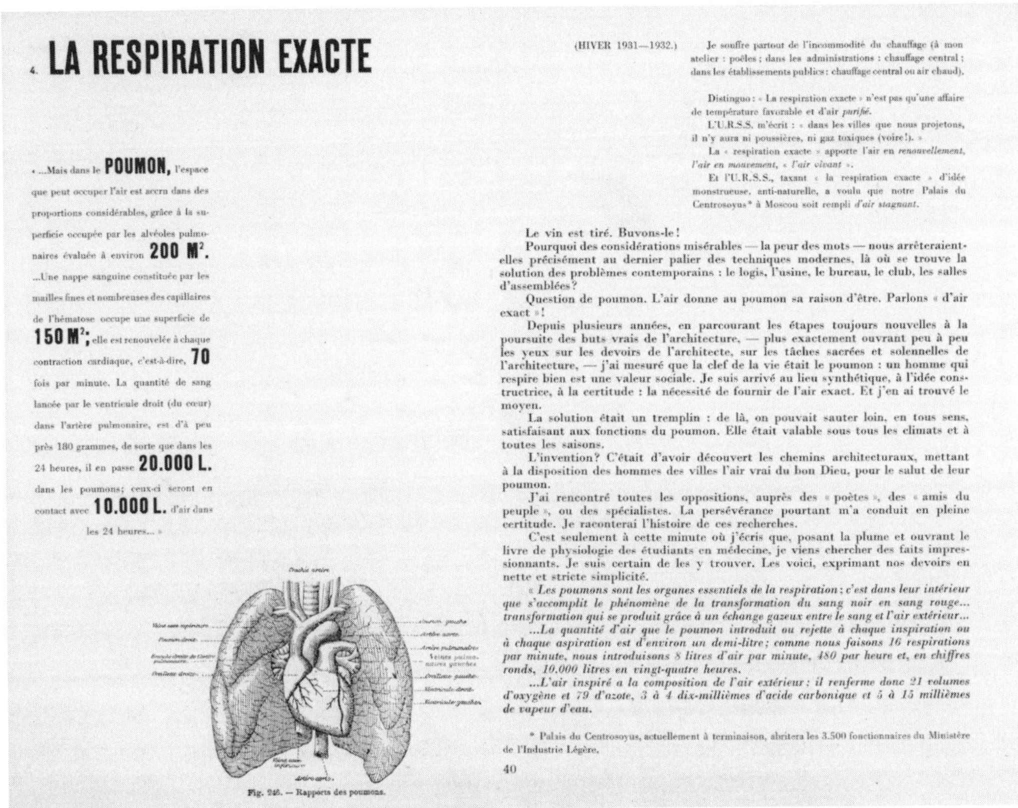

4. LA RESPIRATION EXACTE

(HIVER 1931—1932.) Je souffre partout de l'incommodité du chauffage (à mon atelier : poêles ; dans les administrations : chauffage central ; dans les établissements publics : chauffage central ou air chaud).

Distinguo : « La respiration exacte » n'est pas qu'une affaire de température favorable et d'air *purifié*.

L'U.R.S.S. m'écrit : « dans les villes que nous projetons, il n'y aura ni poussières, ni gaz toxiques (voire!). »

La « respiration exacte » apporte l'air en *renouvellement, l'air en mouvement, « l'air vivant »*.

Et l'U.R.S.S., taxant « la respiration exacte » d'idée monstrueuse, anti-naturelle, a voulu que notre Palais du Centrosoyus* à Moscou soit rempli *d'air stagnant*.

« ...Mais dans le **POUMON,** l'espace que peut occuper l'air est accru dans des proportions considérables, grâce à la superficie occupée par les alvéoles pulmonaires évaluée à environ **200 M².**

...Une nappe sanguine constituée par les mailles fines et nombreuses des capillaires de l'hématose occupe une superficie de **150 M²;** elle est renouvelée à chaque contraction cardiaque, c'est-à-dire, **70** fois par minute. La quantité de sang lancée par le ventricule droit (du cœur) dans l'artère pulmonaire, est d'à peu près 180 grammes, de sorte que dans les 24 heures, il en passe **20.000 L.** dans les poumons; ceux-ci seront en contact avec **10.000 L.** d'air dans les 24 heures... »

Fig. 246. — Rapports des poumons.

Le vin est tiré. Buvons-le!

Pourquoi des considérations misérables — la peur des mots — nous arrêteraient-elles précisément au dernier palier des techniques modernes, là où se trouve la solution des problèmes contemporains : le logis, l'usine, le bureau, le club, les salles d'assemblées?

Question de poumon. L'air donne au poumon sa raison d'être. Parlons « d'air exact »!

Depuis plusieurs années, en parcourant les étapes toujours nouvelles à la poursuite des buts vrais de l'architecture, — plus exactement ouvrant peu à peu les yeux sur les devoirs de l'architecte, sur les tâches sacrées et solennelles de l'architecture, — j'ai mesuré que la clef de la vie était le poumon : un homme qui respire bien est une valeur sociale. Je suis arrivé au lieu synthétique, à l'idée constructrice, à la certitude : la nécessité de fournir de l'air exact. Et j'en ai trouvé le moyen.

La solution était un tremplin : de là, on pouvait sauter loin, en tous sens, satisfaisant aux fonctions du poumon. Elle était valable sous tous les climats et à toutes les saisons.

L'invention? C'était d'avoir découvert les chemins architecturaux, mettant à la disposition des hommes des villes l'air vrai du bon Dieu, pour le salut de leur poumon.

J'ai rencontré toutes les oppositions, auprès des « poètes », des « amis du peuple », ou des spécialistes. La persévérance pourtant m'a conduit en pleine certitude. Je raconterai l'histoire de ces recherches.

C'est seulement à cette minute où j'écris que, posant la plume et ouvrant le livre de physiologie des étudiants en médecine, je viens chercher des faits impressionnants. Je suis certain de les y trouver. Les voici, exprimant nos devoirs en nette et stricte simplicité.

« *Les poumons sont les organes essentiels de la respiration ; c'est dans leur intérieur que s'accomplit le phénomène de la transformation du sang noir en sang rouge... transformation qui se produit grâce à un échange gazeux entre le sang et l'air extérieur...*

...La quantité d'air que le poumon introduit ou rejette à chaque inspiration ou à chaque aspiration est d'environ un demi-litre ; comme nous faisons 16 respirations par minute, nous introduisons 8 litres d'air par minute, 480 par heure et, en chiffres ronds, 10.000 litres en vingt-quatre heures.

...L'air inspiré a la composition de l'air extérieur ; il renferme donc 21 volumes d'oxygène et 79 d'azote, 3 à 4 dix-millièmes d'acide carbonique et 5 à 15 millièmes de vapeur d'eau.

* Palais du Centrosoyus, actuellement à terminaison, abritera les 3.500 fonctionnaires du Ministère de l'Industrie Légère.

40

Figure 2.2. Lungs as shown in Le Corbusier's *La ville radieuse* (Boulogne-sur-Seine: Éditions de l'architecture d'aujourd'hui, 1935), p. 40.

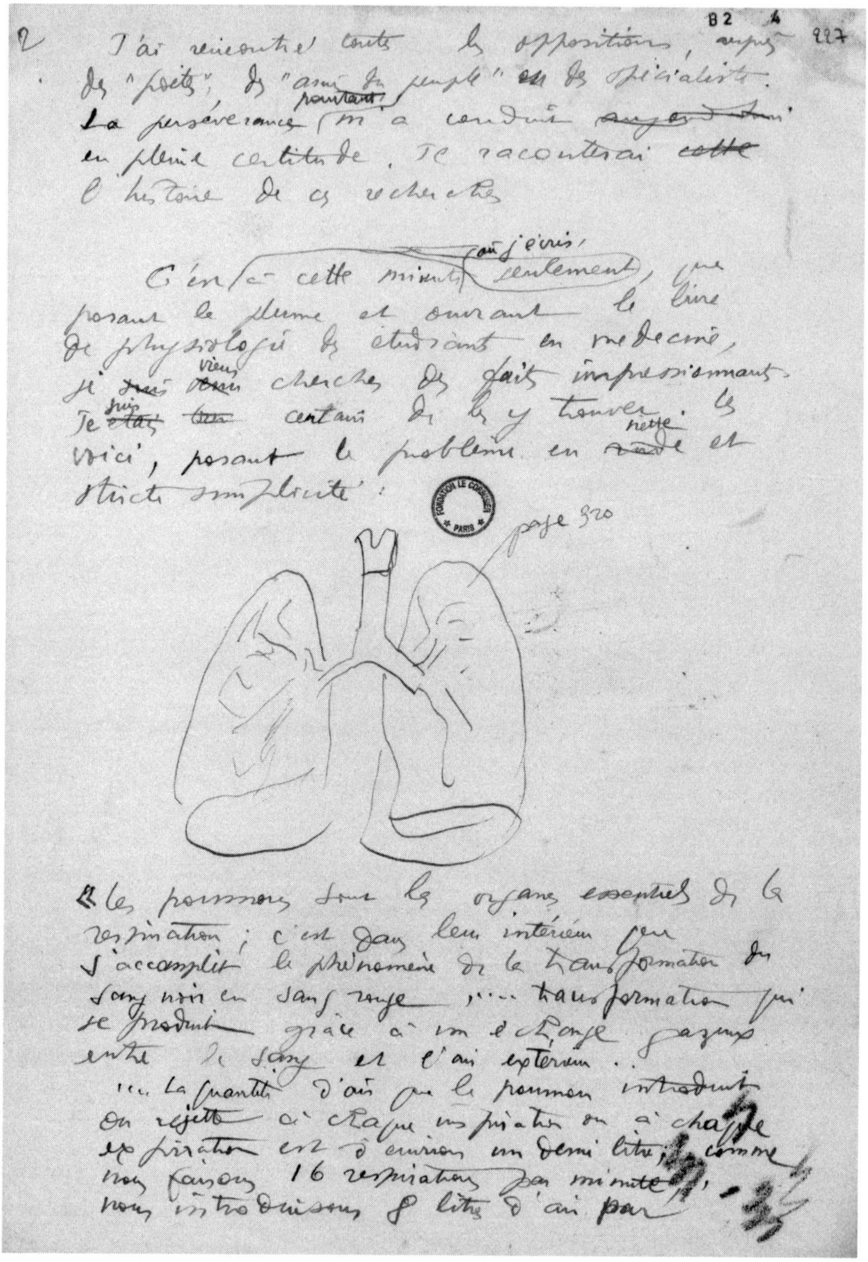

B2 4 227

2 J'ai rencontré toutes les oppositions, auprès des "poètes", des "amis du peuple" ou des spécialistes. La persévérance pourtant m'a conduit aujourd'hui en pleine certitude. Je raconterai l'histoire de ces recherches

C'est à cette minute, où j'écris, seulement, que posant la plume et ouvrant le livre de physiologie des étudiants en médecine, j'y vais chercher des faits impressionnants. Je suis certain de les y trouver. Les voici, posant le problème en nette et stricte simplicité :

FONDATION LE CORBUSIER PARIS

page 320

Les poumons sont les organes essentiels de la respiration ; c'est dans leur intérieur que s'accomplit le phénomène de la transformation du sang noir en sang rouge, ... transformation qui se produit grâce à un échange gazeux entre le sang et l'air extérieur. ...

... La quantité d'air que le poumon introduit ou rejette à chaque inspiration ou à chaque expiration est d'environ un demi litre ; comme nous faisons 16 respirations par minute, nous introduisons 8 litres d'air par

Figure 2.3. Manuscript page for *La ville radieuse* with lungs sketched by Le Corbusier. Fondation Le Corbusier, B2-4-224-004.

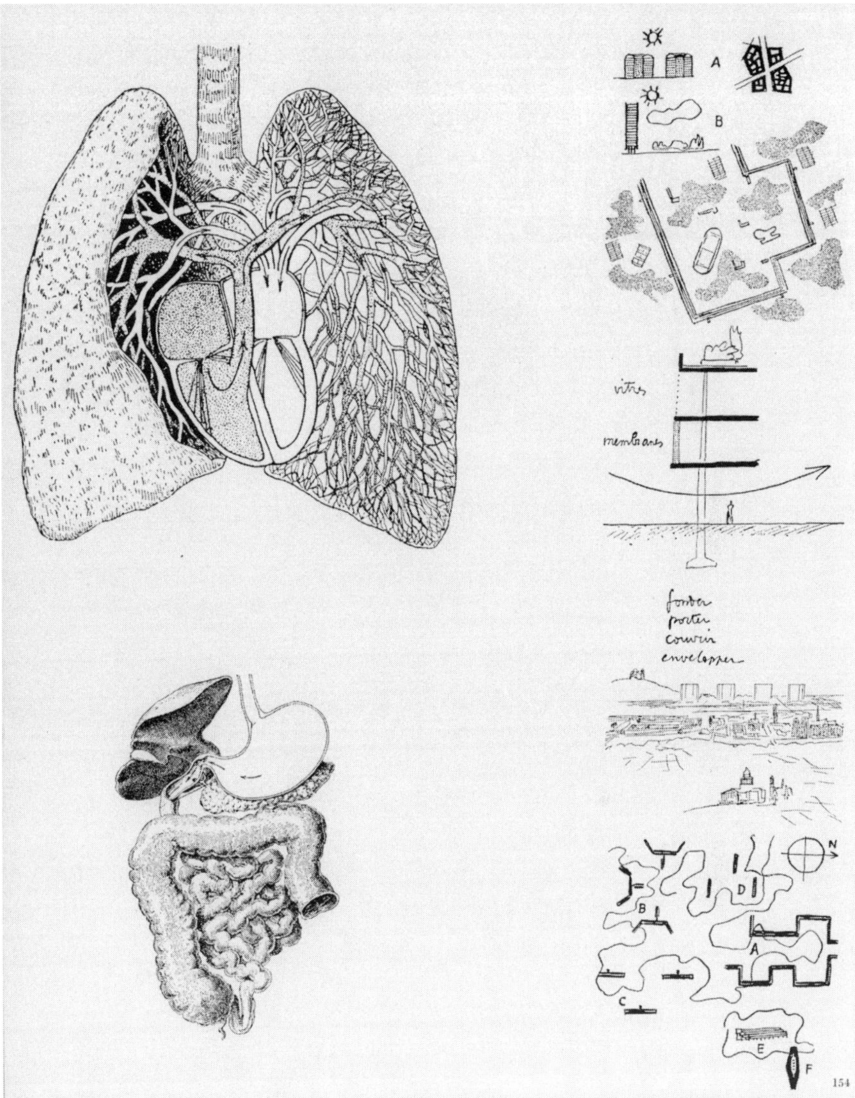

Figure 2.4. Lungs with vector arrows illustrating blood flow as shown in Le Corbusier's *L'Atelier de la recherche patiente* (Paris: Fréal, 1960), p. 154. © F.L.C./ Bildrecht, Wien 2025.

entirely dissected.[16] These lungs are connected to a heart and show detailed features such as pulmonary arteries and veins, with arrows indicating the direction of blood flow. More than thirty years later, in 1960, he included this same drawing in *My Work* (fig. 2.4). The time span between these two publications clearly indicate Le Corbusier's obsession with the lungs and the role respiration played in his vision of modernism.

The shift from breathing taken for granted as an unconscious background process to an activity worthy of thought began in the second half of the nineteenth century for two reasons, both engendered by modernization. One is material, relating to the quality of air, and the other is moral and spiritual, concerning proper breathing technique. The material effects of urbanization, from overcrowding to air pollution, exacerbated challenges to the health of city dwellers and overstrained their lungs. In addition, the increased pace of life and external stimulations of urbanization and modernization were seen as overwhelming inner sensations. As modern subjects began to feel out of sync with the increasingly industrialized world, body and mind gradually disengaged, widening the gap between physiology and intellect. Breathing techniques promised to resynchronize them: through active practice, breathers could tap into their hidden potentials, express their emotions, and realign body and mind.

The new attention to breathing was not merely an invention of a few physicians and sectarian crackpots, but a widespread attitude shared across cultural boundaries. The consciously breathing subject was perceived as a refined personality, indicating that this focus on breathing was a significant cultural phenomenon. Across different disciplines, the fact that breathing operates in the background or could be in jeopardy prompted a wide range of reactions, often converging in claims that it required attention, care, and practice. Overshadowed by the effects of modern life, breathing was endowed with an almost numinous power not only in medical circles, but also in art history, evolutionary theory, and popular culture.

Around the turn of the twentieth century, European culture developed a broad-based fascination with the act of breathing: empathy theory, modern dance, avant-garde pedagogy, and physical culture all put breathing at the heart of modern life, turning society into a world of pneumatic beings.[17] This tendency was corroborated by a concentrated effort, both serious and illogical, by physicians to theorize the physiology of breathing. Whether in the context of avant-garde art practice or popular cultural habit, naturopathy or art history, an increasingly refined sensitivity to the problems and possibilities of breathing was inspired by an increasingly sophisticated understanding of the body's relationship to the environment more broadly, but also to architecture more specifically.

Because breathing is vital, it is controlled by the autonomic nervous system and cannot be willfully overridden—at least in principle. However, unlike our other organs, with our lungs, we have the ability to exert some control over their activity if we choose to do so. The same is true for buildings. We can imagine different ventilation patterns, opening mechanisms, and ways that allow a building to engage with the atmosphere through airflows or perfect stillness. Lungs thus can be seen in direct analogy with architectural elements, for instance, when in 1883, the German anthropologist Moritz Alsberg (1840–1920) called windows "the lungs of a dwelling."[18]

Lungs as Space

In this period, theories of breathing gained increasing importance, and just as the education of breathing promoted full and deep respirations under a tight regime of discipline, architecture also responded to this new sensibility in both discourse and actual buildings. The amount of oxygen intake, the number of inspirations per minute, the average number of pulsations of the heart, and the size of the lungs were all scientifically established values, though there was sometimes disagreement among experts. Lungs are spatial organs, a quality evident in the outcomes of numerous attempts to measure and statistically analyze their function and capacity in anthropometric studies.

Developed in the mid-nineteenth century, the spirometer was one important instrument used to determine the amount of air flow that can enter and leave the lungs. As a diagnostic tool, it was hailed at the time for its ability to determine the lung capacity of individuals affected by lung diseases such as TB, and during its earlier use, mainly by experimental physiologists, it rendered different data based on a body's physiology and anatomy including posture, but also age and gender.[19] However, measuring lung capacity was far from an objective endeavor, and pulmonologists in the United States, for instance, operated under the misguided notion that volumetric properties of the lungs vary across different racial groups.[20]

Often credited as the inventor of the spirometer, the British surgeon John Hutchinson published an extensive article on respiratory organs in 1846 in which he distinguishes between two major aspects of respiration: the chemical and the mechanical.[21] What Hutchinson calls the "vital capacity" is essentially the lungs' respiratory proficiency that determines the amount of air drawn in and thrown out. This air for him is not uniform, but consists of onionlike layers that together constitute vital capacity: residual air, reserve air, breathing air, and complemental air. Residual air, the innermost layer, is the amount of air that always remains in the lungs, regardless of respiratory movements.

Hutchinson illustrated these respiratory divisions in a series of diagrams, speculative cross sections through a human torso, that show his interest lay in the mechanical processes induced by the thoracic movement, rather than in the chemical part of respiration (fig. 2.5). The article demonstrates a spatial understanding of the organ of breath. The so-called "reserve air" he calls the "space for all that air left in the lungs at the termination of an ordinary expiration."[22] Hutchinson's primary objective with the spirometer was to measure the lungs' vital capacity, as evinced by the numerous tables and diagrams throughout the article.

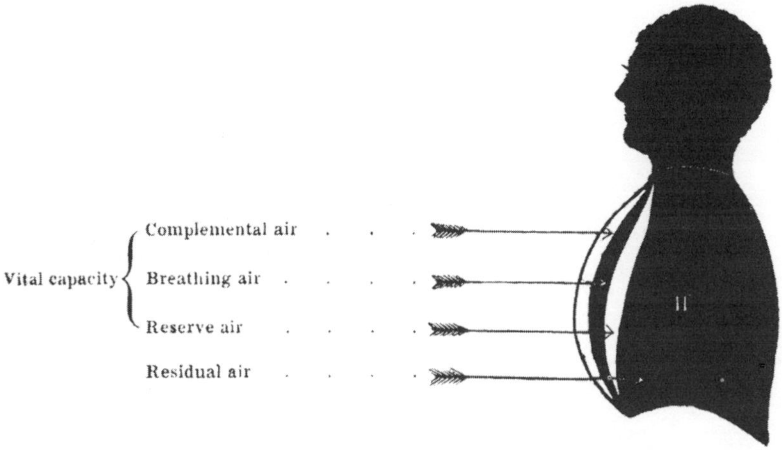

Figure 2.5. Thoracic movements divided into specific portions of air as shown in John Hutchinson, "On the Capacity of the Lungs, and on the Respiratory Functions, with a View of Establishing a Precise and Easy Method of Detecting Disease by the Spirometer," *Medico-Chirurgical Transactions* 29 (1846), p. 143.

In the same line of inquiry, in the 1880s, French physiologist Étienne-Jules Marey (1830–1904) began to measure the physical extent of exhalations through experiments with soldiers, whose torsos he harnessed in a mechanical corset (fig. 2.6). The apparatus girds the upper part of the body to track photographically the lateral expansion of the thoracic cage and thus its external form through iron rods set in motion by human respiration.[23]

Such instruments seek to measure and visualize the expansion and contraction of the human lungs in space, and in the second half of the nineteenth century, space itself also came to be understood in relation to respiration. Since lungs require a specific amount of air, inhabitable space was measured in terms of air volume. In

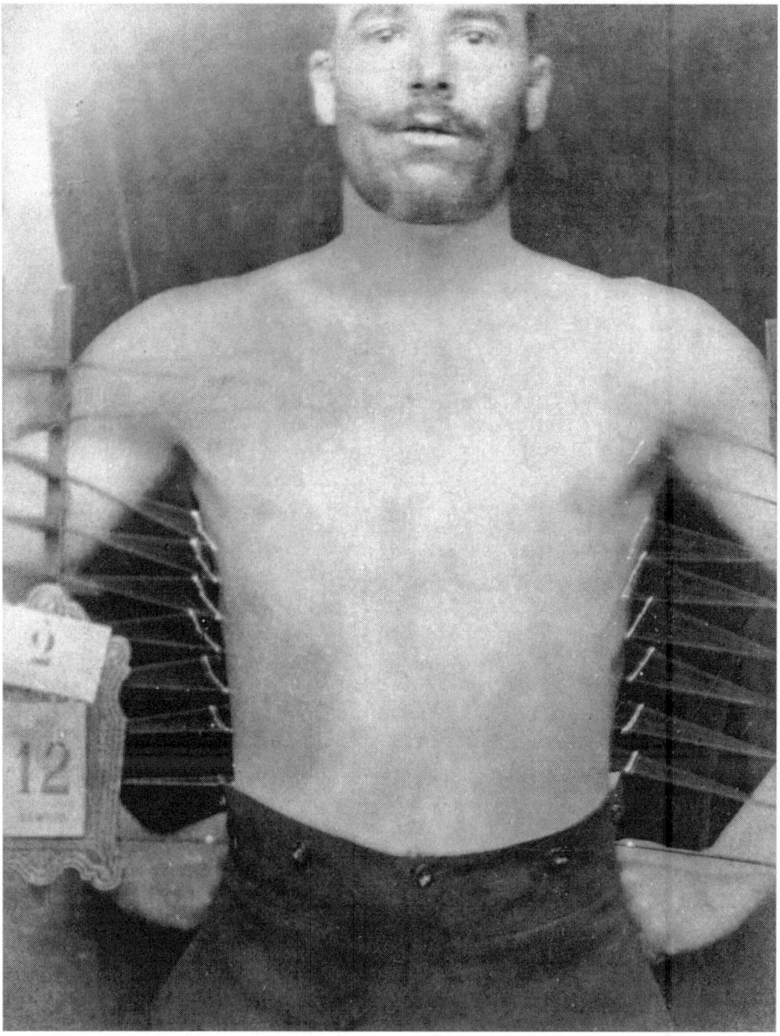

Figure 2.6. Apparatus for measuring chest expansion during breathing at Marey's physiological station. Étienne-Jules Marey, Album Sans Titre 2, Service des archives du Collège de France, Fonds Marey (13 Fi 8), https://salamandre.college-de-france.fr/archives-en-ligne/ark:/72507/r344znxn7zcw6k/f1?context=ead::FR075CDF_00Fi0013_de-8.

the context of health reforms, efforts to combat overcrowding and unsanitary living conditions directly focused on the measurement of air space.[24]

By 1889, for instance, a set of propositions was drafted in Germany, the so-called "Reichsgesetzliche Vorschriften zum Schutze des gesunden Wohnens" (Government regulations for the protection of wholesome living), and presented to the Imperial Chancellery.[25] To manage the overcrowding so prevalent at the time, air became a key indicator of the dwelling space necessary for health: a minimum quantity of ten cubic meter of air per person (or 353.15 cubic feet) was codified and enforced by municipal inspection authorities.[26] Almost inevitably, these emerging health regulations clashed with the interests of landowners and real estate developers, because they required an increase in air volume per resident, making it increasingly difficult to maximize the use of existing floor space.

These poor conditions primarily affected the lower social classes, and the quest for vital oxygen was dictated by the logic of quantitative space—or by what might best be described as economies of air. In May 1890, German civil engineer Reinhard Baumeister published a draft for healthy living conditions to be legally regulated, the so-called "Entwurf zu gesetzlichen Vorschriften zum Schutze des gesunden Wohnens" (Draft for legal provisions to protect wholesome living).[27] To explain the difficulty of the socially underprivileged to acquire healthy living conditions, Baumeister remarks that "adequately healthy dwellings are unaffordable, and cheap ones are unhealthier, or are being exploited in more unhealthy ways than social welfare and charity must desire."[28] Financial constraints within the lower classes had a direct impact on the quantity of available air space and entailed a limitation of oxygen in the breathable air for each pair of lungs.

Today, we know the lungs' surface area spans somewhere in the neighborhood of 1,000 square feet (100 square meters). Owing to advances in the medical sciences, the accepted figure for the size of the human lungs gradually grew. In 1869, for instance, they were

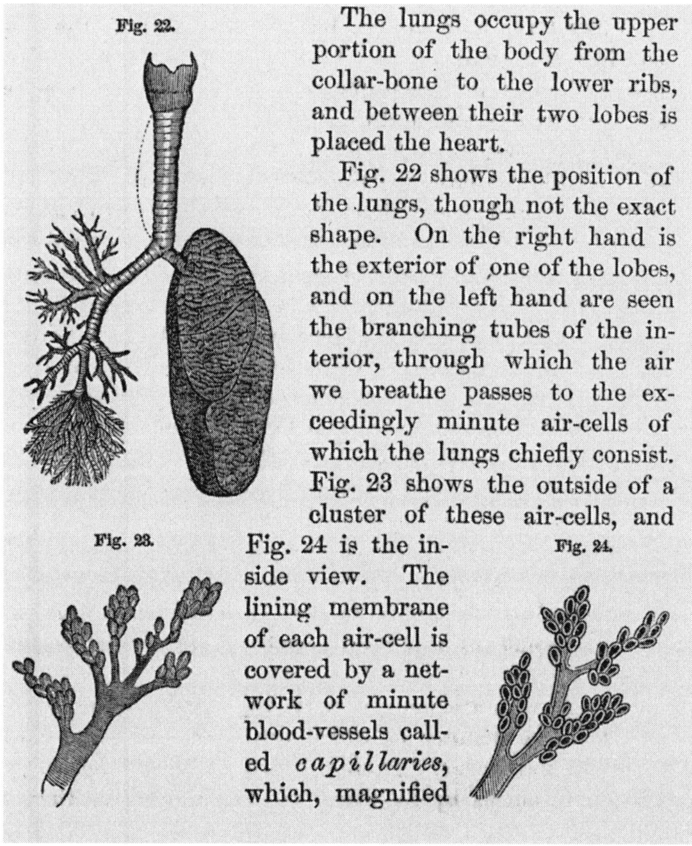

Fig. 22.

The lungs occupy the upper portion of the body from the collar-bone to the lower ribs, and between their two lobes is placed the heart.

Fig. 22 shows the position of the lungs, though not the exact shape. On the right hand is the exterior of one of the lobes, and on the left hand are seen the branching tubes of the interior, through which the air we breathe passes to the exceedingly minute air-cells of which the lungs chiefly consist. Fig. 23 shows the outside of a cluster of these air-cells, and

Fig. 23.

Fig. 24 is the inside view. The lining membrane of each air-cell is covered by a network of minute blood-vessels called *capillaries*, which, magnified

Fig. 24.

Figure 2.7. A pair of lungs as envisioned by the Beecher sisters, including the trachea and revealing the bronchi on one side, as well as a close-up of pulmonary alveoli. Catherine E. Beecher and Harriet Beecher Stowe, *The American Woman's Home: Or, Principles of Domestic Science* (New York: J. B. Ford, 1869), p. 44.

considered significantly smaller than that, but their size seemed daunting nonetheless. When the Beecher sisters envisioned the lungs spread out across the floor, transposing an internal organ to the spatial dimensions of architecture, they wrote "the membrane that lines the multitudinous air-cells of the lungs in which capillaries are, should it be united in one sheet, would cover the floor of a room twelve feet square."[29] These and other of the lungs' specifics served them as a model for the ventilation of rooms in a section accompanied by an illustration of the lungs, the left side of which is uncovered to expose the respiratory tract, showing the trachea and bronchi. As if to attune house and lung, this image gives a good idea about the extent to which the interior surface of the lungs interacts with the interior air of a room, especially when considering a breathing rate of twelve to twenty breaths per minute. This level of detailed data is further reflected in two contiguous visualizations of pulmonary alveoli, where the air sacs are covered by a membrane that plays a crucial role in the transport of blood through the organ (fig. 2.7).

Breathing Visualized

Contrast the spatial comparison in *The American Woman's Home* with an illustration from architect and illustrator Fritz Schüler, included in a 1931 collection of postcards issued by the *Berliner Morgenpost*, in which bronchi of a lung extend octopus-like into a room, with their alveoli spilling onto the floor to form a carpet (fig. 2.8). At the edge of this carpet, an expert lectures on the organ's surface area.[30] In 1931, some sixty years after the Beecher sisters, the organ had grown by over sixty times, to roughly 800 square feet (75 square meters).[31] Perhaps owing to Le Corbusier's propensity for hyperbole, the surface area he quoted in 1933 spans even more—an estimated area over 2,000 square feet (200 square meters, more than twice what it actually is.[32] Apparently Schüler's sources got the facts straight. Schüler contributed a number of illustrations to Fritz Kahn's renowned book series *Das Leben des Menschen* (Human life,

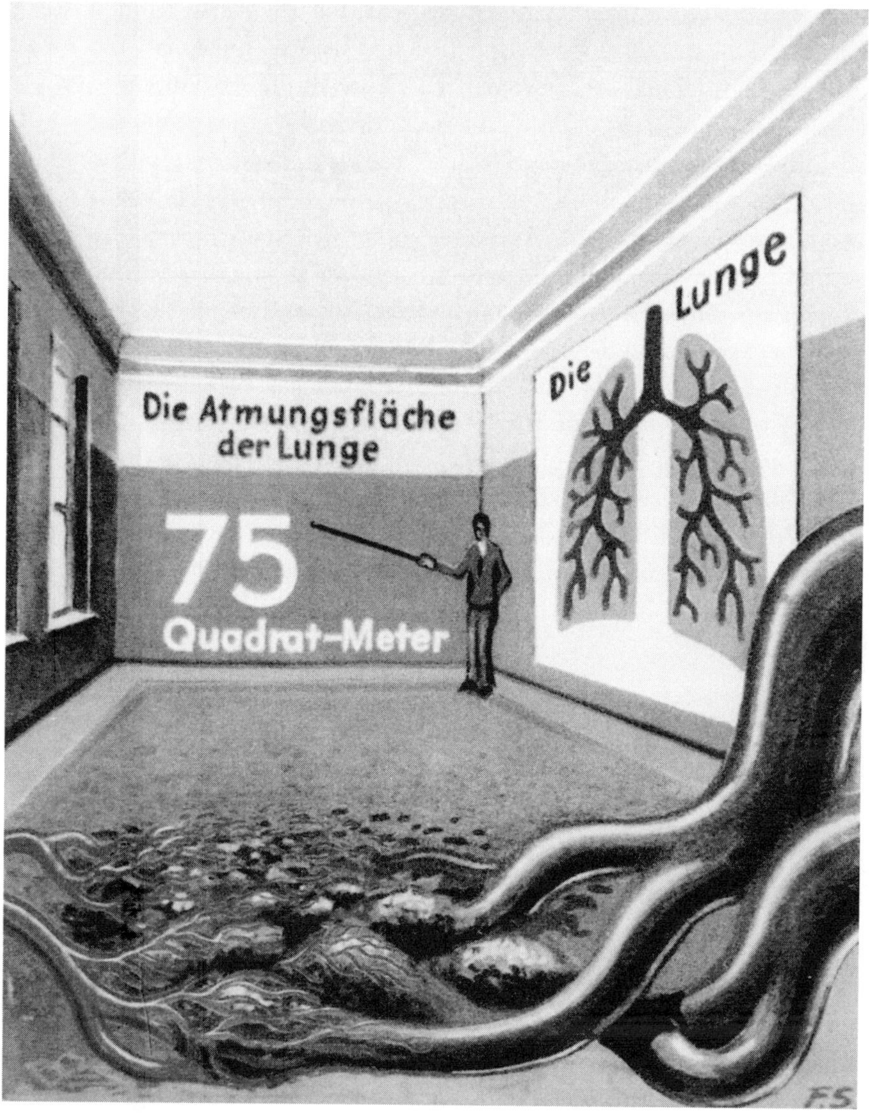

Figure 2.8. Lungs dissolving into a room-sized carpet to indicate their extent. "Bilder vom Menschen," *Berliner Morgenpost*, postcard set, 1931. Axel Springer SE, Unternehmensarchiv.

Figure 2.9. A pneumatic contraption, the *Pneumotor*, transports coal during sleep. Fritz Kahn, *Der Pneumotor*, in *Das Leben des Menschen: Eine volkstümliche Anatomie, Biologie, Physiologie und Entwicklungsgeschichte des Menschen*, 5 vols. (Stuttgart: Franck'sche Verlagshandlung, 1922–1931), vol. 3, p. 53.

1922–1931), an exuberant five-volume account on the human body. A German Jewish gynecologist and popular science writer, Kahn is widely celebrated for his contributions to visual culture, which shed light on the complexities of human biology. Rich in metaphors and laced with visual analogies, *Das Leben des Menschen* unpacked the complex metabolic operations for a general readership and was trendy in Weimar Germany.

Kahn's arresting world of infographics holds a number of stunning illustrations associated with the workings of the lungs. A pneumatic engine, the so-called *Pneumotor*, allegorizes the potency of human respiration. A mechanical engine capitalizes on the lifting power of a sleeping person's thoracic cage as it converts the power of breathing and its up-and-down movements to ferry five hundredweight of coal during one night into the attic of an adjacent house (fig. 2.9). An erect iron bar with saw teeth, positioned on the sleeper's rib cage, impels a belt drive's small gear wheel, which in turn is connected to the coal cart parked in between the two houses. One could hardly think of a visual rhetoric more staggering to illustrate the lifting power of the breathing rib cage.

The visual tropes Kahn employs are ostensibly architectural, illustrating an otherwise barely visible process that is inherently spatial. This spatial aspect is not solely due to the corporeal movement involved in breathing, which contracts and expands an organ in space. It is because this organ calls into question the separation between body and space, between inside and outside. This characteristic also makes it genuinely modern.

Among the most famous illustrations produced in the German interwar period is Kahn's more than three-foot-high poster *Der Mensch als Industriepalast* (Human as industrial palace). This image, akin to an architectural cross section, lays bare the internal secrets of the human body in a visual idiom much closer to the world of industry than that of anatomy. Cutting through torso and head, it presents the human body as an inhabited factory. The illustration blends notions of modern mechanization and medical science; it is also a product of various disciplines—architecture, graphic design, painting—that Kahn's collaborators brought to the table. Still today, the image's appeal is unshaken: as a front cover, it emblazons various books and exhibition catalogues as much as it stimulates scholarly research.[33] A similar illustration, monochromatic and less known, thematizes human respiration by dissecting the breathing process into ten steps and the cardiovascular system into seven sequences: *Die Atmung des Menschen* (Human respiration) (fig. 2.10).

What makes this representation architectural is not just its cross-sectional character, but also the way in which rooms are connected

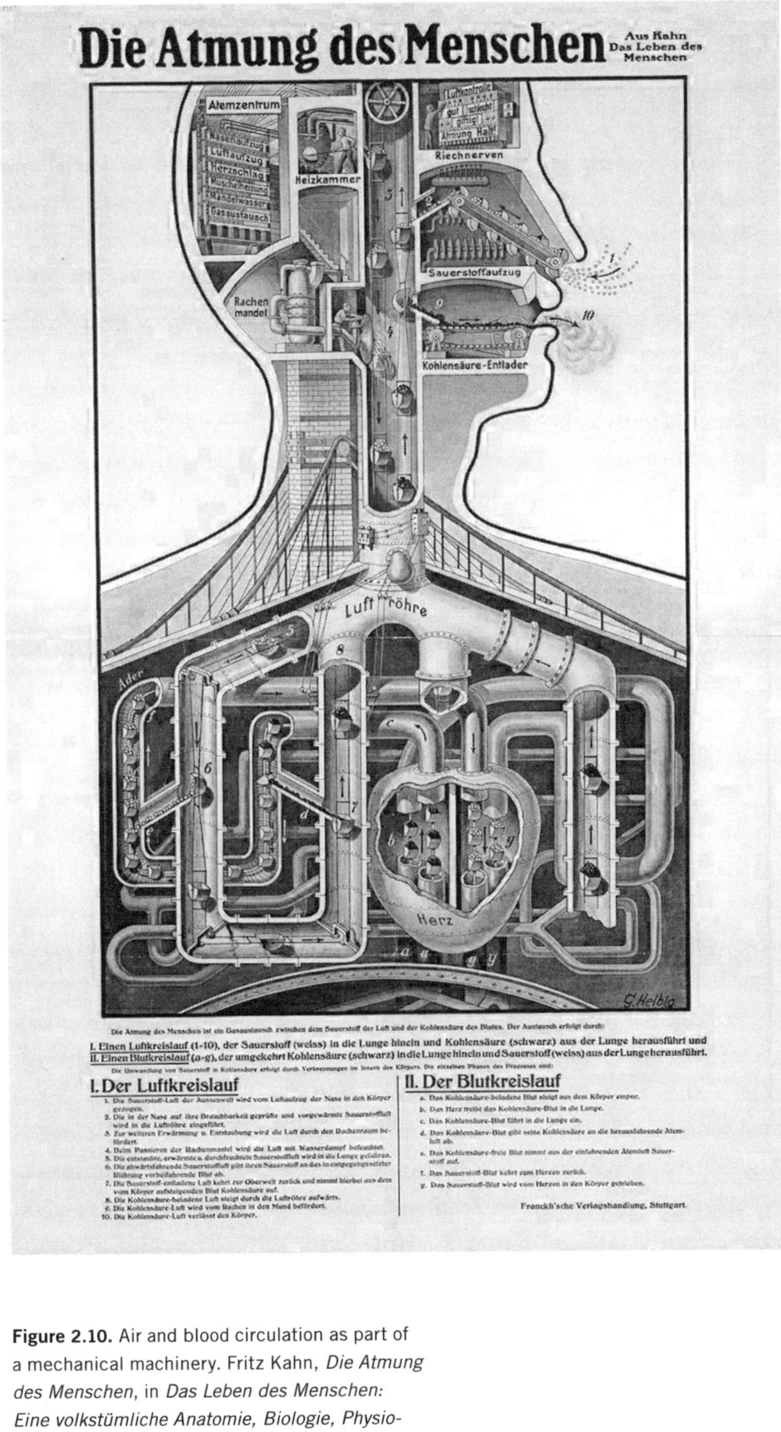

Figure 2.10. Air and blood circulation as part of a mechanical machinery. Fritz Kahn, *Die Atmung des Menschen*, in *Das Leben des Menschen: Eine volkstümliche Anatomie, Biologie, Physiologie und Entwicklungsgeschichte des Menschen*, 5 vols. (Stuttgart: Franck'sche Verlagshandlung, 1922–1931), vol. 3, plate 12.

through stairs, and bricks form a shaft in place of the spine. From this spine, steel cables reminiscent of those on the Brooklyn Bridge are suspended to support the thorax. While regions of the brain resemble the factory's control center — where figures in pants are busy fiddling with knobs and opening valves — riveted steel elements form the heart and trachea below. The lungs are conspicuously absent, or rather, abstracted into a gigantic tubular apparatus that transports cages of oxygen and carbon dioxide via a looped belt. The two gaseous substances, represented as black and white globules, are discharged and absorbed through the mouth and nose, respectively, forming the beginning and end of the breathing cycle. Where "the oxygen air from the outside world is drawn into the body by the nasal air elevator," "the carbonated air leaves the body" through the "carbon dioxide unloader." Efficient and industrious as in a coal mine, driving wheels propel a belt in order to channel the two components of the breathing process throughout the depth of the thorax. Inhalation and exhalation are rendered as part of a mechanical machinery, working properly on the basis of good structural design.

Owing to the nature of the perspective, the individual elements are depicted with extreme plasticity; the skin, in contrast, is rather flat, represented merely by a thick, undulating black line. Everything seems to stay within this line except for the air, which breaches the body's perimeter. The degree of realism is less striking than is the unconventional presentation of human anatomy in the form of an imaginary factory.[34] The illustration speaks volumes about the human physical relationship with its environment. Only small, spherical particles relevant for breathing cross the torso's outline, while everything else remains within the body's silhouette. The illustration also speaks volumes about a technical conception of breathing that emerged during the machine age, a conception that, in the context of architecture, evolved into mechanical ventilation and air-conditioning systems.

Disciplining the Breath

If there is one organ tied to modernity as closely as the eyes are to the Renaissance, it would undoubtedly be the lungs, with breathing as the concomitant activity. A case in point is found in the ten breathing commandments published in 1914 with biblical connotations by the German physician Friedrich-Beda Stubenvoll (1877–1961), the first of which emphasizes the importance of not forgetting to breathe in the first place, as if one could ever dismiss the activity from one's mind.[35] And "sloppiness in breathing leads to anarchy in breathing." While the third commandment urges us to "always breathe in time," the final commandment calls for consistent "deep diaphragmatic breathing."[36] While the Beecher sisters, like many others at the time, had seen breathing as a way to consume atmospheric energy, others came to understand it as a body technique within frameworks related to health, spirituality, or occultism.[37] Regulating one's breath was a way to achieve a certain degree of control over a variety of aspects of life by enforcing order on an activity so ordinary as breathing: life and breath alike, could be managed, commanded, and disciplined, and disciplining the breath became a concern in areas as diverse as regulating workers' physical existence and expressing inner feelings in fields as different as modern dance and architecture.

Workers

A locus for exerting this kind of control over pneumatic human beings arose, in part, with the emergence of garden cities, model towns, and artists' colonies. The social consequences of the machine age were "barbarizing," as historian and architectural critic Lewis Mumford (1895–1990) put it, and often, it was industrialists who, alert to the strained labor conditions in cities and factories, decided to take countermeasures.[38] During his three-year-long sojourn at Dresden, Vienna-born author and architecture critic Josef August Lux (1871–1947) directed classes for arts-and-crafts training in the newly founded preparatory school in the garden city at Hellerau. An assiduous writer and active promoter of the influential Werkbund, an association of artists, architects, designers, and industrialists seeking to combine traditional craftsmanship and industrial mass production techniques, Lux maintained his own media outlet in the form of the art magazine *Hohe Warte* (High watch), in which he reproduced a code of health in an issue of 1905, a code originally put forth by the English Quaker and cocoa industrialist George Cadbury (1839–1922).[39] A committed reformer, Cadbury was deeply concerned with the well-being of his employees and sought an alternative to the implacable urban life of the modern world. Together with his brother Richard, he ran a chocolate and cocoa factory, and with production on the rise, they relocated their business from Birmingham to the nearby countryside. The resulting model town, Bournville, included a wide range of facilities such as hospitals, schools, parks, recreational areas, and libraries. It also featured cottages to accommodate their employees and workers from the surrounding area.

And yet, beneath the image of this idyllic settlement lay a stringent code of conduct designed to enhance the workers' health and fitness. Cadbury's rules, intended to orchestrate the daily routines of Bournville's residents, were well-intentioned, but benevolently repressive. The policy instructed residents not to sleep on feather beds, avoid tight clothing, and rest for at least eight hours a day. From suggestions concerning the preparation of milk to advice on natural lighting in bedrooms, Cadbury's health code prescribed a comprehensive set of objectives that Lux also introduced to his German readership.

Some of the policy's succinct expressions directly addressed exposure to fresh air, insisting that residents breathe through their noses and keep their mouths properly closed.

> Stay in the fresh air and warmth of the sun as much as possible.
> Take a breath through your nose and keep your mouth closed, especially at night.
> Take a walk or exercise in the open air for at least half an hour a day.
> If the weather is not very humid, keep the windows open day and night.
> In each room you will find a Tobin fan that you can leave open so you can breathe fresh air even in the rain and snow when the windows are closed.[40]

In an open landscape, unconstrained by urban life, Cadbury wanted his workers to regulate their breathing practices to achieve maximum efficacy. So among all the protean fantasies about bucolic life, there was no place in Bournville for individuals to breathe as they desired. Rather, as part of a system of discipline and control, Cadbury's regulations were intended to keep working-class bodies fit for production. The expression of concern that caused workers to believe their health mattered was in fact intended to maintain their labor force in good condition.

Modern Dance

While at Hellerau, the first German garden city, Émile Jaques-Dalcroze (1865–1950) pursued the rhythmization of human life by virtue of his Eurythmics movement, Johannes Itten (1888–1967) attempted to align his students' bodies and minds through breathing exercises at the Bauhaus. Both pedagogies placed breathing at the core of their teachings and claimed to allow pupils to release their own feelings by dint of artistic expression. Jaques-Dalcroze had devoted his life to the experimental teaching of rhythm and in 1912 observed how the lack of rhythm in young children was "almost like a disease."[41] To countervail this degeneration, he argued, rhythm should be given the rank of a "social institution" at Hellerau, to which Jaques-Dalcroze relocated his school of rhythmic gymnastics from Geneva.[42]

He established his pedagogy based on a marriage between gymnastics and popular outdoor activities (fig. 2.11). The resulting Eurythmics played an important role in the development of modern dance, in which breathing served as a propellant to bring to the fore the vital emotions latent in each student. Modern dance expresses rhythm through "harmonious movement" for which it is crucial to interconnect "the mental and physical powers" inherent to the modern body.[43]

For Jaques-Dalcroze, a rhythmic sense of time was essential to bridge the professed gap between inner sensations and their

Figure 2.11. Synchronization of dance and breath through Eurythmics, 1912. "A Plastic Exercise," in Émile Jaques-Dalcroze et al., *The Eurythmics of Jaques-Dalcroze* (London: Constable, 1912), p. 65.

corporeal enclosure.[44] In his 1920 book *Le rythme, la musique et l'éducation* (published in English the next year as *Rhythm, Music and Education*), a compilation of essays, he defines the difference between rhythm and meter in terms of their fundamentally divergent origins: while rhythm is internal, arising from underlying emotions, meter is external, imposed by the cultural matrix of modernity.[45] Personal freedom is inextricably tied to rhythm. If the internal drive to breathe can be uncoupled from the regulating disciplines that modernity had imposed externally, he believed, then freedom of movement could be facilitated in an organic way. Conversely, he writes that "the submission of our breathing to discipline and regularity of time would lead to the suppression of every instinctive emotion and the disorganization of vital rhythm."[46] As a powerful expression of deep inner emotions, respiration is also able to skirt conscious rationalization. The forces unleashed to fix a derhythmized society in which the "natural powers of expression" were missing would emerge from within the human body itself.[47] Of the two most conspicuous bodily rhythms, the heartbeat is beyond our grasp and thus of little value for the reformation of modern individuals. The lungs, however, offer a way to combat the regulation of life that the likes of Cadbury tried to impose. In Jaques-Dalcroze's words, "the respiratory muscles being subject to the will . . . we are able to operate them rhythmically."[48] Breathing rhythms are a direct function of the varying "muscular tension" that offers countless ways to stretch out or speed up time. For Jaques-Dalcroze, to incorporate time into the body systematically by breathing techniques quite literally means to inhale and exhale it.

Architecture

A post–World War I student of art and architecture at the Bauhaus in Weimar crosses the Ilm Park, where Goethe's garden house stands, and enters the school's main building to begin his daily studies in the preliminary course. Upon arrival, the first routine would be the daily breathing exercises that all of Itten's students had to perform. This scene entailed corporeal activities such as circular movements of the arms in tune with thorough breath work.

Less than a decade after the publication of *The Eurythmics of Jaques-Dalcroze*, an approach to breath work related to that of Jaques-Dalcroze loomed large in Itten's course at the Bauhaus, where experimental pedagogy acquainted students with the use of vegetarian diets, as well as breathing exercises. The body played a vital role in the education of young Bauhaus students, but while Walter Gropius and Marcel Breuer often challenged the students physically in swimming contests, it was Itten who encouraged them to embrace their own emotions as a basis for their creative work.[49] The underlying connection between rhythm, feelings, and breathing rested on precepts similar to Eurythmics. To harmonize body and mind, Itten began his daily classes with exercises in concentration, breathing, and relaxation "to establish the physical readiness which make intensive work possible."[50] Perplexed at first, Itten's students soon took part in these activities with enthusiasm. He understood the body as an instrument and corporality as the prerequisite for any art. Perhaps the most charismatic of all Bauhaus masters, "there was something demonic about Itten," as one of his students later recalled.[51] When Austrian Bauhaus student George Adams arrived in Weimar, "there was no question that . . . Itten was the outstanding personality among the teachers."[52]

Instead of merely teaching his students the art of copying the great masters, as was common at the time, Itten grappled with ways to discharge their inner emotions, free their artistic minds, and overcome their inhibitions through esoteric practices informed by the Mazdaznan cult, an American sect whose European headquarters was a school near Zurich. Itten's own philosophy was polyvalent, informed by several esoteric practices,[53] but long before joining the Bauhaus, Itten had come under the sway of this Neo-Zoroastrian religion, founded by Otoman Zar-Adusht Hanish (1856–1936), a charlatan and German immigrant who later lived in Chicago, where he was jailed for mailing obscene literature, and Los Angeles, where he was also jailed for contributing to the delinquency of minor children.[54]

Mazdaznan embraced all things metaphysical, including Jewish and Christian mysticism, old Persian and Egyptian myths, as well as Hindu-Tantric beliefs, and its racial theory emphasized eugenics and the supremacy of the Aryan race as the climax of evolution.[55] It also rested on profound breathing techniques Hanish introduced in his 1902 *Health and Breath Culture*. Not unlike *pneuma*, the so-called Ga-Llama stood for "the capacity or power of Breath," whose accumulation was central to Hanish's doctrine.[56] Ga-Llama was said to be a breathable force able to set up a connection with the life-giving universe, inexplicable, but a reality nonetheless: "As soon as you become conscious of it and feel the desire to draw it unto you," he observes, "you become filled with it, and through its accumulating presence get into harmony with the universe which unfolds your individuality to infinity."[57] Breath was believed to be charged with extra vitalizing power, drawing from a nondepletable source. If, with every inhalation, Hanish's followers took on new life, upon exhalation this force was simply returned to the universe much like in a circular economy, as if the transfer between oxygen and carbon dioxide did not exist. Mazdaznan would not be so esoteric if it was not for this occult force. But unlike *pneuma*, which was held to be omnipresent and which predated the findings of modern science by millennia, Ga-Llama could be elicited once desiring students learned "to breathe consciously in order to attract this vital essence."[58] The breathing exercises central to cultivating this force proved essential at the Weimar Bauhaus.[59]

Mazdaznan employed seven different rhythmic breathing exercises, all conducted in the same vein.[60] At the start, inhalation and exhalation were supposed to take four seconds, while one was asked to hold one's breath for one second in between. After some practice, one would slowly advance to breath intervals held for seven seconds. Utmost concentration was required during these exercises, and Hanish urged, "keep your mind centered on breathing only."[61] Distinguished simply by different body postures, the seven exercises were often complemented by rhythmic arm and body movements whose goal it was to draw ideal circles into the air.

No wonder such exercises would appeal to Itten. As preparatory activities, gymnastics and breathing exercises were consistent with Hanish's premise to overcome the division between spirit and body.[62] In Itten's system, breathing served as a gateway to both body and mind, bridging between the two realms to discharge maximum artistic energy.[63] Overcoming this separation, students in the preliminary course could ultimately give themselves over to their individual passions. While these exercises offered a promise of emancipation, they did so by forcing students into specific breathing rhythms, imposing discipline and order on their bodies. In Itten's view, gaining control of the body was an imperative for artistic production.

A sound architect such as Gropius was open-minded enough to have someone so eccentric as Itten run the most important Bauhaus course, at the end of which students were either fully admitted or rejected, but in the face of this occultism, his patience had its limits, and Itten left the school in 1923.[64] While Gropius was less concerned with the activities Itten conducted during class, he soon came to disagree about the school's strategic orientation: where Itten postulated a life in isolation, detached from the world of economics, Gropius increasingly called for closer ties with the industry. In 1921, Oskar Schlemmer observed two almost opposing worldviews in the culture of the Weimar Bauhaus. On one hand, there was a desire for self-realization, evinced by a fascination with Indian culture, a back-to-nature trend, and vegetarianism, and on the other hand, a gushing enthusiasm for American culture, technological progress, and the modern metropolis. The breathing activities Itten adopted from Hanish clearly belonged to the former.

Itten attracted a group of devoted followers and was vigorously hated by some of his adversaries. A kind of force field, possibly fueled by the literal and figurative inspiration of Ga-Llama, shielded Mazdaznan adherents within the Bauhaus circle, but the spell of this cult soon isolated Itten's disciples. Thanks to this growing eccentricity, his apprentices breathed more and more in solitude. Once, a guest was present during one of the seemingly grotesque exercises, and as Paul Citroen, one of Itten's students, infers, he "must really have thought us mad."[65] Breathing was also a covert strategy for defense when an unwelcome character appeared, and Citroen recalls: "I remember meeting a disagreeable person. Muche introduced him to me, and I started the appropriate breathing exercises immediately to make any contact with him impossible, to undercut any influence he might possibly have on me. The fellow noticed nothing of this, but Muche, who saw my nostrils flaring, was amused."[66]

Whereas breathing could be engaged in clandestine ways only noticeable by the initiated, the concomitant dietetic restrictions where more overt, with the smell of garlic penetrating the classrooms.[67] The Bauhaus canteen was under the spell of Mazdaznan rules too, and not necessarily a place to eat one's fill. The food in general was impeccable, although students often lacked the means to eat enough of what their bodies called for. Some students were less tolerant toward Mazdaznan cuisine; "a general undernourishment was the result, stomach and intestinal trouble the rule" and, as Citroen remembers, "our appearance what one might expect."[68]

The nutritional shortcomings in this orchestrated approach to life are no surprise, for Hanish, like others around that time, believed air by itself to be a kind of nourishment, and all it took was faith in his tenets and the cultivation of conscious breathing techniques. Some Bauhaus students began to look gaunt and frequented a local kitchen nearby, which, for little money, offered a large portion of barley soup.[69] The breathing exercises might have helped to loosen up muscles and gaits, tapping organically into the student's rhythm, but they did not compensate for an inadequate diet. These shortcomings notwithstanding, Itten corroborated the importance of breathing decades later. "As we breathe, so we think and conduct the rhythm of our daily routine," and breathing well has direct consequences.[70] Just as Wilhelm Flam declared, "As you breathe, so do you live," he claimed, "People who have achieved great success in their lives always breathe quietly, slowly, and deeply."[71] There was no need to expound the consequences for those who are short of breath.

Jaques-Dalcroze and Itten taught their students to breathe quietly and more deeply with the objective to tap into their inner rhythms, overcome inhibitions, and free their emotions.[72] Yet by characterizing the breathing rhythm as an essential component of avant-garde education, Jaques-Dalcroze and Itten introduced a major tension between freedom and discipline. For them, every act of artistic liberation was founded on a body politics that was also regulatory.

The Dissemination of Breathing Systems

The reform pedagogies at Hellerau and Weimar allowed art students to cultivate their own feelings according to their natural rhythms, and popular breathing systems for the general public emerged from a similar spirit. However, these systems were driven by more pragmatic concerns about health and fitness, focusing on body culture and voice. The purpose here is not to provide a comprehensive account of breathing techniques and their sociohistorical context around the turn of the twentieth century, nor is there room to discuss all publications on breath work from that period. Instead, the aim is to concentrate on a few exemplary cases that illustrate the almost obsessive theorization of breathing in respiratory modernism, often framed as an art and sometimes advanced in a dogmatic, formulaic style.[73] A contemporary critique of one book that likely applies to all similar works notes: "Whether they are the outcome of experience, or merely of a vivid therapeutic imagination, is not very clear."[74]

Concomitant with the development of breathing technologies designed to aid inhalation and exhalation, independent breathing techniques and physical exercises, which have a long tradition, experienced a significant resurgence in the second half of the nineteenth century. This revival was primarily intended to counteract lung diseases such as TB and various bodily ailments caused by modern lifestyles. These techniques often correlated with naturist practices and a proclivity for nudism, or the German *Freikörperkultur*, prevalent at the time—something I will mention only in passing. "Back to nature," the patent slogan of the *Lebensreform* movement, certainly heralded a return to the pristine countryside and an increasing estrangement from the industrialized city.[75]

But it also implied a return to the body. From the nineteenth century onward, proponents began to reiterate the importance of deep breathing, a practice forging particularly strong ties between the lungs and one's immediate environment.[76] In this line of thought, space was synonymous with air, and deep breathing implied taking in large volumes of it. The argument, broadly construed, is this: ordinary breathing occurs unconsciously and, without technique, remains too shallow to capitalize on the full volume of the lungs. A case in point is the German physician Daniel Gottlob Moritz Schreber (1808–1861), a pioneer of the allotment garden movement, who called for a return of children to nature as well as prescribing physical exercises, including shoulder lifts, to combat early signs of TB by improving upper thorax ventilation.[77] His 1855 book contains countless exercises, all of which are illustrated showing the body in motion as if in a double exposure. *Tiefathmen*, or deep breathing, he argued, is particularly suited to those pursuing a sedentary lifestyle. Although the overwhelming number of breathing systems were developed by men, around the turn of the twentieth century, body and breathing pedagogies were often advanced by bourgeois women such as Clara Schlaffhorst (1863–1945) and Hedwig Andersen (1866–1957). Despite publishing little, these women, who also adhered to Hanish's Mazdaznan doctrines, were no less influential.[78]

The Art of Breathing

Jørgen Peter Müller (1866–1938) was a Danish author and gymnastics educator who developed his own system of comprehensive exercises geared toward better health.[79] Franz Kafka, before succumbing to TB in 1917, was an avid follower. First published in 1904, Müller's self-help book *My System* advocates "moderation in smoking," getting eight hours of sleep, and deep-breathing exercises whose main objective it is to maximize the amount of air drawn in and out of the lungs.[80] The benefits of fresh air and proper breathing thus underpin Müller's physical exercises, which Kafka practiced in the nude twice a day in front of an open window. Emblazoned with an image of the Greek athlete Apoxyomenos, *My System* sought to transform its readers into iron men. In the corresponding section, Müller provides detailed instructions for deep-breathing techniques, especially with regard to the proper flow of air:

> Learn to move the lower ribs sideways, and also to "lengthen" the chest straight upwards like a concertina which is pulled out, by one handle being held put, the other down. The arms should help in this movement, the hands pressing upon the cup bones in a downward direction. A vacuum will thus be created, into which the air will rush of its own accord. The air then should not be drawn in by using the nose as a suction pump. The nose should only be a *passive* passage and that both for the inhaled and exhaled air.[81]

Müller compares this movement to an umbrella being opened. Exhalation follows the same logic in reverse order and is said to be even more important than inhalation, especially when performed deeply enough. To induce expiration, one simply relaxes both diaphragm and rib muscles, thereby reducing the space in the chest cavity. But then Müller goes on to detail how exhalation can be further deepened by engaging the small muscles between and beneath the lower ribs, "or quite mechanically by pressing the ribs together with the palms of the hands."[82]

The idea was not to offer something unusual, but to create an ordinary system that could seamlessly integrate into daily life, incorporating breathing exercises into everyday routines. Müller's bestsellers propose time-efficient sequences that could be easily adopted at home, making them accessible and practical for everyone. Thus tailored to a domestic scale and accessible to a broader audience, these daily exercises require no more than five minutes to be performed before breakfast or before going to bed.[83]

This system is entirely predicated on the premise that limbs are inevitably engaged in everyday activities, thereby placing emphasis on the human torso, which is to be strengthened by developing a "muscular corset" surrounding the main organs. As a refuge from the detrimental effects of modern society, gymnastics in Müller's system is but one strand of a more holistic approach to life that also involved regular meals, functional clothing, baths and exposure to air.

Despite its focus on health and fitness, the system inevitably fell short of guarding against "the germ of death itself," as Kafka described his TB.[84] Even if to breathe with deliberation could maintain "the elasticity of the respiratory organs," as Müller claimed, it was no cure for bacterial infections.[85] But Müller believed consumption could be prevented "merely by teaching the children proper breathing," as he maintains in one of his subsequent books.[86] *My Breathing System* (1921) focuses more specifically on deep breathing and its associated "machinery," featuring numerous illustrations in the form of cross-sectional cuts through the human torso and photographs of Müller demonstrating the correct and incorrect techniques of breathing (fig. 2.12). "Of course everybody *does* breathe after a fashion," Müller confesses, "otherwise they would die. But few understand how to breathe, inhale and exhale, correctly." Time and again he reminds us to "inflate and empty the lungs to their utmost limits," incidentally stressing the importance of breathing through the nose (fig. 2.13).[87]

Most of Müller's concerns are common knowledge today. A good breath, after all, is still one that almost effortlessly supplies the body with fresh air in a short amount of time. But one hundred years ago, his instructions fell on fertile ground: promoting free access of air to the lungs, introducing different breathing techniques, drawing attention to the diaphragm and its role inside the thorax, strengthening the thorax, and inflating and emptying the lungs to their utmost extent. By the 1920s, his approach was so rooted in German culture that the verb *müllern* was used synonymously for doing gymnastics.

For example, Mülleresque deep breathing was promoted in the popular 1925 silent movie *Wege zu Kraft und Schönheit* (Ways to strength and beauty), a documentary about healthy lifestyles in Weimar Germany that sought to countervail the detrimental effects of life in the modern metropolis.[88] Promoting gymnastics and an active lifestyle more generally, many of the film's tenets are in accordance with the *Lebensreform* movement, but are also more specific in other regards. To improve poor posture in modern citizens, the film proposes crawling exercises for children and discourages slouching at work, recommending daily physical exercises—especially using wall bars—as an effective countermeasure. What is more important,

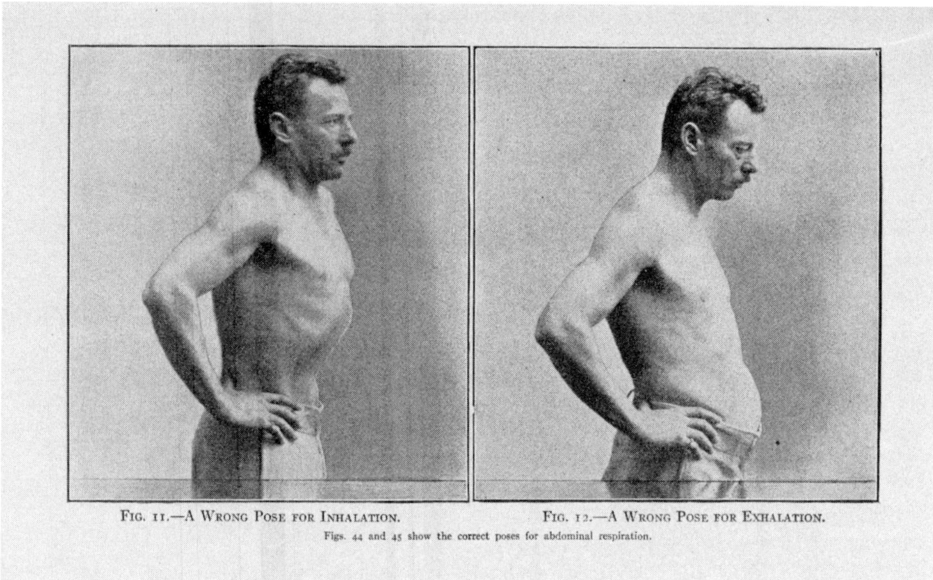

Figure 2.12. Incorrect breathing, demonstrated by Jørgen Peter Müller. J. P. Muller, *My Breathing System* (London: Link House Athletic Publications, 1921), figures 11–12, p. 39.

however, is the attention drawn to breathing, an activity heavily strained in the event of slouching, a posture that restricts the body's ability to perform deep breathing. An animated juxtaposition of two cross sections through the torso—one upright and the other slouched—demonstrates the extent to which the diaphragm's movement is enabled in one case while hindered in the other. "Regular breathing," a title card states, "is an interplay of movements between the rib cage and the belly that should be practiced every day."[89] Two subsequent sections vividly illustrate the movements involved in chest breathing and belly breathing through parallel montages of a real body and an animated drawing, both expanding and contracting

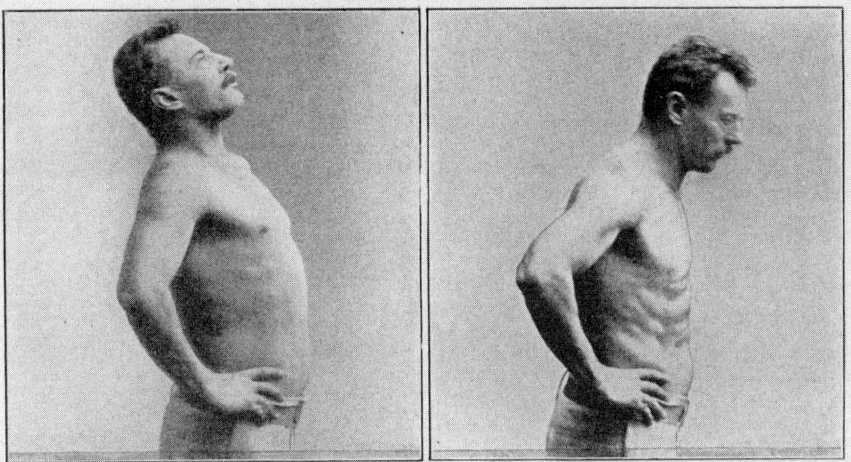

FIG. 15.—THE CORRECT POSE FOR INHALATION, SIDE VIEW.

FIG. 16.—THE CORRECT POSE FOR EXHALATION, SIDE VIEW.

Figure 2.13. Correct breathing, demonstrated by Jørgen Peter Müller. J. P. Muller, *My Breathing System* (London: Link House Athletic Publications, 1921), figures 15–16, p. 43.

in synchrony. While the former, depicting the body from the outside, serves a descriptive purpose, the latter, revealing the body from inside, operates on an analytical plane. The viewer thus gains an understanding of the interplay between the rib cage and diaphragm, almost as if watching an X-ray film penetrating the body.

While Müller's concept of breath work is more rooted in health than in occultism, esotericism, or spiritual ideas of rhythm, it propagated similar notions of air as a vital nutrient and introduced physical activities to a general audience outside the purview of avant-garde schools, notions that were not unlike those taught by Itten. Müller's theories of breathing were disseminated through his numerous books, many of which were reprinted in multiple editions. Despite their multifaceted nature, all these theories essentially boil down to one key concept: *deep breathing*. And breathing itself could involve more than just expanding the lungs.

Enhanced Deep Breathing: Skin Breathing

Müller was so influential at the time that many trailed behind him, amplifying his ideas, even when they critiqued them. All their books aim to counteract shallow breathing, promote deep breathing, and highlight the complexities of the respiratory tract. This complexity is illustrated by statistical data, numerous depictions of lungs, ribs, trachea, and alveoli, and, more importantly, bodies demonstrating the correct breathing techniques (fig. 2.14).

One example of a critic wo nevertheless expanded upon Müller's work is the Swiss physician and naturopath Adolf Keller-Hoerschelmann (1879–1969), who both acknowledged Müller's merits and found fault with his focus on physical exercises. Müller's work primarily focused on exercises engaging the trunk muscles crucial for health, and Keller-Hoerschelmann sought to rectify this purported shortcoming by placing even more emphasis on breathing—literally expanding on his work by emphasizing a role not only for the lungs, but for the skin in healthy breathing.

From 1907 on, Keller-Hoerschelmann directed the Fellenberg sanatorium in Erlenbach, near Lake Zurich, where Kafka briefly sought recovery in 1911 from hypochondria and a general sense of physical weakness.[90] During his tenure, Keller-Hoerschelmann published several works, including *Mein Atmungssystem* (My breathing system) in 1911, where he advocates deep breathing, ideally in the nude, not just to aerate the lungs, but also to allow the skin to perform its function as an excretory organ, thereby cleansing the blood and the body. Keller-Hoerschelmann holds that deep breathing could activate the body from inside out, enhance resistance to weakness and ailments, properly ventilate the lungs, and ultimately prevent disruptions in metabolism and blood circulation.

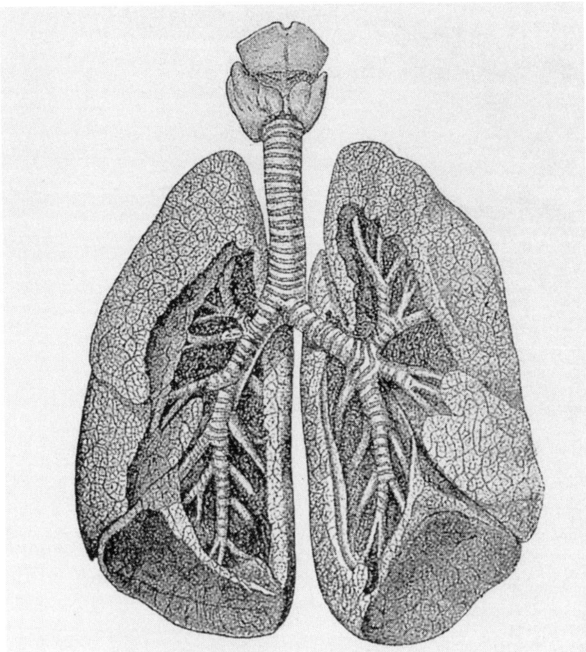

Figure 2.14. Lungs as shown in Keller-Hoerschelmann's *Mein Atmungssystem* with superior, middle, and interior lobes cut open to reveal internal anatomy. Adolf Keller-Hoerschelmann, *Mein Atmungssystem: Bestes Buch praktischer Gesundheitspflege!*, 2nd ed. (Olten: Herm. Hambrecht, 1911), p. 40. Urs Boschung, personal copy.

Like Müller, Keller-Hoerschelmann stresses thorough exhalation for proper lung function and overall health. The best lung is one that can exhale the most air and the longest, for only this ability prepares the organ to take in a good dose of oxygen. He also emphasizes the importance of breathing clean air, a quality not always prioritized in other systems. Keller-Hoerschelmann urges that "deep breathing during strenuous work in a dusty, poorly ventilated workshop inside would be a kind of slow suicide and no one will be tempted to do this. My breathing system should therefore always be carried out in the best air," something Switzerland was blessed with.[91]

This focus on the skin as an organ of respiration was also characteristic of the work of the most widely read physical culturist in Germany at the time, Hans Surén (1885–1972), a major proponent of the naturist movement in Weimar Germany influenced by Müller,

Figure 2.15. Hans Surén posing like a bronze sculpture, inhaling effortlessly. Hans Surén, *Atemgymnastik*, 42nd ed. (Stuttgart: Franck'sche Verlagshandlung, 1935), plate 62, p. 100. Staatsbibliothek Berlin.

and later a member of the Nazi Party. This affiliation was perhaps foreshadowed in his *Atemgymnastik* (Breathing exercises) and was explicitly disclosed in many later editions of his books, some of which he renamed accordingly.[92] Surén was a former physical training instructor in the army, and his breathing system was the most formulaic of all, even if he himself was rather disdainful of military discipline. His renowned books are filled with photographs of his own body, sometimes partially covered and at times nude, often isolated from the background. Idealized through his glossy skin, the images aestheticize his postures, making Surén appear statuelike. The oily coating of the male model speaks directly to the weight Surén places on the skin as a mediating surface central to his ideal of the pneumatic body (fig. 2.15). In the absence of skin oil, he avers, the skin's functioning could be significantly impaired, a condition to be prevented at all costs: "The skin has great influence on the respiratory center. The forces working in it are so wonderful that they are not yet fully recognized in their wealth and depth. The skin breathes too! . . . Even if its portion in the total respiration is small, it is nevertheless inevitable that a person dies if it fails."[93]

You may recall the scene in James Bond's *Goldfinger* where Sean Connery, as Bond, is in a hotel room attempting to retrieve a bottle of chilled Dom Pérignon from the refrigerator. Goldfinger's assistant, Oddjob, knocks him out with a karate chop to the neck. When Bond regains consciousness, he finds the faithless secretary, Jill Masterson, dead in bed, her skin entirely covered in gold paint. This scene is founded on that cultural trope.

The skin is the ultimate interface between an individual's inside and outside, between the human organism and the environment.[94] The obsession with deep breathing and its extension to this interface reveals a desire to engage fully with and absorb the external world, beyond just a naturist practice, as a way to rekindle our connection with nature. This desire deeply ingrained in the body culture of the turn of the century, also became emblematic of the modern movement in architecture, as we will see next.

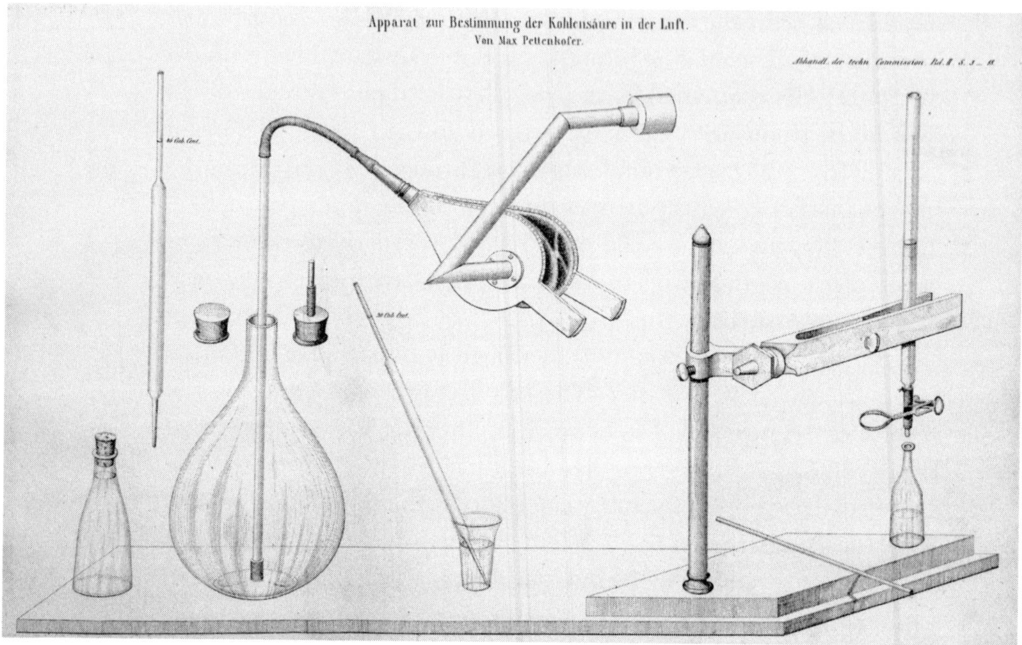

Figure 3.1. Apparatus to determine the amount of carbon dioxide in the air. Max Pettenkofer, *Über den Luftwechsel in Wohngebäuden* (Munich: Literarisch-Artistische Anstalt der J. G. Cotta'schen Buchhandlung, 1858), foldout.

CHAPTER THREE

Breathing Walls

In December 1857, "on a chilly and hazy day," Pettenkofer locked himself in his office, the crevices of which he had meticulously sealed with glue-soaked writing paper.[1] His objective was to determine how well the solid elements of architecture—floor, ceiling, and walls—facilitate air exchange by virtue of diffusion. As an index of bad air, Pettenkofer took the measure of carbon dioxide and its gradual replacement by outside air as proof and measure of the air change rate in his office and in interiors more generally (fig. 3.1). To ensure no air escaped through unintended openings, he even sealed the keyhole and door frame upon entering. He was worried about CO_2 poisoning, having nearly experienced it in a previous experiment in which he burned wood charcoal in a small air furnace to monitor airflow in his office by evacuating the room's air and promoting its replacement. To prevent a recurrence of the earlier intoxication, he repeated the experiment using carbonic acid derived from double-carbonated sodium bicarbonate. Despite the meticulous sealing of his office, the fire in the oven continued to burn vigorously, indicating a continuous influx of air from the outside. With an anemometer, an instrument invented by Leon Battista Alberti to measure wind speed and direction, he was able to document the amount of air flowing into the oven, taking painstaking notes and marshaling his empirical findings. When he compared these results with earlier ones recorded without sealing his office, he found only marginal differences. The brick walls of his office must be porous, Pettenkofer conjectured, a property of the material that he had surmised for years. Like skin, he found, walls breathe.

In 1851, Pettenkofer had published an article on the various effects of heating technologies on air quality in which he pondered the porosity of certain building materials, such as plaster.[2] That walls leaked water was fairly uncontested in the mid-nineteenth century—the visible effects of excess moisture, such as mold or cracked paint, were clearly visible on surfaces—but questioning the airtightness of walls was quite uncommon at the time. If anything, walls were thought to be structural elements, not mediators between different atmospheres. Contrary to these common beliefs, Pettenkofer set out to demonstrate the permeability of brick and solid matter, for if water was able to penetrate the pores of building materials, they must contain hidden voids capable of hosting foreign substances, to the detriment of the dwellers within. And if water could penetrate what appeared to be impermeable material, air could do so all the more.

Defining the extreme poles of architectural enclosure, in the article, Pettenkofer observes that dwellings are either "hermetically sealed" or have interiors whose air is "in a diffusion relationship with the free atmosphere."[3] Although he refers to air renewal and gas diffusion, rather than breathing, Pettenkofer hints at epidermic qualities when asserting that "it is a completely erroneous view to consider the cracks in our windows and doors as the sole sources of air renewal in our rooms, and to ignore the myriad pores in our walls."[4]

This analogy of walls with human skin shaped Pettenkofer's thinking. In fact, he himself was straightforward about making the comparison. As he put it, "the pores of our walls can be as important as the pores of the epidermis of our body—as the pores in the limestone shell of the bird egg." An eggshell hermetically sealed with oil would stifle the embryo inside, suspending "the communication between the air in the egg and the outer atmosphere."[5] Replace

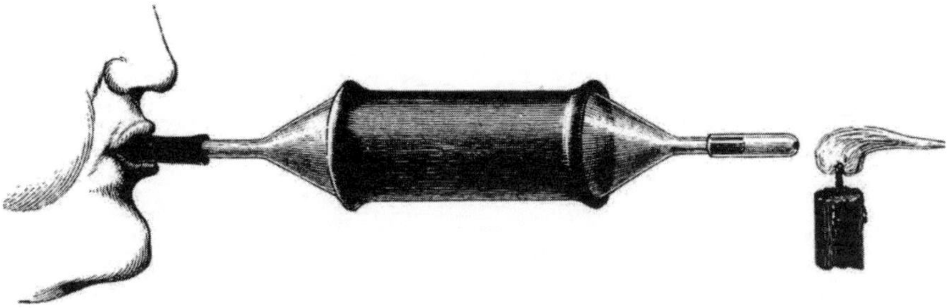

Figure 3.2. Pettenkofer demonstrating the permeability of mortar by nearly extinguishing a candle. Max von Pettenkofer, *Beziehungen der Luft zu Kleidung, Wohnung und Boden: Drei Populäre Vorlesungen* (Braunschweig: Druck und Verlag von Friedrich Vieweg und Sohn, 1872), p. 42.

"egg" with "house," and you get the principal idea of this line of thought. In this chain of analogies at the confluence of physiology and architecture, the problem of the barrier in its potential effects on the well-being of human and animal life was posed.[6]

To bolster his findings, Pettenkofer sealed a brick on four sides with a mix of wax, oil, and resin, leaving the two front faces exposed, which he covered with sheet metal featuring a small hole in the center and a pipe attached perpendicularly.[7] Encased in this airtight seal, the brick allowed air to pass through when it was introduced from either end of the pipes, making the passage of air through seemingly solid matter visible as it bubbled out from the other end when it was submerged in water. In a drawing included in his lectures published in 1872, the experiment is illustrated in different form: a figure with inflated cheeks blows air into a glass funnel, one of which is fixed with an airtight seal on either side of a cylindrical piece of mortar, "covered all over with melted wax."[8] On the verge of being extinguished, a candle flickers at the opposite end (fig. 3.2).[9] Years later,

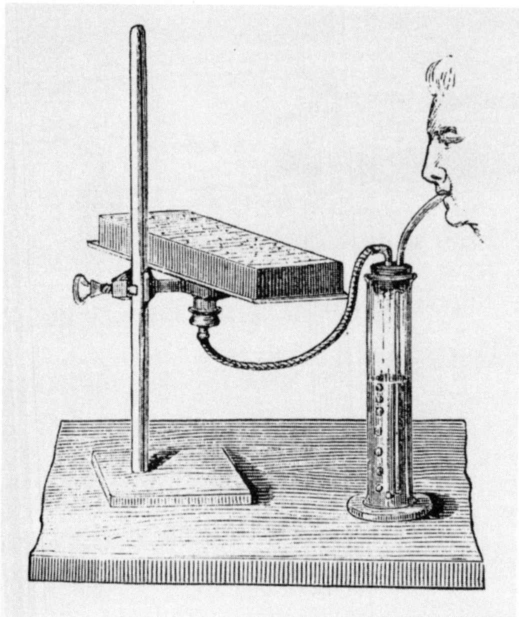

Figure 3.3. Fodor demonstrating the permeability of a brick by inhaling through a rubber tube. Josef von Fodor, *Das gesunde Haus und die gesunde Wohnung* (Braunschweig: Druck und Verlag von Friedrich Vieweg und Sohn, 1878), p. 33.

when Fodor revisited Pettenkofer's findings to emphasize the porosity of certain building materials, he inverted the experiment, asking, "Who would believe that one could breathe through a brick?"[10] Here, it was not a forceful exhalation but the act of inhalation that demonstrated the material's permeability: in the experiment, as air is drawn through the brick and into a glass jar, rising bubbles serve as indexical signs of its porosity (fig. 3.3). In Pettenkofer's writings, the wall, composed of such materials, thus reveals that instead of being a barrier between inner and outer, it has its own workings—like skin. As he put it in one of his lectures, "As you can see, even the wall for me has a life of its own, its own physiology."[11]

The concept of skin in architecture has long been a notion associated with the modern movement, where the use of the term signals the shift from a load-bearing exterior wall to a material layer that simply encloses the interior, wrapping around a structural framework.[12] But while the metaphor of the wall as skin traditionally underscores the structural change that began from the turn of the twentieth century onward, it also retains semantic traces that evoke other organic qualities of skin, especially its permeability, its ability to mediate between inside and outside, as well as its ability to protect against a hostile environment—qualities whose analogical application to architecture have evolved throughout history. In fact, the wall-skin comparison is one that predates modern construction techniques in the nineteenth century and extends beyond the one-dimensional concept of the nonstructural wall. This chapter examines several episodes that reveal the complexities of this metaphoric constellation within a broader cultural context of respiratory modernism and in relation to the breathing culture portrayed in this book.

The focal point of this reflection is a confluence of medical and architectural ideas in the design and critique of architectural enclosures in the modern period. I want to describe not how the status of the wall changed from a load-bearing element to an enclosing building skin, but rather modern conceptions of that shift that focused on breathing walls, protective walls, and the cultural discourses that surround these conceptions. My subject is thus not technology, but the real and perceived properties of skin and wall as understood in medical sciences, architectural theory, and broader cultural contexts. Skin, evoking both corporeal and architectural connotations, may be seen as something anatomically irreducible, organic and vital. At the same time, it can also be metaphorical, implying elasticity, permeability, tensile properties, or thinness, with inescapable associations to the body.

Viewed in these terms, the status of the wall underwent a significant transformation in modernist architecture. It is not just the case that structural advances brought about by new industrial materials—such as iron, reinforced concrete, and large-format glass—combined with standardized design, mass production, and innovative assembly techniques, allowed a shift in architectonic composition from solid walls to building skins, often seen as transparent in nature. This transformation in construction also was accompanied by a change in language. When the term "wall" was replaced by "skin," modernist architecture also introduced a flurry of terms that denoted the same phenomenon such as, "curtain wall," "screen," "glass skin," and "membrane" among them, each of which conceptualizes a building as an enclosure that can be stretched around a supporting structure.

"Theoretically," as Curt Walter Behrendt (1884–1945), architect and editor of *Die Form*, remarked in 1927, "a material of membrane-like strength would be sufficient for this purpose."[13] The underlying model of the house as skeleton is expressed nowhere better than in Le Corbusier's famous diagram of the Maison Dom-Ino from 1914, a prototype whose open floor plan and modular structure entails all primary architectural elements except for enclosing walls—concrete slabs, thin posts, foundations and a stairway for vertical circulation (fig. 3.4). This model is also expressed in Mies van der Rohe's dictum of skin-and bones-architecture, which draws on yet another biological analogy.[14]

There is of course an inherent difference between actual skin and the metaphorical "building skin": materials such as brick infill, curtain walls, large glass panes, and cement plaster applied on the exterior of a building lack the stretchiness and sensory qualities of true skin. The comparisons at the heart of any metaphor always can be disaggregated into the differences between what the metaphor melds into a single term. While the metaphor of the wall conceived of as skin retained the functions of permeability and communication as the basis of this comparison while still also retaining its role as a boundary, skin's numerous other properties—elasticity, sensation, pigmentation, the potential for self-renewal, and its alleged role as mirror of the soul—are not so easily attributed to the building wall. But the use of metaphors can have material consequences and inform programs for action.[15] A metaphor becomes a conceptual model.

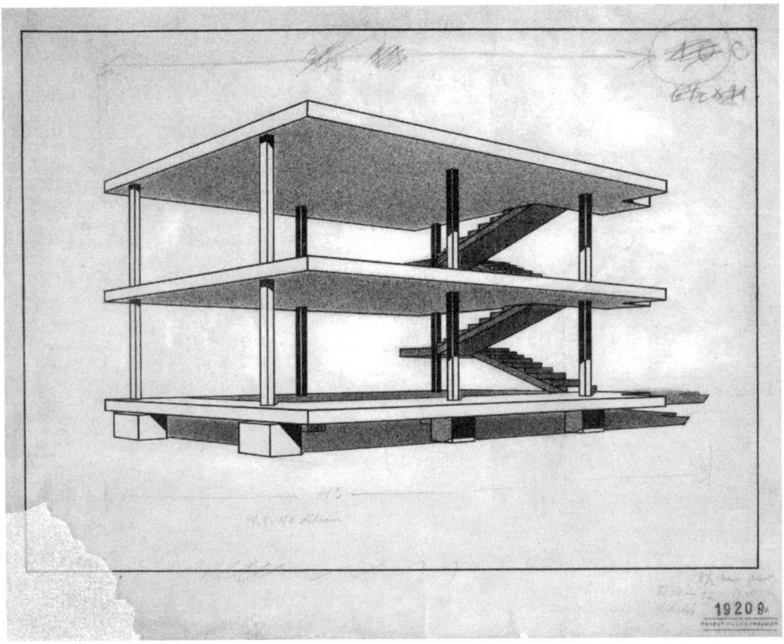

Figure 3.4. Maison Dom-Ino as a skeletal house waiting to be wrapped by a membrane. Le Corbusier, Maison Dom-Ino © F.L.C./ Bildrecht, Wien 2025.

The Wall as Skin: Permeable Walls

The metaphor of wall as skin functioned as a conceptual model in this way in a variety of domains and disciplines: those dealing with walls often refer to them as skin, while others dealing with skin frequently draw analogies to walls. In the case of the former, we can think of architects and architecture theorists; for the latter, we can think of physicians and philosophers. To see this, we can look to the works of Alberti and Plato, but also to how the metaphor has been employed since then, from the eighteenth and nineteenth centuries to the twentieth.

The metaphoric use of skin in architectural theory had been already employed by Alberti. In book 3 of his *On the Art of Building in Ten Books* (*De Re Aedificatoria*, 1452), he offers prescriptions about the composition of walls with an eye toward the longevity of a structure: "There are two types of skin, the inner and the outer. If the outer skin is made of hard stone, the durability of the building will be improved."[16] Between these two skins, an infill serves to hold together both layers, and Alberti admonishes his readers to take great care in ensuring "that the courses on either side are bonded together and level."[17] But it is not just skin, but its permeability that serves as the basis of comparison in many of these metaphorical conceptualizations. Such was the case in the *Timaeus*, where long before Alberti, Plato had conceived of skin as a "body wall"—Heinrich Boruttau called it a *Körperwand* or *Leibeswand*, in his 1909 synopsis of breathing theories—the part of the body that Plato held to be permeable to air.[18] Plato saw the relationship between the universe and the human organism as governed by a cyclic process of elements flowing in and out of the body, air being a crucial agent, and saw what we now refer to as skin as a "net" with which God "enveloped all the hollow parts of our body." The body thus is essentially porous:

> the net he made to find a way in and out through the pores of the body, and the rays of fire which are bound fast within followed the passage of the air either way, never at any time ceasing so long as the mortal being holds together. This process, as we affirm, the name-giver named inspiration and expiration. And all this movement, active as well as passive, takes place in order that the body, being watered and cooled, may receive nourishment and life.[19]

The skin breathes. and upon inhalation, external air merges with the inner fire residing in every human body, sustaining this fire's ability to aid in the digestion of nutrients in the abdomen through the continuous intake and expulsion of air. Exhalation then causes the surrounding air to penetrate the skin: "Seeing that there is no such thing as a vacuum into which any of those things which are moved can enter, and the breath is carried from us into the external air . . . the breast and the lungs, when they emit the breath, are replenished by the air which surrounds the body and which enters in through the pores of the flesh and is driven round in a circle; and again, the air which is sent away and passes out through the body forces the breath inwards through the passage of the mouth and the nostrils."[20]

"The image of the skin as a wall" is a literary and cultural topos with a deep "iconographic and metaphorical" heritage, as literary scholar Claudia Benthien has shown.[21] Generally, the basis of comparison has been its impermeable, protective function. The skin is often imagined not as "sacklike and soft," but rather as a "static and solid" boundary that envelopes the body, "a hollow, vessel-like space." Seen in this way, both skin and a house provide shelter, and both are "inhabited." This metaphor extends to the body's openings, which are likened to doors and windows, allowing selective sensory interaction with the outside world,[22] an image that renders the skin as "a stony wall, a static and impermeable boundary between the self and the world."[23]

However, Benthien shows, in the eighteenth century, the metaphor based on the permeability of skin prevailed, with its various openings distinguished only by size, not by function, so that pores and other bodily orifices — eyes, mouth, ears — were all seen as serving similar purposes, acting as exits for something that had to be channeled out of the body. The skin thus was seen less as a solid wall with operable windows and doors and more as a "porous tissue," much like Pettenkofer's wall, that could have openings anywhere.[24]

In the mid-nineteenth century, as we've seen, a similar understanding emerged, when walls and skins were conceived as interfaces where ostensibly independent systems — inside and outside — meet and interact. When Pettenkofer, the physiologist, refutes the idea of the stony wall as an impermeable boundary in

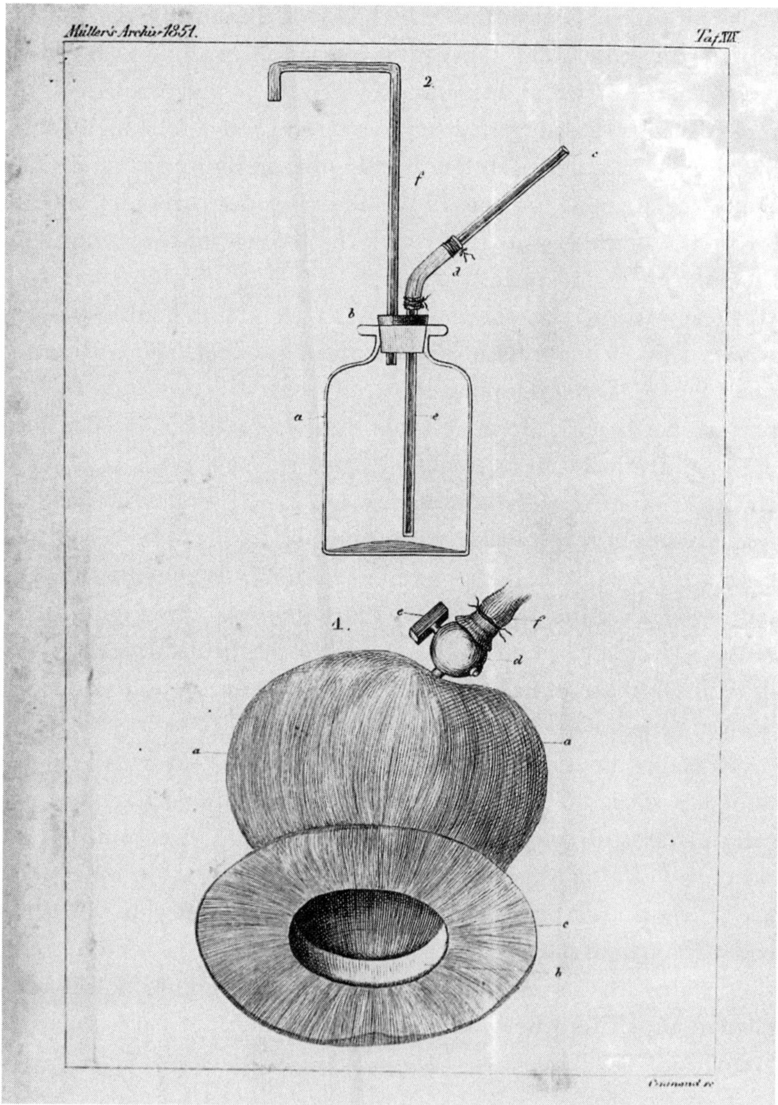

Figure 3.5. Sealed horse bladder to demonstrate cutaneous breathing. Joseph von Gerlach, "Über das Hautathmen," *Archiv für Anatomie, Physiologie und wissenschaftliche Medicin* (1851), table 19.

his writings, he also cautions us to ignore the numerous tiny pores present in the walls.[25]

Pettenkofer's experiments put a modern, scientific foundation under the comparison, as old as Plato's, of walls to skin. In 1851, the same year Pettenkofer formulated his conception of the porous wall, experiments conducted by the German professor of anatomy Joseph von Gerlach (1820–1896) provided the first modern scientific evidence that, like walls, skin breathes. Despite the lungs actually being the largest organ directly exposed to the surrounding air, thanks to their vast internal surface area, Gerlach presumed some involvement of the skin in the process of gas exchange, a presumption he sought to verify in a variety of ways, including by trapping atmospheric air inside a horse bladder (fig. 3.5). Gerlach also sealed the skin of rabbits and horses with warm linseed oil and measured their respiration and pulse rates, both of which increased during his tests.[26] Animals coated twice with oil had no chance to recover, and rabbits died in less than two days.[27] Epidermic involvement in breathing, he demonstrated in these experiments, even if it appears to be only slight, "is nevertheless always considerable enough in the long run to regard it as indispensable beside the actual respiratory process."[28]

It was indispensable, because while the lungs take in more oxygen than they release carbon dioxide, the opposite holds true for the skin. Gerlach diagnosed two opposing trends that together formed the driving force behind breathing: an "affinity" (*Verwandtschaft*) between oxygen and the human blood, and carbon dioxide's "ambition" (*Bestreben*) to escape from the blood, leading him to the conclusion that "only the blood breathes, technically speaking," and the skin, like the lungs, is nothing but a permeable boundary, like Pettenkofer's wall.[29]

Prior to Gerlach's scientific confirmation, David Boswell Reid had also intuited the then-speculative connection between the skin and the respiratory system, noting that the condition of the skin and the process of transpiration have a significant impact on respiration. In his *Illustrations of the Theory and Practice of Ventilation* from 1844, he notes that "the surface of the skin has the power, like the surface of the lungs, of absorption and exhalation."[30] Reid assumed that the condition and function of the skin can vary greatly among individuals, with some exhibiting very low levels of skin perspiration, which leads to an excessive amount of perspiration from the lungs. When the skin's functions are suppressed, however, the lungs often compensate with increased activity, a situation that can be alleviated once the skin's normal functions are restored. To gain a better understanding of ventilation, architects and engineers first needed to understand the process of breathing. Physiological conceptions offered a framework that extended beyond the technicalities of construction, introducing universal ideas directly tied to an understanding of the human and animal body—ideas that were simultaneously epistemic, social, and political in nature. The skin is a selective boundary, open to certain things while impenetrable for others. In this way, the body offered a medico-scientific framework for conceptualizing the house. As a scientific product of the 1850s, this conception of the openness of the human body and the house is a discernible shift in modern architecture's approach to the wall, an approach informed by an underlying awareness of all things respiratory and pneumatic. This was one paradigm that informed the ways people thought about walls, skin, and health as the era of modern architecture began. This is why, in *The American Woman's Home*, the Beecher sisters could explain that

> in the skin of every adult there are no less than seven million minute perspiration tubes, each one fourth of an inch long. If all this were united in one length, they would extend twenty-eight miles. These minute tubes are lined with capillary blood-vessels, which are constantly sending out not only carbonic acid, but other gases and particles of decayed matter. The skin and lungs together, in one day and night, throw out three quarters of a pound of charcoal as carbonic acid, beside other gases and water.[31]

The Wall as Skin: Protective Walls

A quintessential example of the paradigm of walls and skin as permeable membranes is to be found, also in 1851, in the Caribbean hut that Gottfried Semper (1803–1879) found in Joseph Paxton's renowned Crystal Palace — a temporary structure in London's Hyde Park constructed for the Great Exhibition mounted there that year, the first of the nineteenth century's world's fairs, and often said to be the beginning of modern architectural history in many traditional Western accounts and syllabi. In his famous *Die vier Elemente der Baukunst* (The four elements of architecture, 1851), in which Semper elaborates on the analogy, the wall's forerunner appears in form of a braided rug, a piece of textile used to enclose interior space,[32] and as braided tree branches or woven grass blades, which Semper sees as the primordial manifestation of space especially in favorable climates.[33] As architectural historian Ákos Moravánszky pointed out, the most important element in architecture for Semper is thus the product of a lightweight, unstable material with no connection to the ground, but one instead associated with the air, architecture flapping in the wind.[34]

For Semper, the etymological proximity between the German words *Wand* (wall), and *Gewand* (garment), attests to this genealogy and conforms to a set of conceptions of human skin;[35] it is permeable, elastic, flexible, nonstructural, and unconnected to the ground. But etymology indicates another proximity Semper did not think about: that between the German words *Haus* (house) and *Haut* (skin), the common root of which implied to cover or protect something.[36] The linguistic and functional kinship suggests that the house, with its walls, protects the human organism from external conditions. Like skin, the wall also was seen as protection against what is outside — in architecture, a barrier between the interior of the building and the city, between a welcoming space and the vicissitudes of the exterior atmosphere.

That conception of the metaphor of walls as skin could exist as a complement to the paradigm of walls as permeable, as allowing

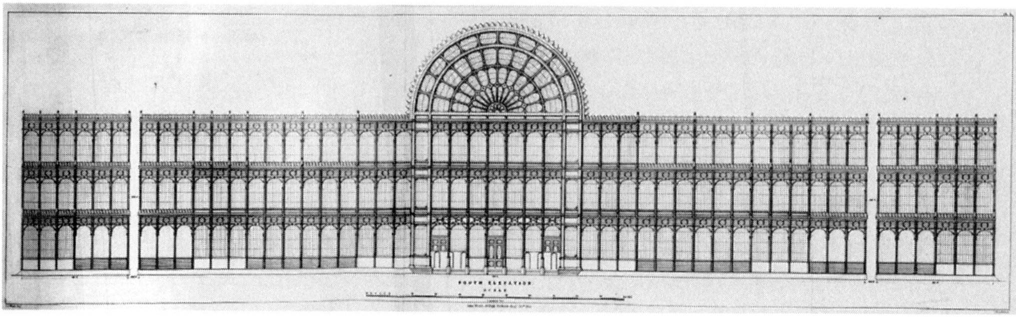

Figure 3.6. Crystal Palace, south elevation. Charles Downes and Charles Cowper, *The Building Erected in Hyde Park for the Great Exhibition of the Works of Industry of All Nations, 1851* (London: John Weale, 1852), plate 4.

the outside inside and the inside outside. Indeed, at the Great Exhibition, walls deployed as barriers literally enclosed the permeable walls that Semper found on exhibit in the Caribbean hut.

The boundary wall of the Crystal Palace was nearly an all-glass envelope (fig. 3.6). Although much discussed in other ways, the Crystal Palace warrants special attention in the context of walls as skin and the relations of buildings to public health. In many respects, the structure was first and foremost about climate, air, and eventually about breathing, but in a way that segregated healthy from unhealthy environments. As a modular, prefabricated construction made of timber, cast iron, and plate glass, the Crystal Palace drew from a lineage of modern greenhouses, which can be viewed as early models of architectural climate control.[37]

Joseph Paxton (1803–1865), a horticulturist and architect with experience in constructing greenhouses, designed the Crystal Palace to house international exhibits ranging from art and technology to colonial raw materials while also accommodating three preexisting elm trees. His objective was to create a space with more genial air than the polluted atmosphere of London at the time, essentially shielding visitors from the outside world.[38] Paxton was an astute observer of all things climatic and knew about the insalubrious air of London, which he observed over many months as "impure, murky, and unfit for healthy recreation and enjoyment."[39] Because the exhibition was intended to be temporary, the structure was impermanent, and despite Paxton's appeal to retain it at its original site after the world's fair, the Crystal Palace was translocated to South London, where it survived until its destruction by fire in 1936.

Prior to this relocation, Paxton proposed what we now call adaptive reuse—repurposing a structure for a different program—in his short piece *What Is to Become of the Crystal Palace?* In this instance, the proposition entailed converting an exhibition venue into a winter garden to provide a safe and healthy environment for London's residents with the city's perilous atmosphere in mind.

The nineteenth century was an age of overcrowded workers' housing, air pollution, and cholera outbreaks. Dwellings, especially those for the poor, were built so "that the clammy air cannot escape," a condition that Friedrich Engels (1820–1895) bemoans in his study on the working class in England. Depleted of oxygen, the metropolitan atmosphere of industrial cities was not only strained by "two and a half million pairs of lungs," as in the case of London, but also by the many burning fires whose carbon dioxide remained in the streets, because of its specific weight.[40] Coupled with the unsanitary conditions endured by the lower classes, who were often crammed into overcrowded rooms with bad air, the polluted atmosphere outside compounded the suffocating environment for many workers, so much so that "the air which they breathe at night is enough to stifle them," Engels writes in 1845.[41]

This repurposed version of the Crystal Palace as Paxton envisioned it, could be taken as a way to give Londoners literal breathing space, a structure designed to sustain an artificial environment distinct from the polluted air of London. Through oxygen-producing photosynthesis of CO_2, the atmosphere inside would have been thoroughly oxygenated, invigorating Londoners visiting this public space while also buoying their spirits.

For Paxton, this proposed "*Winter Park and Garden* under glass" was far more than a simple reprogramming of an exhibition space soon to be abandoned: it was part of a socio-ecological strategy.[42] Indeed, "climate would be the principle thing studied," as Paxton declared, a climate that is heated and ventilated solely for the promotion of health and what he had in mind specifically was the climate of Southern Italy.

> Here vegetation in much of its beauty might be studied with unusual advantages and the singular properties examined of those great filterers of Nature, which during the night season, when the bulk of animal life are in a quiescent state, inhale the oxygen of the air, whilst in the day, when the mass of animal existence have started into activity, they drink in the carbonic supply, given out by man and animals, which goes to form their solid substance, at the same time during forth streams of oxygen, which mingling with the surrounding atmosphere, gives vigour to man's body and cheerfulness to his spirits.[43]

It was against this backdrop that Paxton offered his recommendation to convert the former exhibition hall into a breathing space, the boundaries of which were nearly all glass — a greenhouse for the cultivation of Londoners.[44] This vision was not just a response to the immediate needs of the industrial era, but also a forward-thinking attempt to create a healthier, more sustainable environment in the heart of London. It also meant that, despite the numerous operable vents incorporated into the glass-skin of the Crystal Palace, Paxton envisioned its reused interior as a bubble climatically isolated from London's atmosphere.

Glass Skins and Airtight Buildings

But as Pettenkofer had proved, no building is airtight — no building *can* be airtight — nor should it be. The genealogy of glass-enclosed building after the Crystal Palace, brought that lesson home to architects in the early twentieth century. The Fagus shoe-last factory in Alfeld-an-der-Leine, designed by the young architects Adolf Meyer (1881–1929) and Walter Gropius (1883–1969) when they established their own practice after working in the Berlin office of Peter Behrens (1886–1940), is a classic case in point, owing to its extensive use of glass in which "the role of the walls," Gropius notes in his classic *The New Architecture and the Bauhaus* (1937), "becomes restricted to that of mere screens stretched between the upright columns of the framework to keep out rain, cold, and noise."[45]

The great founding myth of modern architecture in Western accounts, when not ascribed to the Crystal Palace from 1851, has frequently been attributed to the Fagus Factory. It was the factory's facade, its use of glass as skin—that elevated the building into one of the most influential structures of the modern movement. But there was a problem with the building that had not been anticipated by Meyer and Gropius. Drafty from early on, the main production hall suffered from a partial vacuum caused by a "high suction pressure of the shavings exhaust," resulting in effects of the facade that have little to do with how it is commonly described: Whenever someone opened the door of the main hall, the facade would sag inward due to abrupt changes in air pressure, and correspondingly, it would balloon outward when the door closed.[46] Through this swelling and sagging movement was the building literally breathing.

This constant breathing of the structure, while otherwise invisible to the naked eye, placed unnecessary strain on essential parts of the building. Over time, these undesired effects caused several more problems, wearing down the materials used for the facade. The movement gradually compromised the rustproof coating on the mullions, leading to water seepage and significant condensation inside. This excess moisture accelerated the corrosion, damaging the facade from both the inside and outside at the same time. Ideally a straight line in section, the facade soon began to undulate toward the bottom, "like a sack of potatoes."[47] The protruding floor slabs sagged over time with changing wind pressures, further spurring the deformation of the facade. This material deterioration of the factory's enclosure resulted from the Fagus Factory's sense of *pneuma*, animating one of early modern architecture's seminal works. Seen in the context of respiratory modernism, it was precisely this quality that made the Fagus Factory truly modern.

The project served as a stepping stone to an architectural career for Gropius and led to a kind of sequel: the Bauhaus Dessau, which opened its doors in December 1926 after the institution's earlier years in Weimar. The workshop wing is doubtless remarkable with its all-glass corner becoming the most iconic feature, so much so that it inspired the Swiss architectural historian and critic Sigfried Giedion (1888–1968) to juxtapose a photograph of it, butterflylike, with *L'Arlésienne*, one of Picasso's cubist works of art, implying a kinship between the transparent qualities of the building and those of the painting.[48] The glass facade wrapped around three sides of the workshop wing and was composed of thin glass panes held by a grid of iron mullions and muntins (fig. 3.7). Looking back on his own achievement, he affirmed that there, "for the first time, the problem of dissolving the wall by bracing a continuous glass skin in front of the load-bearing building skeleton was carried out to the last consequence."[49]

The rise of glass facades excited a flurry of different terms, often used almost interchangeably both then and today.[50] In *Bauhausbauten Dessau* (Bauhaus buildings in Dessau, 1930), Gropius himself used the terms "outer skin" (*außenhaut*), "glass skin" (*glashaut*), and "outer glass skin" (*glasaußenhaut*).[51] The idea of the skin as wall is absorbed into this use, he writes about the exterior wall of the workshop wing as being entirely dissolved in plate glass and glazing bars, while "inside, the supporting pillars stand behind the glass wall."[52] The workshop wing's facade is first described as an "iron window network closing off the spaces," and then as a "glass wall," but ultimately also as "glass skin."[53]

The environmental performance of this all-glass corner and its adjacent surfaces left much to be desired. Too hot in the summer

Figure 3.7. Bauhaus workshop wing with three open vents that act as metaphoric pores in the building skin. Gelatin silver print, Lucia Moholy, 1927. Bauhaus-Archiv Berlin; index number 12434/14.3.

Figure 3.8. Opening mechanism inside the workshop wing. Gelatin silver print, Erich Consemüller, 1925–1926. Bauhaus-Archiv Berlin; index number 5995/5.

and bitterly chilly in winter, the workshop wing quickly became a climatic disaster, with its glass skin offering poor insulation and no shading, thus causing the building's energy demands to skyrocket due to the "aggressive heating system."[54] The Fagus Factory could have served as a warning because it had produced similar conditions of poor insulation and thermal drain more than a decade earlier, necessitating retrofits with external blinds and curtains to mitigate its adverse climatic impacts. Gropius, however, was focused on solving a different problem that had plagued the Fagus Factory: allowing the Bauhaus building to breathe.

What sets the Bauhaus Dessau apart from other early modern buildings with curtain walls, such as the Steiff Factory (1903) by Richard Steiff, or the Fagus Factory, is the unprecedented number of opening mechanisms. These mechanisms provide variable control over the building's airflow, thanks to a conspicuous variety of nifty window handles, metal chains, and sophisticated hinges (fig. 3.8). From straightforward to advanced contrivances, including now-common vertical casement windows, hopper windows (inward-opening windows hinged at the bottom) above and below, ingenious chain-pulley systems, and retractable panes activated by control wheels, as seen in the cafeteria, the Bauhaus Dessau performs like a trade fair for windows and flamboyant opening mechanisms.[55]

Between the concrete slabs and the curtain wall of the workshop laboratories, a gap of roughly 5.9 inches (15 centimeters) allowed air to circulate across individual floors—an airspace that united all the floors of the building. Architectural historians have noted the unnecessarily small-grained fenestration, asserting that Gropius could have easily applied larger glass panes, but he obviously sought to give a strong expression to the openings and their mechanism as a distinct architectural element.[56] This is in contrast with his claim in a 1926 essay on glass buildings that fifty years ago, "a seamless shop window" was a captivating object that garnered public admiration, and today it is commonplace to showcase commodities "behind windows without muntins"—that is, without precisely the small grid pattern he then employed.[57] As an aesthetic choice, the decision to reintroduce an abundance of muntins, despite their technical redundancy, could only have been made by someone intent on defying the prevailing norms of their era. But this was not Gropius's intention. The lattice's subdivision aligns with the operation of the opening panels, suggesting that this tessellation was essential for integrating multiple vents into cohesive units. The tessellation was Gropius's attempt to subdivide the metaphoric building skin into smaller vents—metaphoric pores that allow the skin to breathe.[58] The meticulously adjustable vents regulate the flow of air between the interior and the exterior and outside (fig. 3.9).

Merged on each floor into two rows of either six or ten rotating sheets—bundles of six on the long west facade of the workshop wing and bundles of ten on the shorter north facade—the vents (*Lüftungsflügel*) can be engaged using chain pulleys and locking rods. While functionally similar to a block and tackle, the chain pulley system here is simpler, utilizing a single chain looped around two gear wheels, without amplifying the input power. The result is an immediate and direct transfer of motion. Composed of intricate steel elements, the original chain pulley featured gear wheels with visible teeth, allowing the chain links to engage with the mechanism seamlessly, each component prominently displayed for observation.

However, this design also allows all vents to remain fixed in any position. A caption in *Bauhausbauten Dessau* succinctly notes that "the vents are vertical pivot windows coupled together, which stop in every position."[59] This level of control over air movement parallels the contemporary interest in regulating human respiration, as seen in the work of Gropius's contemporaries. Just as Itten and Jaques-Dalcroze sought to discipline the human breath through regulated breathing practices, Gropius aimed to discipline the undisciplined breathing of a building with a glass skin wall through design and technology.

Figure 3.9. Workshop wing with open vents seen from inside. Gelatin silver print. Photo probably taken by Gertrud Arndt. Bauhaus-Archiv Berlin, index number 2007/13.60.

Figure 3.10. Canteen windows featuring a single hand wheel to adjust the vent opening. Photo by Erich Consemüller, 1928. Bauhaus-Archiv Berlin, index number 5995/1.

Indeed, the outer surface of the school appears haunted by turn-of-the-century Europe's concern with breath and breathing, particularly reflecting the medico-scientific models articulated by physicians such as Gerlach. In the Bauhaus Dessau canteen, a single hand wheel triggers three to four windows, each subdivided into four horizontal pivots that are coupled together. Built into the wall, a locking rod transmits the wheel's circular motion, engaging a system of hinged steel bars that allow for smooth and simultaneous adjustments of all the windows (fig. 3.10). Much like the chain pulley machinery of the curtain wall, the iron windows in the canteen can be precisely controlled and locked in any position. Grouping the windows into bundles of smaller vents surely simplified their management and facilitated the simultaneous operation of multiple apertures with a single, efficient motion. The frequent depiction of open windows in historical images not only reflects the season when the photographs were taken, but also speaks to the students' preference and need for ventilation.

But if that was all that there was to it, the controls needed only to offer prompt adjustments through ample gestures. In fact, however, if merely affording ventilation was the concern, the design of the apparatus is overdetermined. Instead, the gear ratios involved allow for stunningly fine-tuned modifications within a hair's breadth. Banks of windows open smoothly and continuously, without being confined to a set number of increments, and the fluidity of these systems remains impressive to this day. And there is even more to these mechanisms. Unlike the inward-opening types Gropius used elsewhere, such as hopper windows that extend fully into the interior, the horizontal pivot vents in the canteen and the vertical pivot windows of the curtain wall reassert the authority of the facade's geometric plane. When these windows are opened, they symmetrically extend both inward and outward from the central axis, effectively blurring the boundaries between inside and outside of the facade's liminal space.

In one of the well-assorted photographic binders included among the files of the Bauhaus Archiv in Berlin, a self-portrait

Figure 3.11. Helmut Schulze breathing inside the open vents. Helmut Schulze, self-portrait. Bauhaus-Archiv Berlin, index number 12443/114.1.

by Helmut Schulze (1903–1995) stands out for its apposite depiction of this in-between. Schulze, a former mechanic and lathe operator employed in the aviation industry in Dessau, enrolled in László Moholy-Nagy's preliminary course at the Bauhaus in 1926, became a journeyman in the metal workshop, and later collaborated with Marianne Brandt for the design of several pots and light fittings. A photo taken between 1926 and 1930 is marked with an index card, hinting at its connection to Schulze's tenure at the Bauhaus prior to his graduation in 1931. Schulze's composition puts him center stage, partially obscured by the veil of Gropius's gridded facade, with his head carefully aligned to create a striking composition where the mullions and muntins conspire to frame him like a picture, locking Schulze in place within a graphic cacophony of superimposed lines (fig. 3.11). Schulze finds himself *inside* the open glass skin, breathing. Seemingly at ease, his eyes look keen, if not altogether cheerful. The reflections on the glass pane cloud his face slightly, but do not mask his expression. The photograph is at once a self-portrait, head shot, and statement of the time, capturing a Bauhaus member enmeshed within the glass skin's liminal space, symbolizing the atmospheric interplay between interior and exterior environments.

In giving substance to the machinery that could gracefully set in motion significant parts of the building envelope, Gropius not only empowered the Bauhaus building to breathe, but also encouraged occupants to participate in the pneumatic process, connecting a sublime breathing machine to the surrounding *Allraum*—his term for a new spatial concept where his buildings could seamlessly dissolve into the exterior by dint of overcoming the notion of an enclosing wall.[60]

Plasmatic Architecture: Membranes and Atmospheres

For Siegfried Ebeling (1894–1963), what Gropius was doing with the design of the Bauhaus Dessau was not nearly enough, because it was based on too limited a conception of walls as breathing skin and of the atmosphere that inhabitants breathe.[61] In *Der Raum als Membran* (Space as a membrane),[62] a short manifesto published on December 4, 1926, and thus coinciding with the Bauhaus's official opening in Dessau, Ebeling argues that the conception of the traditional building that still informed structures such as Gropius's, the building as a "relatively rigid, multi-celled spatial entity" that shields its inhabitants from external conditions, ignores the wide range of elements and energies present in the surrounding atmosphere, energies from "the radiating space of the sky" and "innumerable measurable (or as yet immeasurable) minute flows stemming from the breathing earth," elements and energies that either rebound off the walls without being harnessed or are "neutralised within their cavities."[63] As a result, buildings as traditionally conceived and executed fail to tap into the myriad energy potentials that surround them, the chimney being the sole exception.[64] "Thus, while the so-called 'breathing' wall skin [*Wandhaut*]—made of wood, mud, stone or substitutes—may be able to regulate in a very crude way the relation between the natural climate and the artificial interior climate, it does nothing to prevent the human occupants from being exposed to the detrimental effects of subtler atmospheric fluctuations (such as thunderstorms, blizzards or the Foehn or Scirocco winds)." Nor does it make positive use of the energies and forces omnipresent in the atmosphere. Ebeling argues that a permeable wall is no longer sufficient to address the delicate atmospheric elements uncovered by the natural sciences during the rise of the Bauhaus.

In an earlier essay titled "Kosmologe Raumzellen" (Cosmologist space cells), Ebeling expressed the conviction that the "revolutionary orientation of our whole epoch" led to a "vital structural change" of the human species, a "state of formation within which disintegration and decay are blatantly 'ingrained' [*durchwachsen*] with a new rhythm system."[65] He argued that knowledge of material relationships alone no longer met the expectations of his generation, and only a synthesis of what he called the "three moments"—industry, biology, and psychology—could become "constitutive for the spiritual constitution of our time." While design and building could have the potential to express the cultural transformation he desired, space, in turn, had the capacity to establish an "absolute harmony" between human and material substance; it refined the former (*Menschensubstanz*) and helped to "attune it to the vibrations of the life-constituting matter."[66] Endowed with a mediating agency, Ebeling's space was no longer seen as an empty container hosting subjects and objects within a nonempirical, a priori framework familiar since Kant. Instead, it calibrated human life and reconciled it with the cosmos at large.[67]

For Ebeling, the by-now classic scientific notion of permeability established by Pettenkofer and other physicians and chemists throughout the nineteenth century was far too simplistic, too coarse. The presence of the manifold, subtle forces Ebeling believed to surround him called not for a porous, breathing wall, but for a space of the future where "the character of the skin" or a "membrane between the exterior space and the dimensions of the body" becomes just as crucial as the spatial dimensions or the "psychophysical" properties of a space.[68]

Ebeling's concept of a membrane was inspired by his reading of philosophical biologist Raoul Heinrich Francé (1874–1943), who in Weimar during the early 1920s proposed a future science based on what he called "plasma."[69] Francé saw plasma as a primordial source material essential to both plant and human life, biochemically similar across species, "an air derivative" (*Luftabkömmling*) that thrives on atmospheric substances — oxygen, nitrogen, carbon dioxide, and hydrogen, but that is ontologically prior to the chemicals that compose the atmosphere. "When plasma decomposes," Francé asserts, "it ultimately seeks to float in the air as clouds and as one more breath for the others." This is a feedback loop of use and reuse, not unlike the general exchange between aerobic organisms and photosynthesizing plants. Hence, "because plasma consists of air components, it must therefore renew itself from them. On the one hand through respiration, on the other hand by ingesting plasma, i.e. components of the air as food." For plasma to exist, it must either breathe or absorb aerial substances directly through itself. And because we are plasma, we are consequently made of air. "Yes, we are 'air'; air is all living things and it becomes air again. This is not a 'witty paradox,' it is a tangible, sober fact."[70]

Membranes are central to the functioning of plasma in Francé's account in the final section of *Die technischen Leistungen der Pflanzen*, which is what truly excited Ebeling.[71] It is across walls conceived of as membranes that plasma absorbs or expels the chemical components of air. Francé himself called upon architects to take inspiration from nature's materials and the structural integrity of plants, which he believed surpassed that of modern constructions, and other architects answered the call, as well — around forty of Francé's books were part of Mies van der Rohe's personal library.[72]

Despite positing this vitalist substance, however, Francé's account remained consonant with the scientific accounts of breathing walls and skins from that were advanced by Pettenkofer and those who followed, beginning in the nineteenth century. This monistic supersubstance contains oxygen — "the most versatile of all elements" and also the most widespread, and plasma thrives on oxidation, a continuous process of transformation.[73] Breathing, which Francé terms "pure oxidation," is essential for plasma, driving swift modifications that are balanced by nutrition: "Respiration and nutrition are therefore technically necessary services of the plasma that are essential for its maintenance in order to ensure its chemical structure remains unalterable over its lifetime."[74]

For Ebeling, however, plasma conceived in this limited way, as physical chemistry, oxygen and its oxidation as carbon dioxide, was merely a "body matter."[75] "A study remains to be done," he wrote, "to which the natural (chemical-physical) forces of the ground and the radiation forces present in open space — specifically those which become reactive under the influence of light — could be exploited to create electrical charges which could then be harnessed via a circuit of resistors."[76] The house, he argues, should be seen as a membrane, but a membrane through which such more extensive energies and forces present in the atmosphere will pass:

> On the whole it should be stressed that the house is to be perceived as a conducting medium (*Durchgangsmedium*) channeling a continuous stream of forces — a stream of forces that is refracted several times in its trajectory, flowing from a ground surface that in geophysical terms is variously defined, through a hollow space, to an open space that is also variously defined, and then back again in reverse direction. In the centre of this play, in each instance, are organisms subject to both physiological and psychological laws.[77]

As part of a larger system yet to be fully understood — what Francé calls "cell architecture" (*Zellarchitektur*), a term that echoes

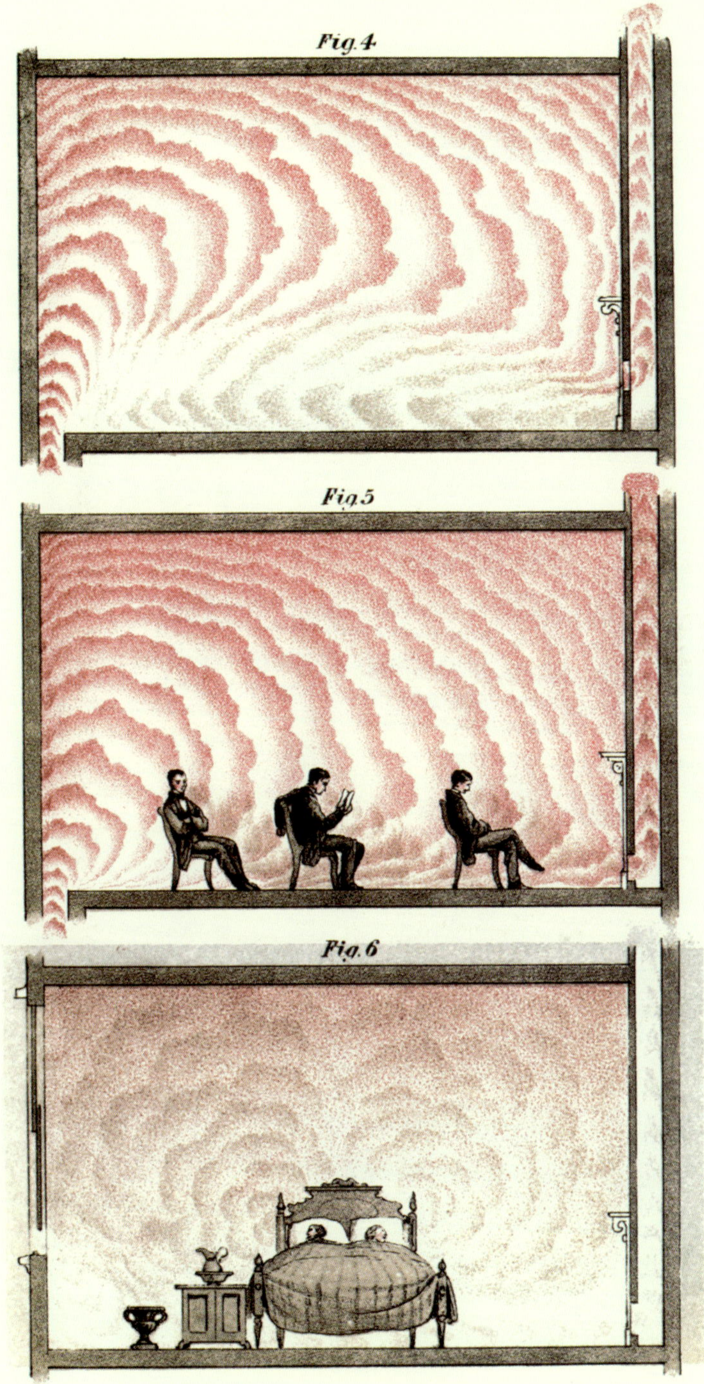

Figure 1.8. Illustration of fresh warm air entering the room. Lewis W. Leeds, *Lectures on Ventilation* (New York: John Wiley & Son, 1869), p. 29.

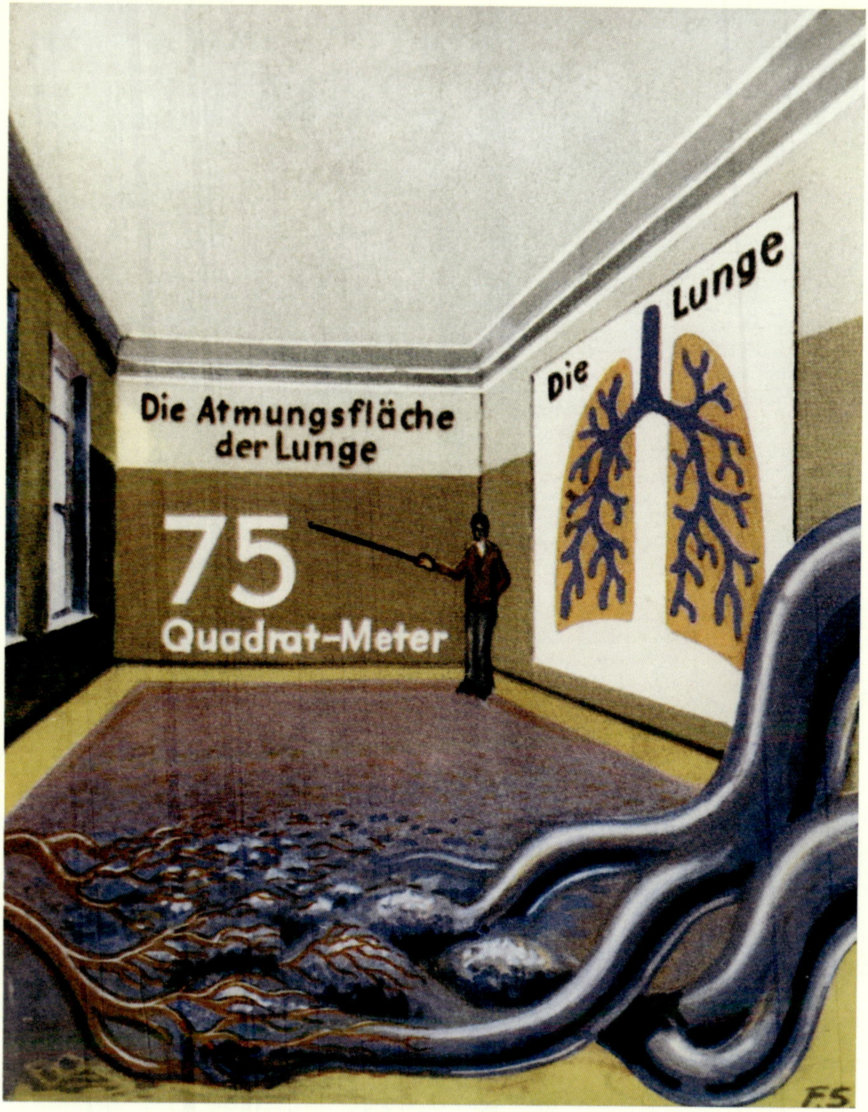

Figure 2.8. Lungs dissolving into a room-sized carpet to indicate their extent. "Bilder vom Menschen," *Berliner Morgenpost*, postcard set, 1931. Axel Springer SE, Unternehmensarchiv.

Figure 3.12. Cover of *Space as Membrane.* Siegfried Ebeling, *Der Raum als Membran* (Dessau: C. Dünnhaupt, 1926), Stiftung Bauhaus Dessau.

Figure 4.2. Fidus exposing himself in the nude to the forces of the atmosphere, 1894. Fidus [Hugo Reinhold Karl Johann Höppener], Lichtgebet, 1894, Deutsches Historisches Museum.

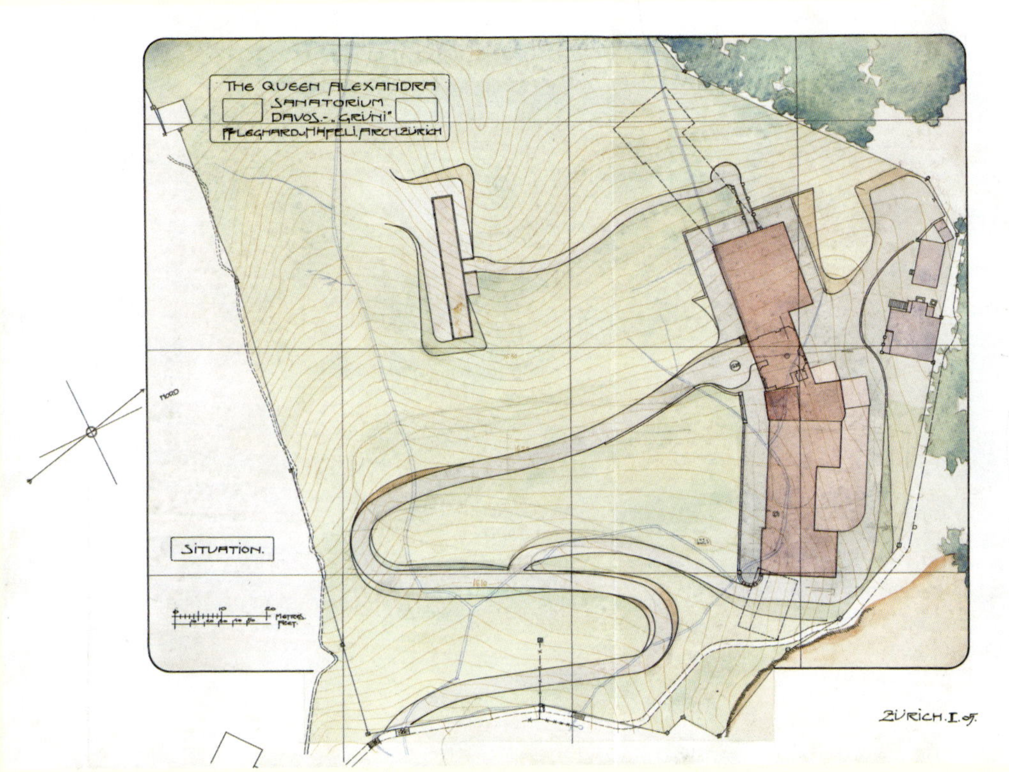

Figure 4.6. Embedded in aromatic pine forests: the scenic approach toward the Queen Alexandra Sanatorium. Site plan, 1905. Pfleghard & Haefeli, Queen Alexandra Sanatorium, Davos. Staatsarchiv Thurgau, 9'11, 5.0.0.1/1.

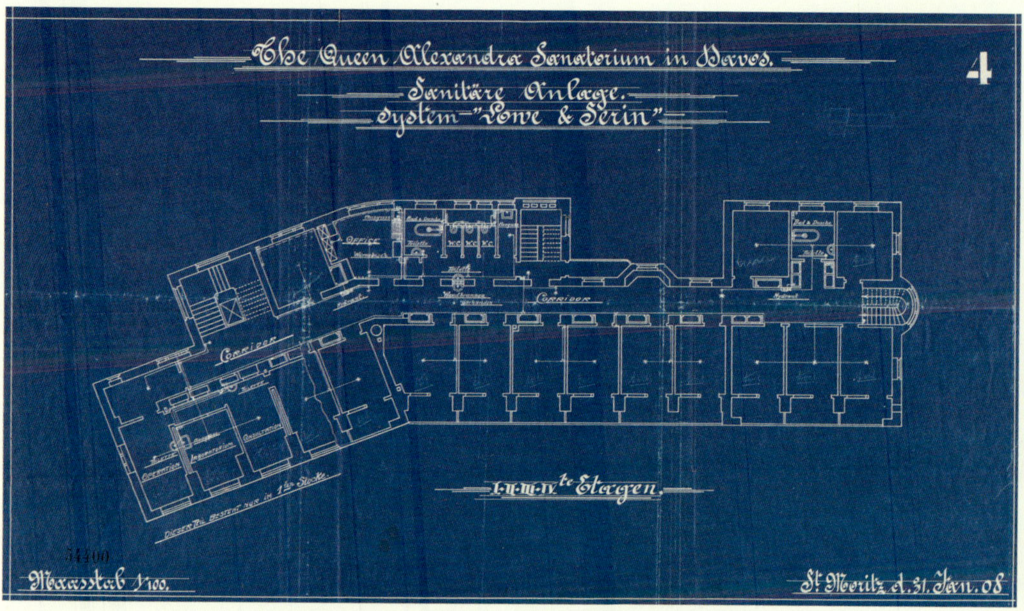

Figure 4.7. Blueprint of the Queen Alexandra Sanatorium dating from 1908, with all patient rooms facing south. Pfleghard & Haefeli, Queen Alexandra Sanatorium, Davos. Staatsarchiv Thurgau, 9'11, 5.0.0.2/5.

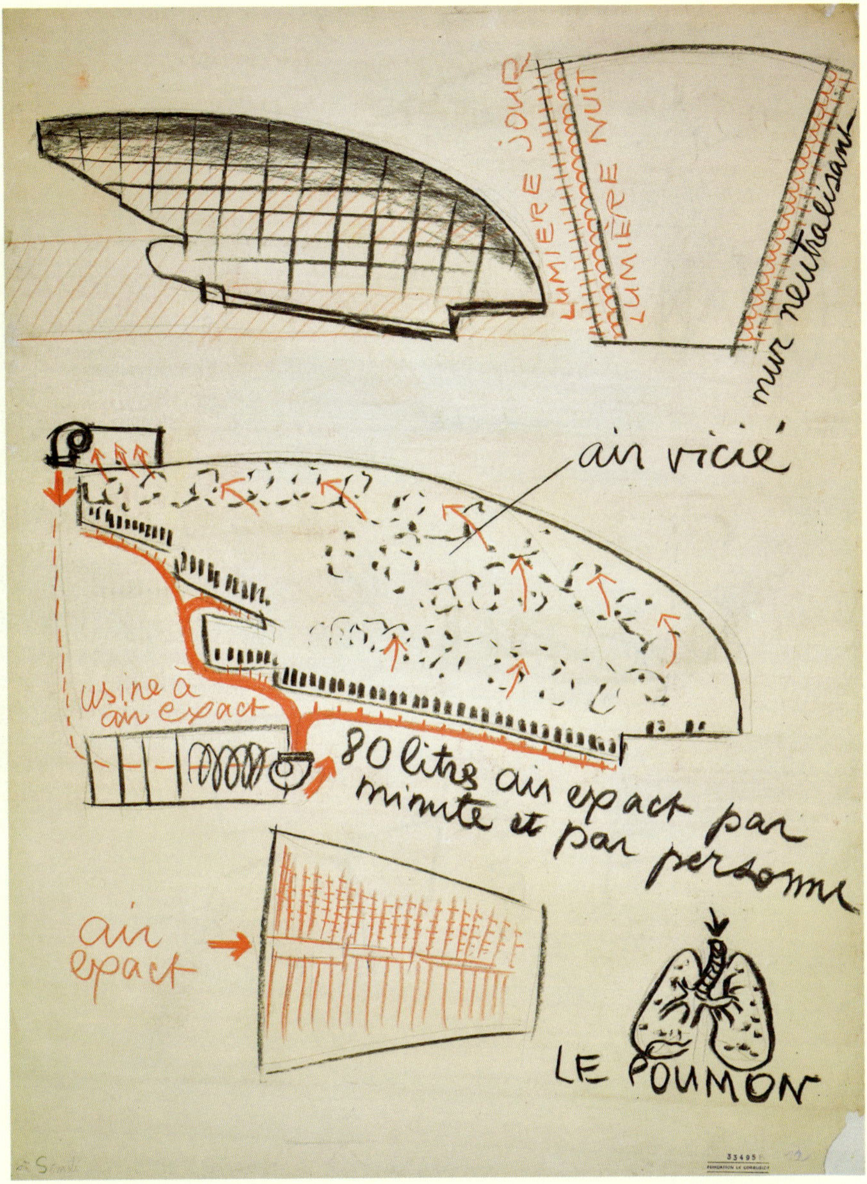

Figure 5.4. The analogy of anatomy and architecture as breathing and ventilation. Le Corbusier, *Precisions on the Present State of Architecture and City Planning*, trans. Edith Schreiber Aujame (Cambridge, MA: MIT Press, 1991), p. 167. Fondation Le Corbusier, Accession Number 33495B

Figure C.3. *Weibliche Figur (Seifenbläserin), auf dem Pegasus über einer Industriestadt reitend.* Watercolor by Karl Friedrich Schinkel, 1837. Kupferstichkabinett, Staatliche Museen zu Berlin Inv.-Nr.: SM 54.12 = KdZ 28498.

in the title "Kosmologe Raumzellen" (for Ebeling), the membrane's material properties are central to his investigation: imbibition, elasticity, tenacity, and adsorption. These characteristics of the colloidal membrane, a tensile substance, sharply contrast with the "crystalline-amorphous" materials commonly used in human constructions, known for their greater pressure resistance.

This nexus of ideas forms one of the foundations of Ebeling's theory, and how he received the new Bauhaus building at Dessau with its "crystalline-amorphous" materials, becomes clear in his polemic when he directly attacks the state of contemporary architecture. Merely relying on new materials—"still defined in physical, static terms" such as iron, concrete and glass—does not constitute a new architecture unless one transcends old principles and unlocks the full potential of creative forces. It is easy to picture the architecture of Gropius when Ebeling caustically observes in *Raum als Membran* that "even those buildings with cubic or cubically dissolving masses—with flat roofs and projecting planes, and windows pushed to the corners—are still being modelled in a sculptural spirit. Everything is still plastic, not plasmatic; everything is still formal, or rather once again merely formal, but not substantial."[78]

Der Raum als Membran was not widely read at the time, yet it did gain recognition among a few leaders of the modern movement, and these included Gropius and Mies—the latter of whom heavily annotated his own copy.[79] Although breathing as a process of exchange and flow remained a central theme in Ebeling's polemic, it raised a question that existing architectural theory and practice had not fully articulated or considered: Nineteenth-century ventilation discourses in architecture tended to treat the metaphor of walls as skin in mechanical terms, based on the chemical theories of respiration carried forward from nineteenth-century science and focused on the physical well-being of inhabitants. Ebeling instead foregrounded the organic connotations inherent in this metaphorical framework, including a much more expansive conception of the relationship of the organism with the environment. In doing so, he proposed a more expansive concept of the well-being of the human organism itself, one that includes not just the body, but also the embodied mind.

Though utopian in concept and elusive in its language, Ebeling's theory as it is briefly set forth in *Der Raum als Membran* is underdeveloped, but what informs this new conception of space is the psychophysiological body with its biophysical constitution. This approach is consonant with the various contemporary body-centered doctrines of health and well-being such as those by Itten, Jaques-Dalcroze, Müller, and Keller-Hoerschelmann, but it expands the physiological framework in which breathing plays a fundamental role to include psychological processes, as well. Because it "relates to the human body more directly than ever," the house should serve as membrane through which the various environmental forces flow, and as Ebeling emphasized, not just "physiological," but "psychological laws stand in the center of this play of forces."[80]

Pettenkofer had postulated the breathing body within interior spaces that communicate with the atmosphere, but a conception of the atmosphere as complex as Ebeling's was beyond his imagination. While Pettenkofer focused on airflow penetrating porous walls, and Gropius designed intricate machinery to engage with and regulate how a building could breathe, Ebeling envisioned telluric forces and atmospheric radiation extending far beyond the earlier understanding of the atmosphere as it interacts with humans. Physiology could no longer offer an adequate framework to address the relationship between the body, the building, and the environment.

Ebeling's critique of the architecture of the 1920s appeared at a time when, on the one hand, breath and breathing were popular topics in the discourses of health and, on the other, contemporary science was expanding the concept of cosmic forces and psychology was expanding the concept of the human mind. Ebeling's theory is illustrated, in a nutshell, on the cover of his thin tract, as Spyros Papapetros cogently demonstrates.[81] A so-called "space-cube," both self-sufficient in energy and intricately intertwined with its electromagnetic environment, hovers above the earth,

Figure 3.12. Cover of *Space as Membrane*. Siegfried Ebeling, *Der Raum als Membran* (Dessau: C. Dünnhaupt, 1926), Stiftung Bauhaus Dessau.

penetrated by abstract graphic elements (fig. 3.12). Within this structure, a geometric figure is framed, making the cube appear as a conduit for the myriad forces coursing through the air. "In this way," Papapetros writes, "the body is enveloped by the 'living cube,' but the cube is in turn enveloped by a greater atmospheric body that remains invisible."[82] In Ebeling's polemic the underlying concept of respiratory modernism in architecture remains consistent: walls mediate like a skin or membrane between the atmospheric environment and the inhabitants who depend on it. What was changing however, were conceptions of the body, the atmosphere, and their relation and therefore how the threshold between the body and the atmosphere should be designed.

„Es werde Licht"

oder

Die atmosphärische Cur.

Ein Beitrag zur natur-gemäßen Gesundheitslehre

von

Arnold Rikli,

hygienischer Arzt in Veldes (Krain) und in Triest.

Bekleidung für den Ausmarsch zum Lichtluftbad in Veldes.

1895. Fünfte verbesserte Auflage, 70 Pf.

Im Verlage des Verfassers und bei L. Fernau in Leipzig.

Figure 4.1. The atmospheric cure: a way to bathe in sun and fresh air. Frontispiece in Arnold Rikli, *Die Grundlehren der Naturheilkunde einschliesslich die atmosphärische Cur "Es werde Licht"* (Leipzig: L. Fernau, 1895). Staatsbibliothek Berlin.

CHAPTER FOUR

Immersive Atmosphere

Siegfried Ebeling borrowed key ideas about the psychophysiological body from Willy Hellpach (1877–1955), a German physician and psychologist who explored the effect of climate on the psyche in his 1911 book, *Die Geopsychischen Erscheinungen* (The geopsychic phenomena).[1] Beneath its speculative research, the book is a study of the environmental effects — weather, climate and landscape — on the central nervous system and on the nature of the atmosphere that surrounds us and the soil on which we live, insofar as it has a direct influence on the life of the soul. Drawing attention away from the social milieu — family, status, rank, class — that significantly influences one's psyche, Hellpach emphasizes the natural milieu as it is constituted by the fact that even "the most advanced civilization must exist on earth and within its atmosphere."[2] While the atmosphere is often perceived as an enduring and universal backdrop unbounded by regions and unaffected by time, not only is it never in a stable state of equilibrium, but our conceptions of it are also fluid, and Hellpach's broadened conception of the atmosphere and its effects on humans marks a change of emphasis at the turn of the twentieth century.

The word "atmosphere," despite its root in the classical Greek *atmos* (vapor), actually is a neologism coined in the early seventeenth century with the addition of the Latin *sphaera* (sphere, or globe), signifying a sphere filled with vaporous air. Its meaning was heavily influenced by experiments conducted during that period and also increasingly disseminated across different disciplines, from cosmology and meteorology to botany and medicine. Charged with "terrestrial effluvia and emanations," essentially the byproducts of all breathing bodies, atmosphere in the seventeenth century was already conceived as a volatile fluid enveloping the earth, its configuration and gravity fluctuating with the rarefactions and condensations induced by heat and cold.[3]

While in a rudimentary form, the concept of the atmosphere as a life-sustaining setting appears in Rousseau's novel *La nouvelle Héloïse*, with its promotion of the "society of open-air life," as Anthony Vidler called it, in the context of respiratory modernism, it was psychologists such as Hellpach and, in a different register, the Swiss naturopathic healer Arnold Rikli (1823–1906), who around the turn of the twentieth century intensified efforts to draw attention to this otherwise impalpable, yet life-sustaining medium.[4] Their registration of the various qualities inherent in the atmosphere was an attempt to bring out something we usually take for granted, akin to how fish may not realize the necessity of water unless taken out of it. The work of Hellpach and Rikli and its influence on early twentieth-century architecture thus forms a prehistory of today's efforts to focus on the atmosphere and its degradation as the most urgent issue of the Anthropocene.[5]

Charged Atmospheres and Atmospheric Baths

According to Hellpach, life in the atmosphere had been fundamentally compromised by human dwellings, reaching its apex in urban housing. In cities, especially in their most sophisticated apartments, the presence of weather had been largely eradicated, replaced instead by an "artificial living atmosphere" (*künstliche Lebensatmosphäre*) that replaced natural sensory experiences—such as colors, forms, and scents—with artificial ones.[6] This observation in a way echoes nineteenth-century ventilation expert David

Boswell Reid's view of architecture, as discussed in the first chapter, as a means to create an interior atmosphere through the use of a material shell. Without using the term "architecture," Hellpach framed the way dwellings are constructed as a form of atmospheric technology working to our disadvantage.

While distinguishing between breathing techniques as practices and breathing technologies as material devices, John Durham Peters notes that in order to operate, both techniques and technologies require an agent and an environment—one who breathes and the atmosphere breathed—that together constitute "the media of breathing."[7] Due to the interdependencies between organism, environment, technique, and technology, categories necessarily overlap, and in his systematic effort to outline these media, Peters sees architecture, poison gas, and ventilation as a single technology characterized by the "intentional or unintentional alteration of the atmosphere."[8] This juxtaposition serves as a reminder that building construction necessarily alters the broader atmosphere in which it exists. Isolating and modulating a volume of air is one thing; emitting greenhouse gases is another. And architecture can do both.

Leaving a dwelling means reconnecting with or being partially exposed to the natural milieu, which for Hellpach involved two main components, one of which he believed affects the central nervous system through its hidden properties, while the other enters our body directly through the senses. In the first instance, we experience the earth through its atmospheric and soil elements, which manifest as weather or climate. In the second instance, we encounter the earth through its scenic vistas and natural features—through the landscape. Together, weather, climate, and landscape produce the psychological effects that Hellpach termed "geopsychic."

The key distinction here lies between the sensory effects provoked by the landscape and the tonic effects elicited by weather and climate, effects that could psychophysically affect the body's tissue tension and the metabolism more broadly. The intricacy of the issue lies in the intrinsic connection between body, mind, and environment. Attempting to isolate specific factors to distinguish between the physical and psychological effects of climate and location is virtually impossible, and Hellpach was acutely aware of the challenge. However, what was at stake for him was the way in which the atmosphere itself, conceived as a domain for habitation, is imbued with multiple qualities.

It was this notion of the atmosphere that prompted Ebeling to reconsider the status of the house as an entity deeply intertwined with its environment, as we saw. Hellpach's reassessment of the atmosphere, previously regarded simply as a collection of climatic elements—rain, clouds, sunshine, wind—positioned it as part of a reciprocal system with the earth. In this view, telluric factors influence the atmosphere just as much as atmospheric conditions influence the earth. By the same token, these atmospheric conditions strongly influence our mind and central nervous system with corresponding mental effects. No longer a mute container merely filled with neutral air, the atmosphere assumes an authoritative role in shaping our mental well-being through its elaborate composition, its movement, humidity and air pressure, thermal radiation, and atmospheric electricity. Mediating between the earth and the atmosphere, "the organism is part of the electrostatic earth field and as such constantly participates in the influence equalization between the earth field and the air field."[9] Engaging in this exchange at the threshold between the earth and its surrounding air envelope can lead to electrostatic discharges in some individuals, Hellpach maintained. Due to this complex structure of the atmosphere, it is evident why a conventional breathing wall pervious to air would be deemed inadequate by someone so radical as Ebeling, who sought to harness the full range of atmospheric properties for the house to come.

Hellpach's conception of psychology was somewhat speculative, but in medical circles more generally, climatic considerations of the atmosphere highlighted a host of attributes that treated the atmosphere as highly complex. This is particularly evident in the health resorts that started appearing in isolated alpine regions across Europe in the latter half of the nineteenth century, coinciding with advancements in the *Lebensreform* movement and naturopathy. Here, the naked body was ostensibly presented within the landscape, yet it was actually exposed to the atmosphere.

Toward the end of the nineteenth century, Europe had witnessed a baffling array of views regarding the effects of fresh air on the human body, a fascinating mixture of original and traditional ideas reflected in new understandings of human physiology such as Hellpach's. The context for this transformation was the development of the modern city, whose increasingly unsanitary conditions had triggered the emergence of clean-air health movements as early as the mid-nineteenth century. These campaigns, often dogmatic and quirky, promoted the countryside as a space that could not only host, but actively foster an alternative lifestyle promoting dynamic, healthy bodies. Naturopathy and atmospheric baths thus became essential components of alternative strategies for pursuing a modern, yet healthy lifestyle.

The duality of countryside and city mirrored the tension between two popular conceptions of air: as a recuperative element that flows freely and as something that requires purification. The emergence of the "atmospheric bath" (*Lichtluftbad*) and the establishment of alpine health resorts, along with the treatment of TB in the latter half of the nineteenth century, vividly illustrate the dual role of air as both a life-giving force and a potential cause of death.

If we were to pinpoint the primary organ of focus for naturopathy movements and clinical tuberculosis treatment, it would undoubtedly be the skin for the former and the lungs for the latter. However, medical and lifestyle approaches often overlapped, and the boundaries between them were as porous as physical walls, with the hygienic practices promoted by conventional physicians and those advocated by alternative-life reformers addressing both lungs and skin similarly in their strategies.[10] Essentially, these treatments hinged on two crucial aspects: exposing the human body, particularly its largest organ, the skin, to an atmosphere seen as a source of health-giving radiation and exposing the lungs to pure air free of unhealthful pollutants. Both of these treatments were central to the effort to treat tuberculosis, and to the construction of sanatoriums in which to do it.

Air and Sun, Skin and Lungs: The Rise of the Sanatorium

Although sun and air had been seen as therapeutic since Hippocrates's time, their use as medical treatments largely had fallen into oblivion until the mid-nineteenth century. Christoph Wilhelm Friedrich Hufeland's *Enchiridion Medicum*, published in 1830, had emphasized the importance of periodic air baths as a treatment for nervous disorders.[11] It was with the naturopath Rikli, however, that the sun and air as cures for the diseases of the modern world entered the culture of respiratory modernism. "The most direct and accessible means of achieving the circuitous return to nature through the radiation of air and sunlight," Sigfried Giedion notes, "was rediscovered in 1869 by Arnold Rikli (1823–1906)."[12] Rikli published his treatise *Die Grundlehren der Naturheilkunde* (Principles of naturopathy) in 1895, which included an essay titled "Die atmosphärische Kur" (The atmospheric cure).[13]

This curative practice, focused on thorough exposure to the natural environment, had been promoted by Rikli since at least 1855, when he opened his first dedicated establishment. The treatise is embellished by a frontispiece featuring a resolute young man, Rikli himself, who appears determined to embrace substantial exposure to the elements (fig. 4.1). Adequately dressed, but with his shoes tied around his hips, he stands barefoot and bareheaded in an alpine setting near a rocky lakeshore. His right forefinger points toward one of the adjacent peaks beyond the etching's frame, indicating the direction of his intended activity. A hiking staff, nearly as tall as the mustachioed man himself, is his sole accessory. His shirt, unbuttoned to the navel, is equally revealing as his shorts. Dressed in this manner, he clearly intends to tan and air his skin — the "atmospheric bath" (*Lichtluftbad*) that Rikli considered much healthier than a traditional water bath.

Rikli's belief in the benefits of atmospheric exposure partly stemmed from the notion that humans are born naked, without attire, and thus predestined to live in what he called *Lichtluftmeer*, or "sea of light and air." He viewed humankind as the most developed of all living creatures, or "animal plants" (*Tierpflanze*), and criticized what he saw as an unhealthy retreat from the atmosphere, which he considered our primary habitat. Humans were diminished not only by wearing clothing but also by taking "shelter" (*Bauschutz*) and seeking shade. Rikli expresses regret over the unequal recognition of air and light as "nourishment of the lungs" (*Lungennahrung*), compared with their significance for the skin.

Clothing, much like architecture, increasingly had distanced us from the elements, he believed.[14] Thus, naturopaths such as Rikli valorized "movement of the unclothed body in the open air," as Giedion describes it, as a way to return to a primordial state where "the easily weakened ultra-violet rays take effect."[15] Rikli argued that the optimal exposure could be best achieved in the countryside, far from the detrimental effects of modern cities. However, clothing, like shelter, seldom can be dispensed with, and he also offered strategies for urban dwellers, such as "clothed atmospheric baths" (*Kleidungsluftbäder*), in which city dwellers were to take multiple daily strolls outside in light clothing to cool the skin, because only light clothing allows adequate exposure of the skin. Described as an "organ of circumscription" (*Begrenzungsorgan*), the skin needs to breathe, and such effects can only be achieved when dressed lightly. Upon returning indoors, however, strollers were mimic the return to enclosure by donning warm clothing, irrespective of the initial climatic conditions.

The outside also must be brought inside, and Rikli recommended thoroughly airing out living and working spaces at least twice daily through cross ventilation. This requires opposite-facing doors and windows that lead outdoors to facilitate effective airflow.

In addition to setting the air in motion, sunlight itself can effectively invigorate stagnant air and should be blocked only during periods of intense heat. And while all rooms benefit from regular ventilation, Rikli emphasized that the bedroom is crucial, insisting that sleeping with open windows enhances sleep quality, and in urban settings, air quality typically improved at night, due to reduced industrial emissions. To prevent drafts and ensure comfort, especially while sleeping, he suggested using a folding screen or drapes, and in extreme cases, wearing more fitted nightwear.

At the time, Rikli championed these curative measures in relative isolation and without widespread public endorsement—no surprise "in the time of parasols, high-collared and corset-like clothes," as Giedion notes.[16] However, pioneers of the *Lebensreform* movement took these approaches to heart. Life reformers such as the artist Fidus (Hugo Reinhold Karl Johann Höppener, 1868–1948) in his famous *Lichtgebet* (Prayer for light), from 1908, depicts a young, slender figure standing nude on a mountain ridge, exposed to the wind and sunlight (fig. 4.2). This image was later reproduced as a small-scale oil print that could be easily carried in a purse, gaining widespread popularity and eventually becoming venerated as a religious icon.[17] The circles influenced by Fidus and other like-minded individuals came to view the skin as a crucial interface between the organism, the soul, and the outside world. These movements fostered an increased awareness not only of the atmosphere, but also of breathing. The small illustration became emblematic of the *Lebensreform* movement, symbolizing its core principle, the renegotiation of the body's interaction with its environment. Conceptually, it was believed that only through the skin and lungs could the untainted exterior be fully absorbed into the body.[18]

Rikli and other naturopaths emphasized the role of the skin, but medical pathologists were more concerned with the role of the lungs, especially in the treatment of one of the nineteenth and early twentieth centuries' most widespread and lethal disease, tuberculosis. While tuberculosis can affect various parts of the body outside

Figure 4.2. Fidus exposing himself in the nude to the forces of the atmosphere, 1894. Fidus [Hugo Reinhold Karl Johann Höppener], Lichtgebet, 1894, Deutsches Historisches Museum.

the lungs, pulmonary TB, which directly affects the upper lobes of the lungs, was and still is by far the most common form. Deemed one of the world's deadliest diseases at the beginning of the twentieth century and still considered so today, TB is caused by inhaling an infectious agent, the often lethal *Mycobacterium tuberculosis*.

Until the discovery of streptomycin in 1943, air was regarded as both a disseminator of TB and an essential part of its treatment for the pulmonary version. The medical practice of relocating patients to different regions with salutary atmospheres became increasingly institutionalized, and sanatoriums emerged as the primary sites for this type of treatment. Their location in isolated regions far from urban agglomerations, surrounded by better air, were believed to make them ideal for aiding the recovery of infected lungs, although even with the benefit of hindsight, it is impossible to determine accurately the relative success of TB management in sanatoriums.[19] And regarding these buildings, as recently as 2000, British pathologist Thomas Dormandy observed in his sweeping history of tuberculosis that "no comprehensive monograph chronicles one of the strangest episode in the history of medicine: the rise, dominance and fall of the tuberculosis sanatoria."[20]

While scholars from various disciplines have examined this rich spatiomedical history from diverse, and at times diverging, perspectives, architectural historians such as Beatriz Colomina and Margaret Campbell have specifically emphasized the influence of sanatorium design on the development of modernist architecture.[21] Here, I focus on the unique role that the rise of the sanatorium played in both the history of this medical practice and the historiography of modern architecture because of the way it redefined architecture not as a protective wrapper, but as a facilitator of the atmosphere itself as the primary space of human habitation. As we will see, the Queen Alexandra Sanatorium in Davos occupies a special place in the history of that development.

Despite appearing in numerous publications, the building was only recently examined in depth, having first gained prominence in 1929, by virtue of Giedion's small pamphlet *Befreites Wohnen* (Liberated dwelling) and Richard Döcker's book *Terrassen Typ* (Terrace type).[22]

Davos and Sanatorium Architecture

Although efforts to curb the spread of TB extended beyond sanatoriums, eventually influencing other cultural practices and building types, the rise of the sanatorium was the principal response to TB as the most fatal disease in Europe and North America during the nineteenth century, offering hope through various treatment methods developed over time. A sanatorium was essentially a shelf for the storage of recumbent patients in specific aerial regions, and TB management was not confined to remote mountain regions. As Susan Sontag observed, "the most contradictory destinations were proposed. The south, mountains, deserts, islands—their very diversity suggests what they have in common: the rejection of the city."[23]

In the mid-nineteenth century, physicians thought they understood the pathology and progression of TB.[24] Some physicians considered poor nutrition as a sole cause of the disease,[25] but genetic predisposition and later the harmful impact of indoor air were considered primary factors in its development since the disease predominantly affects the lungs. It was in this context that three physicians planted the seeds for the evolution of the modern sanatorium: the German Hermann Brehmer (1826–1889), his patient, convert, and later assistant, pulmonary specialist Peter Dettweiler (1837–1904), and American physician Edward Livingston Trudeau (1848–1915). All of them eventually contracted and successfully treated the disease themselves, inferring that their recovery methods could be conferred to others.

Brehmer played an important role in scientifically systematizing open-air treatment by establishing a facility in Görbersdorf, Silesia, in 1854. He is widely regarded as the founding father of the modern sanatorium, a building type that soon epitomized radical discipline and extreme hygiene. Brehmer administered his establishment rigorously, enforcing a strict regimen on patients' daily routines that included physical exercises, enhanced hygiene, a strict diet, and thorough medical supervision. Over time, Dettweiler's therapeutic approach shifted the focus from active exercises to restorative rest. A prevalent hypothesis suggested that strengthening the body's immune defenses could significantly improve treatment outcomes.

In 1876, some two decades after Brehmer founded his establishment, Dettweiler inaugurated his own institution, known as the Falkenstein Sanatorium. Located in the Taunus, a mountain range in Hesse, Germany, this sanatorium pioneered the implementation of the "rest cure" (*Liegekur*), a therapeutic cure conceived by Dettweiler where patients reclined in specifically designated areas for the open-air treatment. Taking Bremer's therapeutic emphasis on the benefits of the atmosphere one step further, Dettweiler advocated staying in fresh air, albeit under a protective roof. Thus covered, these so-called "lying-down halls" (*Liegehallen*)—an example of psychosomatic measures applied to a fundamentally organic disease—hosted patients wrapped in layers of wool blankets, later replaced by blankets made of camel hair, positioned neither indoors nor outdoors, but in between, throughout the day. They rested in chairs specially designed by the institute's director.

Isolated mountain resorts with open-air decks for the treatment of reclining patients came into fashion based on empirical evidence, because physicians practicing in such regions incidentally observed fewer cases of TB among people living at elevated altitudes. According to the German physician and expert on climatology Sir Hermann Werner (1848–1918), by virtue of their "highly stimulant and tonic" qualities, high altitudes could promote many physiological benefits, including "amplification of the respiratory movements," "strengthening of the muscles of respiration," "strengthening of the heart and circulation," "increase in the amount of watery vapor and carbonic acid given off from the lungs," "increased activity of the skin," "increase of appetite and of the amount of food taken," "improvement of the digestive functions," "improvement in the quality of the blood, and in the nutrition of the organs, particularly of the lungs," and "increased activity of the nervous system."[26] But Werner repeatedly stressed that climate in itself was insufficient without necessary medical supervision and attention to hygiene and diet, procedures for which the sanatorium provided the spatial matrix based on a highly controlled exposure to the atmosphere, where climate could do its magic only in conjunction with a tightly managed medical regime.

But not all high-altitude climates are the same. Cultural historian Eva Horn notes that climate can be a local phenomenon, inflecting cultural practices and routines as much as it shapes architecture.[27] Davos, a Swiss mountain village situated in the canton of Graubünden, at an elevation of 5,120 feet (1,560 meters) above sea level, emerged as a prime location for situating sanatoriums, and there were reasons for this, which also prompted more thorough scientific analyses of the atmosphere there than in many other parts of Europe and which even led Ebeling to visit the local Physical Meteorological Observatory.[28] While Werner, for instance, favored the Peruvian Andes thanks to the "great dryness and rarefaction of the atmosphere," they were a long way from TB patients in Europe.[29] And where the Rocky Mountains were seen as "somewhat drier and warmer than Davos and St. Moritz," at the same time, they were "also more windy," a condition that patients and physicians alike found a nuisance.[30] What made Davos so special was its location at the bottom of a valley, wide and flat, whose dimensions and relationship with adjacent valleys and mountains created absolutely ideal conditions, with the surrounding peaks, spectacular and numerous, low enough to allow the low winter sun to touch most of the valley.

The valley's relative lack of wind and exposure to abundant sunlight were crucial for the treatment of TB patients, according to contemporary medical understanding of the disease. Historic weather data published in 1907 reveals how calm Davos was, with a mostly northeasterly wind occasionally coming in at speeds of around 1 on the Beaufort scale. Between 1887 and 1904, wind speeds averaged just 0.3 on the Beaufort scale.[31] The winds brought patients just enough fresh air. Even the prevalent southwesterly winter wind was so light that it went virtually unnoticed, and most winter days exhibited a complete absence of wind. There also was minimal cloud cover to obstruct the available solar warmth, which helped to shield patients from the actual air temperatures. The water vapor content in the atmosphere was so low that when inhaled air reached body temperature, its vapor pressure significantly decreased, leading to the extraction of humidity from the lungs, a factor deemed favorable in the case of TB, which was considered a wet disease. Compared with other nearby resorts, Davos also was virtually free from fog.[32] Summer days were moderately warm, while the nights remained pleasantly cool.

Similar conditions had already been inscribed as prerequisites into the foundational texts of Western architectural theory. In the first of his *Ten Books on Architecture*, Vitruvius dedicates several paragraphs to the performance of winds. With an eye to medical concerns, he contends that places with less wind are healthier, implying that wind sweeps away everything beneficial.[33] The "shutting out of the winds" not only protected patients suffering from diseases such as "catarrh, hoarseness, coughs, pleurisy, consumption, [and] spitting of blood," but also healthy citizens, and Vitruvius speculated that patients with these diseases could be cured only in windless locations, because the wind would take "all the sap of life out of their diseased bodies."[34] Likewise, in *On the Art of Building*, Leon Battista Alberti observes that "the air that we breathe . . . when really pure may have an extraordinarily beneficial effect on health,"[35] and "the healthiest form of air is that which is the purest and least polluted, the most easily pierced by sight, the most transparent and light, and which is always serene and largely constant."[36] Ideally, good air remains in the background and is therefore imperceptible, a claim that is far from settled in architectural discourse, where theories of air remain rather dynamic. Unlike the serene, nearly undetectable air of Vitruvius or in Davos, eighteenth-century French hospitals, for instance, aimed to induce "a powerful draft" to flush their interiors with fresh air.[37] In contrast, the turn-of-the-twentieth-century sanatorium in Davos was precisely not about ventilation. Instead, it served as a device to enable tubercular patients to be enveloped in the ideally calm and invisible mountain air. When Hans Castorp, the protagonist of Thomas Mann's *The Magic Mountain*, first ascends to the sanatorium where his cousin resides, he suddenly finds himself over five thousand feet above sea level. Mann engages the distinctive qualities of the Davos air not through a meteorological lens, but through a literary one, translating atmospheric peculiarity into narrative form. The air is portrayed as strangely devoid of qualities, except for one: "And in his curiosity, Hans Castorp took a deep breath, testing the alien air. It was fresh—that was all. It lacked odor content, moisture, it went easily into the lungs and said nothing to the soul."[38]

Today widely known for the annual meeting of the World Economic Forum, the spectacular ascent of Davos from a small farming village into an international health resort in the 1860s is largely attributed to Alexander Spengler (1827–1901), a local doctor who noted the absence of TB among Davos residents and advocated stays in such high-altitude settings as a cure. His pioneering work paved the way for the development of advanced treatments and for Davos to become the epicenter of high-altitude medical treatment in Europe, a place where the construction of sanatoriums brought together architects and medical pioneers.

Karl Turban (1856–1935), a pulmonary specialist, played a pivotal role in establishing Davos as a disciplined health colony governed by an elaborate regime of spatiomedical supervision. Prior to his arrival as medical supervisor of a newly founded sanatorium, Davos had simply been one of the many places where patients, left to their own devices, could recover on their own terms under the benevolent gaze of local doctors. Turban, who had previously worked as an assistant to the German microbiologist Robert Koch (1843–1910), the discoverer of the *Mycobacterium tuberculosis* bacterium, contracted

TB himself during his time at Koch's institute in Berlin. He sought relief in Davos, but first spent a brief period at Dettweiler's institution to study the rigorous methods he imposed on his patients. In Davos, the era of relying solely on the pristine alpine climate to do all its magic quickly came to an end as the discipline Turban introduced soon materialized into architectural form. In 1889, he established his own health-care facility in Davos, featuring a distinctive internal design where all rooms faced south, and circulation areas such as the corridor and stairwell were situated to the north (fig. 4.3). This layout was designed to maximize each room's exposure to sunlight and fresh air, thereby enhancing the therapeutic effects of alpine respiration. As a design scheme, it emerged as a pioneering model, with inflections repeated in numerous sanatoriums, including the one integrated into Tony Garnier's Cité Industrielle, a visionary plan for an ideal city that never came to fruition.[39]

As a manual for the erection of sanatorium buildings, Turban's *Normalien für die Erstellung von Heilstätten für Lungenkranke in der Schweiz* (General principles for the construction of sanatoriums for lung patients in Switzerland) from 1893 provided theoretical underpinnings for the construction of a great number of newly designed institutions.[40] However, there were numerous deviations for his design. According to medical consensus in Davos, it was imperative that all rooms in a sanatorium had direct access to fresh air, but there are other means to this end, and a balcony was not mandatory. However, conflicting opinions jelled around the provision of the individual balconies that became so iconic in many later facilities.

Turban deemed these to be "of little value."[41] The ability to transform each bedroom into a loggia was more crucial for him. Instead of individually bringing patients toward the atmosphere, he decided to bring the air into their rooms. To provide access to dry, pristine mountain air, Turban recommended using French doors instead of conventional windows and using "hopper windows" above them.[42] Almost entirely composed of glass and equipped with sophisticated

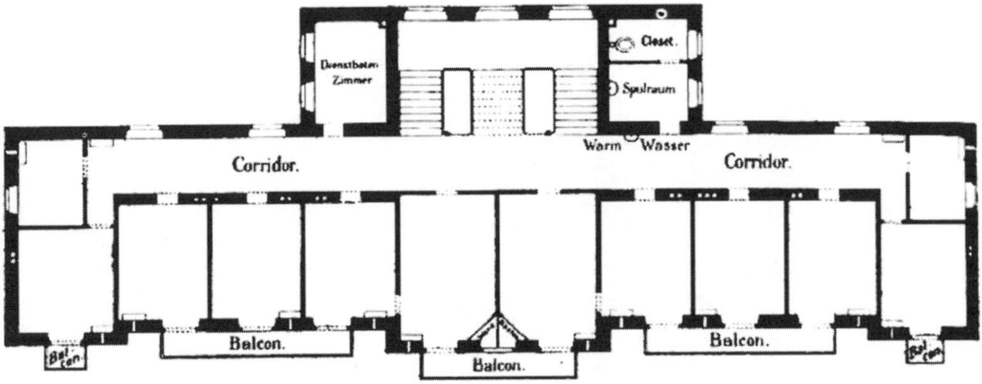

Figure 4.3. Comblike floor plan of Turban's sanatorium, with all rooms facing south. Karl Turban, *Tuberkulose-Arbeiten 1890–1909: Aus Dr. Turbans Sanatorium, Davos* (Davos: Buchdruckerei Davos, 1909), p. 118.

opening mechanisms, this facade foreshadowed modernist curtain walls and rejected the notion of architecture as a barrier to the elements (fig. 4.4). The promise of recovery was made by the rooms' connection to the intimate mountain air, allowing inhabitants to engage fully with the atmospheric conditions of their surroundings.

To open the exterior walls of the patient rooms to the outside atmosphere is a far cry from the idea of architecture as a protective medium, a technology designed to protect inhabitants from it. Turban's scheme also provided for communal decks at least 8.2 feet (2.5 meters) deep to allow patients to move around unobstructed. Essentially resembling a shoebox open on just one side, these decks while roofed and supplied with movable curtains to shield against direct wind and excessive sunlight, also were fully exposed to the south.

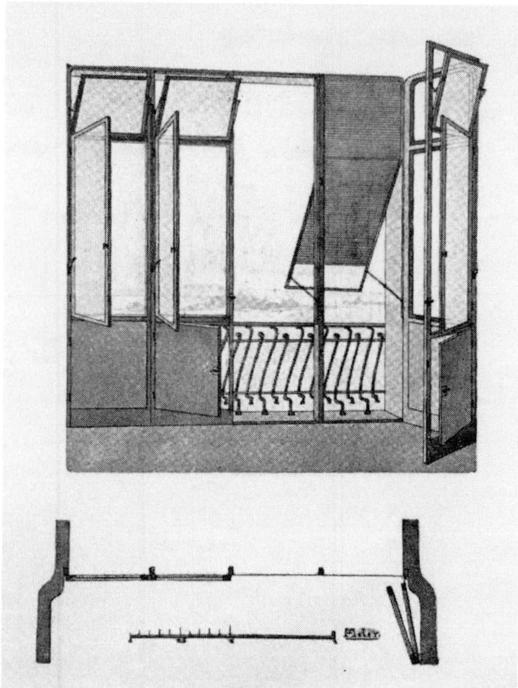

Figure 4.4. Turban's sanatorium windows as a precursor to the modern curtain wall facade. Karl Turban, *Tuberkulose-Arbeiten 1890–1909: Aus Dr. Turbans Sanatorium, Davos* (Davos: Buchdruckerei Davos, 1909), p. 265.

While Turban's design principles were soon realized in subsequent sanatorium schemes, many of the structures built after he published *Normalien für die Erstellung von Heilstätten für Lungenkranke in der Schweiz* incorporated the individual balconies where patients could be parked outdoors that Turban disliked, a trend most notably advanced by the Swiss architectural practice Pfleghard & Haefeli.[43] The firm traced its origins to 1898, when the two architects, Otto Wilhelm Pfleghard (1869–1958) and Max Haefeli (1869–1941), decided to ally after studying at the forerunner of today's Swiss Federal Institute of Technology in Zurich. While their early work was still haunted by the specters of historicist references or use of historical styles and motifs, they soon embraced a modernist approach, and despite their extensive oeuvre spanning a wide range of building types, they developed particular expertise in the burgeoning field of sanatorium design.

The transformation from historicism to modernism is most patent when comparing two of their own schemes located in Davos: the Schatzalp Sanatorium from 1899 and the Queen Alexandra Sanatorium completed ten years later. While the former appears palatial and almost neoclassical, the latter is informed more by the new architectural principles of modernism, exhibiting a rationalized form of alpine architecture driven by medical requirements for the tonic cure and modern construction techniques (fig. 4.5).[44] Although the layout of the Queen Alexandra Sanatorium is reminiscent of the spatial organizations typical of nineteenth-century hospitals in the United States, it is heavily influenced by Turban's recommendations, a two-fold heritage that makes the building at once highly contextual for Davos while also positioning it within a longer tradition of medical facilities.[45] Embellished with the name of the British queen, the sanatorium catered to British and American citizens of little means who could otherwise not afford the costly sojourn in Switzerland.

The Queen Alexandra Sanatorium

Located on the slopes of an alp, described in the institution's annual report as "the last good sanatorium site" available in the valley, the facility benefited from unobstructed morning sunshine, free "from smoke and river mists."[46] By setting the building against a backdrop of sparkling snowy hills and aromatic pine forests, the architects created an imposing stage for the rest cure to follow (fig. 4.6). In 1907, the year of the laying of the foundation stone, one physician exalted the setting's "pure, cold, invigorating air" that is "perfectly still," and noted "the cold, absolutely very dry air" that improved conditions for consumptives.[47] The conditions described by another physician were the sine qua non of contemporary tuberculosis care: "The rarefaction of the air, the purity of the air, the intensity and long duration of the sunshine, the abundance of [ultra]violet rays

Figure 4.5. A structure in which to inhabit the atmosphere: the design of the Queen Alexandra Sanatorium, 1923. Pfleghard & Haefeli, Queen Alexandra Sanatorium, Davos, 1907–1909. Photo ca. 1922. Archiv Photoglob-Wehrli, Eidgenössisches Archiv für Denkmalpflege, Schweizerische Nationalbibliothek.

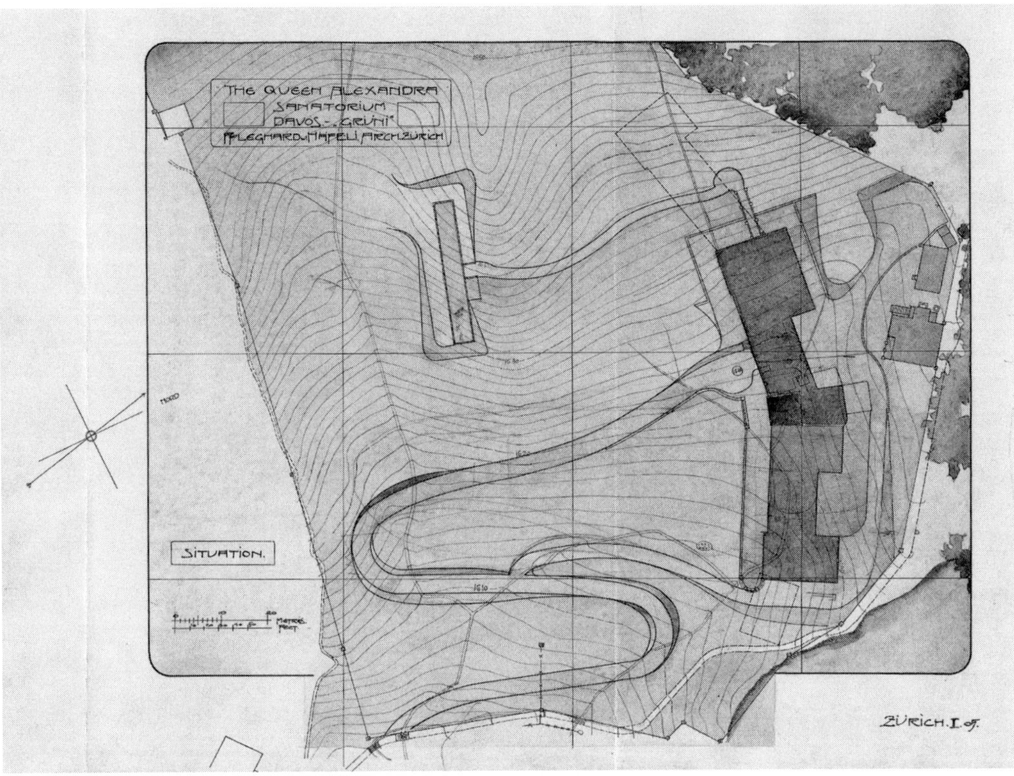

Figure 4.6. Embedded in aromatic pine forests: the scenic approach toward the Queen Alexandra Sanatorium. Site plan, 1905. Pfleghard & Haefeli, Queen Alexandra Sanatorium, Davos. Staatsarchiv Thurgau, 9'11, 5.0.0.1/1.

and of Becquerel rays, the high electric potential, the small amount of cloud and fog, the dryness and coldness of the air, the calmness of the air, especially prevalent in winter—all these, together with some further factors, make up the climate of high altitudes."[48] What added another dimension to the local air was the surrounding pine forests, because their scented emanations were also considered beneficial for infected patients.[49] According to Werner, "there are also exhalations from the trees to be taken into account, especially in pine forests, where the aromatic substances in the air may possess an antiseptic influence."[50] Within this symbiotic coexistence, physicians anticipated a reciprocal effect caused by the joint breathing of trees and patients.

A firsthand account from a patient staying at the Queen Alexandra Sanatorium confirms the ideal conditions:

> Here one may carry out the fresh-air treatment in summer or in the depth of winter amid surroundings that make the cure a joy and not a hardship. Here are no wind-swept rooms or corridors. The valley of Davos is free from wind. In winter, so brilliant is the sunshine and so warm its rays that one may lie out on the balconies in perfect comfort. Of course, when the sun goes in the cold may be intense, but it is always a dry cold, and the freedom from wind prevents us from feeling any discomfort, provided we are well wrapped up. Our doctors do not expect us to live in draughts and icy rooms; each room has its radiator and double windows. We dress and undress in warm, cozy rooms, and once in bed with a hot-water bottle we can enjoy the cold fresh air with our windows open wide.[51]

Pfleghard & Haefeli's scheme for utilizing architectural features to amplify the purported curative benefits of sunlight and air for treating TB was simple. A central part, with allusions to an avant-corpse, a projecting element common in French baroque architecture, was flanked by two slightly rotated wings, one of which was added two years after the opening of the sanatorium in 1909. The general layout of the plan recalls Turban's generative principles: "Although the main elevation of the house should be directed to the south, slight turns to the southwest or southeast are not excluded, as long as careful attention is given to the local sun and wind conditions. . . . For larger buildings, it is advisable to choose a center section with two side wings attached at an obtuse angle, with the *Liegehallen* facing south."[52]

Above a ground floor with communal spaces, including a grand dining hall, there were essentially four floors with patient rooms located toward the south and service rooms positioned to the north, with both series of spaces separated by a corridor, just as Turban mandated (fig. 4.7). Individual balconies, roughly half the size of a patient room, contributed to a cell-like structure that Thomas Mann characterized as "porous as a sponge" in describing "the International Sanatorium Berghof" in *The Magic Mountain*.[53] These reinforced balconies, together with an abundance of openings exploited the threshold or intermediate zone between inside and outside.[54] As a contemporary commentator noted, "The outer wall of each patient's room is nearly all window, the construction having been evidently carefully devised with that end in view" (fig. 4.8).[55]

While the use of individual balconies had significant social implications, such as fostering privacy, their design was primarily driven by a desire for domesticity, rather than for medical reasons, since infected patients all arrived in similar conditions and all would be breathing the same air. A regular patient room contained two sets of casement windows and double doors, each approximately four feet (120 centimeters) wide, with matching hopper transom windows above, which, operated by iron pull handles, could swivel both inward and outward (fig. 4.9). This system, straightforward and easy to use, allowed for varying degrees of exposure to the outside air, based on the different configurations of door leaves and windows. Bundled in blankets with a hot-water bottle, a patient at the Queen Alexandra Sanatorium could experience the conditions of fresh mountain air without drafts, even with their windows wide open. Clearly, these circumstances prioritized health over energy efficiency because radiators ran overnight with all the windows open. This

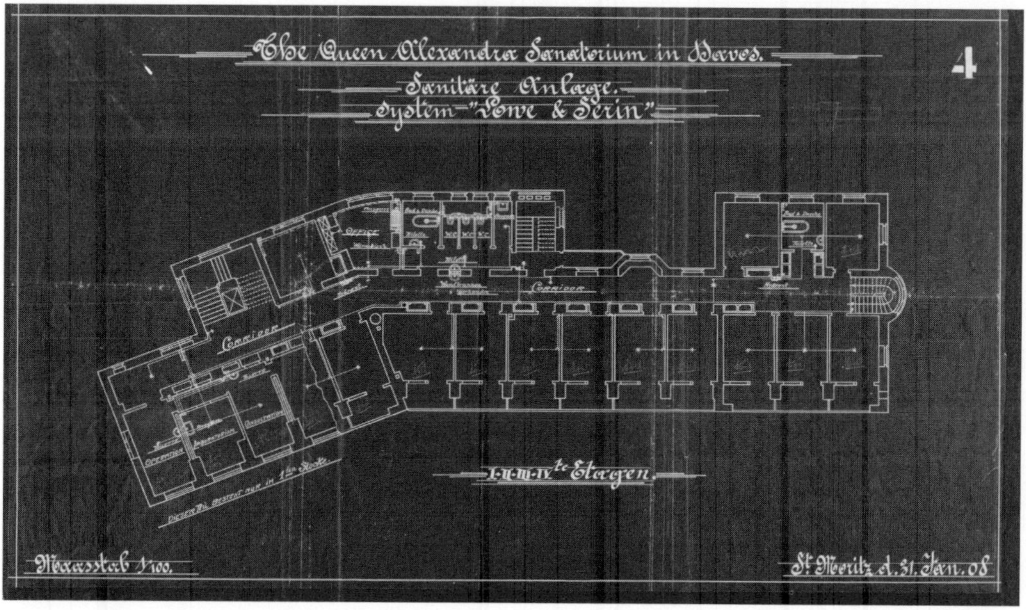

Figure 4.7. Blueprint of the Queen Alexandra Sanatorium dating from 1908, with all patient rooms facing south. Pfleghard & Haefeli, Queen Alexandra Sanatorium, Davos. Staatsarchiv Thurgau, 9'11, 5.0.0.2/5.

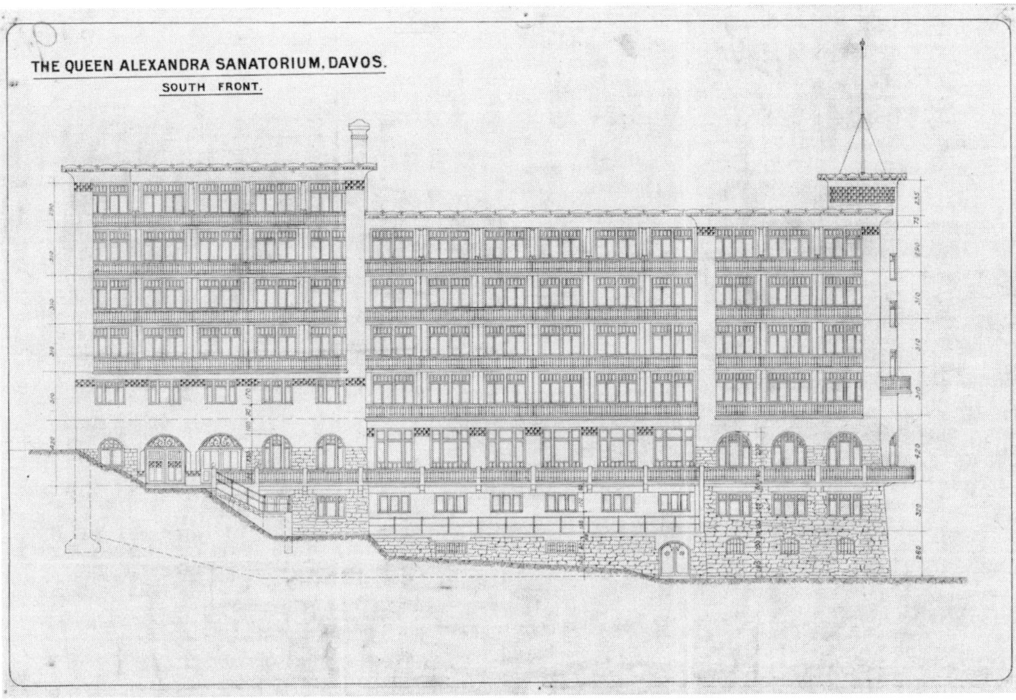

Figure 4.8. South elevation of the Queen Alexandra Sanatorium, without the later extension, featuring patient rooms equipped with individual balconies.Pfleghard & Haefeli, Queen Alexandra Sanatorium, Davos, 1907. Staatsarchiv Thurgau, 9'11, 5.0.0.1/1.

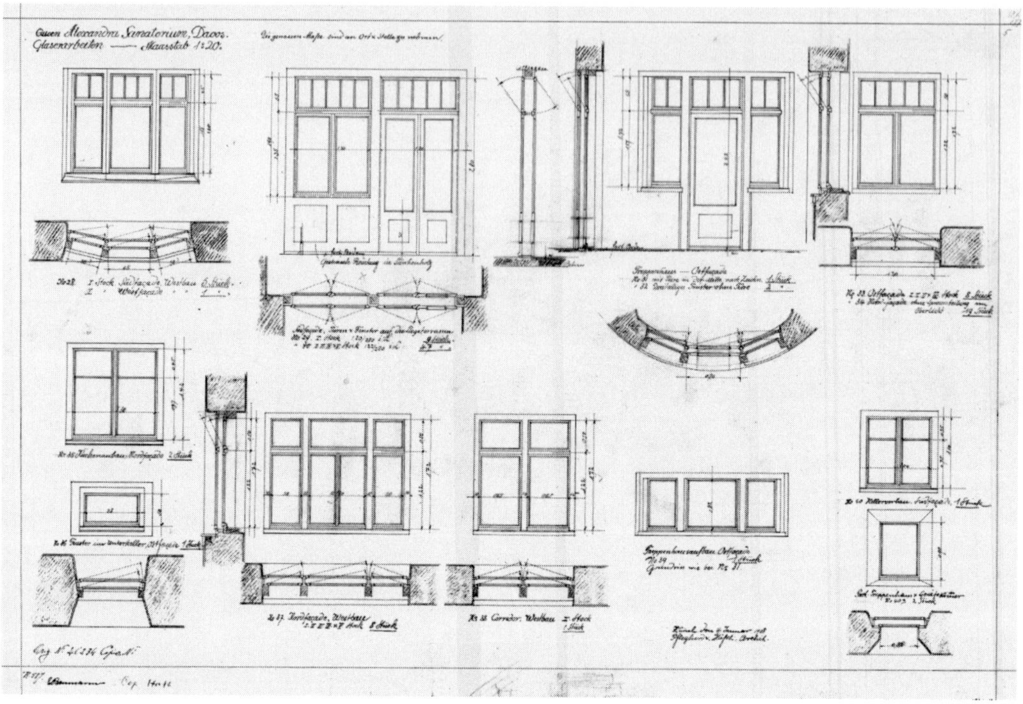

Figure 4.9. Pfleghard & Haefeli, different window types for the Queen Alexandra Sanatorium, Davos, including opening directions, 1907. gta Archive, ETH Zurich, Pfleghard & Haefeli.

building was not designed to temper the interior or induce ventilation. Instead, it rendered drawing outside air inside unnecessary as there was a seamless body of air throughout, creating a fluid environment. Contrary to Hellpach's and Rikli's concerns about architecture as a material shell cutting us off from the physical environment, this structure was deeply enmeshed with it (fig. 4.10).

Giedion was captivated by the way the plan capitalized on sunlight and the elimination of long, bleak corridors. He prominently featured the subsequently added rooftop solarium of the Queen Alexandra Sanatorium in *Befreites Wohnen* and in a 1929 article where he lauded it as "still the best Swiss sanatorium."[56] Both his own photographs, along with his taut, poetic captions, conveyed his enthusiasm for the building: "Solarium. Subsequently added on top of the People's sanatorium (by [Rudolf] Gaberel). The photograph far from reproduces the charm that arises from the interpenetration of landscape; the point of view (which hovers above the ground); and architectural firm framing."[57]

Giedion suggests that the often invisible quality of the atmosphere, as the medium in which everything is immersed and interconnected, has eluded the camera's lens. This is the critical juncture of embodied entanglement where landscape and architecture converge with the perceiving subject. The gta Archive of ETH Zürich contains several photos he took on site, but ultimately excluded from *Befreites Wohnen*, one of which perhaps best illustrates the atmosphere in its engulfing presence. Shot on a rare hazy day, possibly in winter, in this image, the typically impalpable atmosphere becomes a physical envelope for an otherwise exposed structure (fig. 4.11). Due to unusual weather conditions — Davos witnessed little sky cover — the air, at this moment, no longer escaped visibility and became perceptible to the human eye. Here, a translucent, vaporous substance fills the open spans between the roof, posts, and floor, which frame its presence.

With Giedion's photograph in mind, it is easy to envision how the atmosphere effectively formed an envelope for both patients

Figure 4.10. Postcard showing the Queen Alexandra Sanatorium with extensions, including the solarium on the roof of the southwest wing. By then, it had been renamed Thurgauisch-Schaffhausische Heilstätte. gta Archive, ETH Zurich, Haefeli Moser Steiger.

Figure 4.11. The atmosphere as an envelope: photograph taken from the sanatorium's rooftop by Sigfried Giedion around 1922. gta Archive, ETH Zurich, Sigfried Giedion.

and the building, exemplifying the primary objective of the sanatorium movement: to create a space of immersion for patients who benefited from the calm, invigorating mountain air. Much as Giedion's image reveals the otherwise immaterial atmosphere, the gridded structure of the sanatorium asserted its existence by seemingly dividing the aerial substance into equal portions to be inhaled and exhaled by each patient. While architecture often serves as a "protective cocoon" against the weather, the design of the Queen Alexandra Sanatorium inverted this concept.[58] It was constructed not to shield its occupants from the elements, but to expose them to the surrounding environment, facilitating life within the atmosphere.

Air as Habitat and Existential Threat

The particular enmeshment of building, patient, and atmosphere at the Queen Alexandra Sanatorium reveals what philosophers and media scholars today attempt to stress more generally about our relationship with the air. For philosopher Emanuele Coccia, "We are not inhabitants of the Earth; we inhabit the atmosphere."[59] In his philosophical investigation of plants, Coccia emphasizes this ontological interpretation, arguing that the atmosphere relates less to the perception of things and more to their "mode of being."[60] It is "our first world, the medium in which we are wholly immersed: the sphere of breath."[61] And this sphere is charged with byproducts from various sources: gaseous emanations of plants, solid particles such as dust and pollen, germs and microorganisms such as the *Mycobacterium tuberculosis* or the coronavirus, as well as anthropogenic particles created or incidentally produced by human activities such as aerosols or microparticles. Indeed, the composition of air, beyond the gases that chemically constitute the atmosphere, is quite elusive.[62] Seen in this way, air is a substance at once internal and external to us: due to its volatile and immersive nature, it serves as the medium through which we inhale and exhale the world.

With his conception of the atmosphere as a realm to inhabit and air a substance to take in, Coccia helps us understand that this dual notion of air functions as a principle of mixture. It also aligns with our analysis of the Queen Alexandra Sanatorium's relationship to the local climate of Davos, where tubercular patients inhaled pristine mountain air enriched with scented pine aromas while simultaneously being enveloped by this fluid environment. Immersion and breathing coincide in the air, and the sanatorium simply manifests this affair through its architecture.

This idea of dwelling in the air traces back to French philosopher Luce Irigaray's critique of Martin Heidegger — a staple in all recent discussions of air — where she succinctly asks whether air is not "the whole of our habitation as mortals?"[63] Withdrawn from Western thought, air as an invisible substance has been eclipsed by everything solid and conceptually suppressed in its role as our primary space that is "irreducibly constitutive of the whole."[64] That is Irigaray's appeal to architectural discourse: a conception of air as a vast dwelling, as something in which we are "housed."

This existential dimension of the atmosphere as our primary habitat also makes it an existential threat that far extends beyond concerns of comfort or well-being. German philosopher Peter Sloterdijk argues in *Terror from the Air* (2009) that the environment as such was discovered in the trenches around Ypres, where the first use of mustard gas occurred during World War I.[65] The book tells the story of the most dreadful weapons system of its time and in so doing identifies what Sloterdijk claims is a pivotal moment in history when the epistemological framework that defined the breathable atmosphere suddenly entered the collective consciousness: the atmosphere emerged as a critical life-support system on which we all depend. And yet, the manipulation of the atmosphere described so drastically by Sloterdijk could be achieved only through the prior knowledge and long series of discoveries about the atmosphere that we have been exploring.[66] The events at Ypres simply provided the most drastic example in the early twentieth century of the ways in which breathing can come under duress and our lungs can be harmed.[67]

What happened? On the afternoon of April 22, 1915, German soldiers from a newly founded gas warfare regiment carried over six thousand steel cylinders filled with chlorine gas to the front lines, embedding them in the trenches and covering them with earth or sandbags. Lead pipes connected to the valves snaked out beyond the front line.[68] The attack relied heavily on favorable wind conditions, and when the valves were opened, a green cloud of chlorine—half a dozen kilometers wide and nearly a kilometer deep—wafted toward the French-Canadian troops, engulfing everyone downwind and quickly overwhelming the Allied forces, thus clearing the path for the German advance (fig. 4.12). When chlorine gas combines with water, it forms hypochlorous acid, causing severe tissue damage to the lungs and mucous membranes, and ultimately causing suffocation. Many died in agony, gasping for air.[69] Despite prior delays and multiple warnings, French forces were caught completely off guard, and so were the German forces, who ironically failed to capitalize on the devastating effect of their own attack.[70]

Sloterdijk describes the gas attack at Ypres as "the introduction of the environment into the fight between adversaries,"[71] and weaponizing the atmosphere as an instrument for war did not mark any profound epistemological shift or the discovery of the environment as such, but it did lead to new technologies for dealing with the possibility that the atmosphere can be hostile to human health and well-being, just as the development of meteorology and the advent of air-conditioning became new tools for its dealing with its negative effects.[72] From the terror of chemical warfare, one device emerged as a more or less adequate defense mechanism to restore breathable air: the gas mask. Protection by virtue of individual, mobile air filters became a primary military concern during World War I. These devices embodied the heightened awareness of air as a critical element that had been developing since the mid-nineteenth century.[73]

Figure 4.12. German soldiers emerging from a cloud of poisonous gas in Flanders during World War I. Bundesarchiv, image 183-R05923.

When dealing with the threat of gas became a necessity, there were essentially two ways to resist poisonous vapors: first, through self-contained breathing apparatuses based on a closed-circuit system that temporarily detached the human organism from the surrounding atmosphere, and second, through filter respirators that maintained the connection between the human respiratory system and the environment, albeit with a protective screen. The former created an autonomous, hermetic breathing space, constraint by the available supply of "breath nourishment" (*Atemnahrung*), while the latter relied on filtered immersion, unable to generate additional

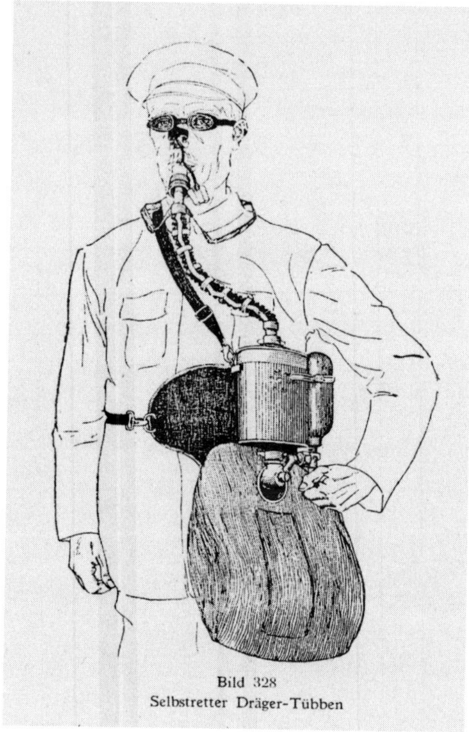

Figure 4.13. Breathing device for survival in unbreathable atmospheres as shown in a book on diving technology from 1933. "Selbstretter Dräger-Tübben," figure 296, in Hermann Stelzner, *Tauchertechnik* (Lübeck: Charles Coleman, 1931), p. 204. Staatsbibliothek Berlin.

breathable air if the oxygen content fell below the minimum threshold (fig. 4.13).[74] Oxygen breathing apparatuses were initially deployed in the mining industry, as Sloterdijk writes, and were only gradually adapted for warfare.[75] The actual gas masks, employing chemical filters, were invented by the German chemist Fritz Haber, who quickly became the leading authority on all matters of chemical warfare.[76]

The lesson of chemical warfare, that an enveloping atmosphere could pose extreme dangers, registered in architectural discourse in 1927, when the German chemist and pharmacist Rudolf Hanslian (1883–1954) idealized the hermetic building envelope as a protective measure. More than seventy years after Pettenkofer warned of the

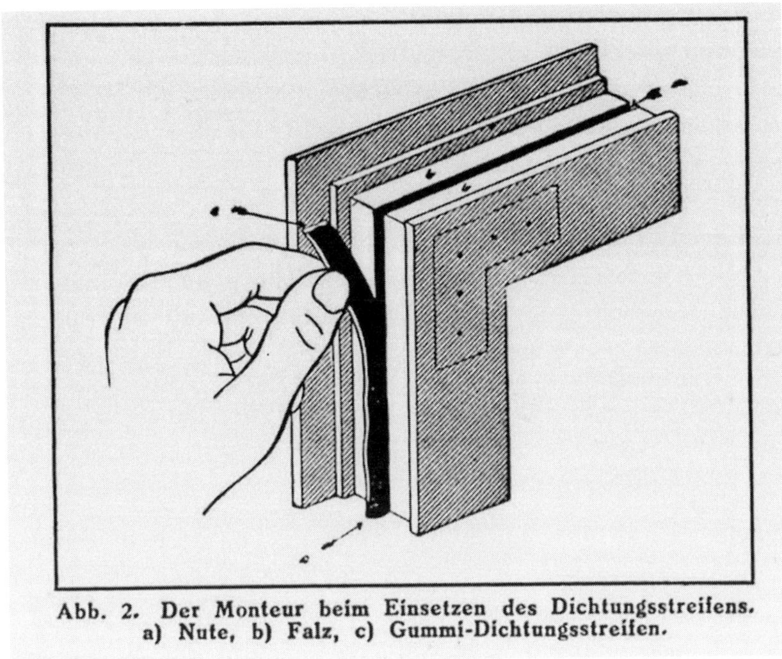

Figure 4.14. How to seal a window frame properly with a rubber band. H. Drucker, "Technik des Luftschutzes," *Gasschutz und Luftschutz* 3.3 (March 1933), pp. 83–84.

dangers posed by sealing in the atmosphere produced by inhabitants of a dwelling, Hanslian focused on the need to seal them in against threats from the atmosphere without.[77] He noted that for new constructions that were going to be designated as protective gas shelters, "the presence of big glass openings implies a handicap hard to resolve" and suggested that this challenge could be mitigated by avoiding windows whenever possible.[78] A building could be made airtight by "lining the entrance door with felt or rubber inserts" (fig. 4.14), as well as by "repeatedly painting the ceiling and walls with oil paint."[79] He also advocated using felt sealings on apartment doors, "particularly those on the first and second floors." The staircase also raised serious concerns because its external wall, especially at the base, was considered the "most susceptible to gas."[80]

Where Hanslian faced this threat from a hostile atmosphere on the scale of door seals and individual rooms, Le Corbusier addressed it on an urban scale in his 1933 masterplan for La ville radieuse (The Radiant City), an unrealized scheme for a highly rational modernist city with anthropomorphic allusions.[81] His exploration of holistic urban designs integrated the looming threat of future atmospheric attacks along with considerations of traffic, noise, and public space in *La ville radieuse*, published in 1933 (fig. 4.15).[82] The Radiant City finds parallels in Le Corbusier's earlier designs—such as his Villa Savoye (1929)—where the use of pilotis, slender concrete posts, "disengages the house from the humid soil," as he claims in a 1930 movie.[83] These commonalities can of course be attributed to the underlying principles of Le Corbusier's architecture (the use of pilotis, the free design of the ground plan, the free design of the facade, horizontal windows, and a roof garden), but the Radiant City was a response to contemporary fears in an era when the previous world war threatened a catastrophe to come: "The magazines and newspapers are full of pictures and descriptions. And the poison gas factories work to build up huge stocks. The chiefs of staff announce: 'Not one existing city will be spared: fire, collapse, death by gas. Nothingness! the city razed to the ground! . . .'"[84] Le Corbusier, asks, "What must be done, to hold out against war from the air?" The answer, which he attributes to "the gist of the unexpected verdict made known by the chief of staff":

> Given the present state of city planning, only those cities which are conceived along the lines of the Radiant City are capable of emerging victoriously from an air war. Because in the Radiant City, 100% of the ground is free and only 5% to 12% of the surface has buildings on it; now, those buildings are 'on pilotis,' which means that air circulates, that there is continuous space, that the wind will be able to dissipate the gas.[85]

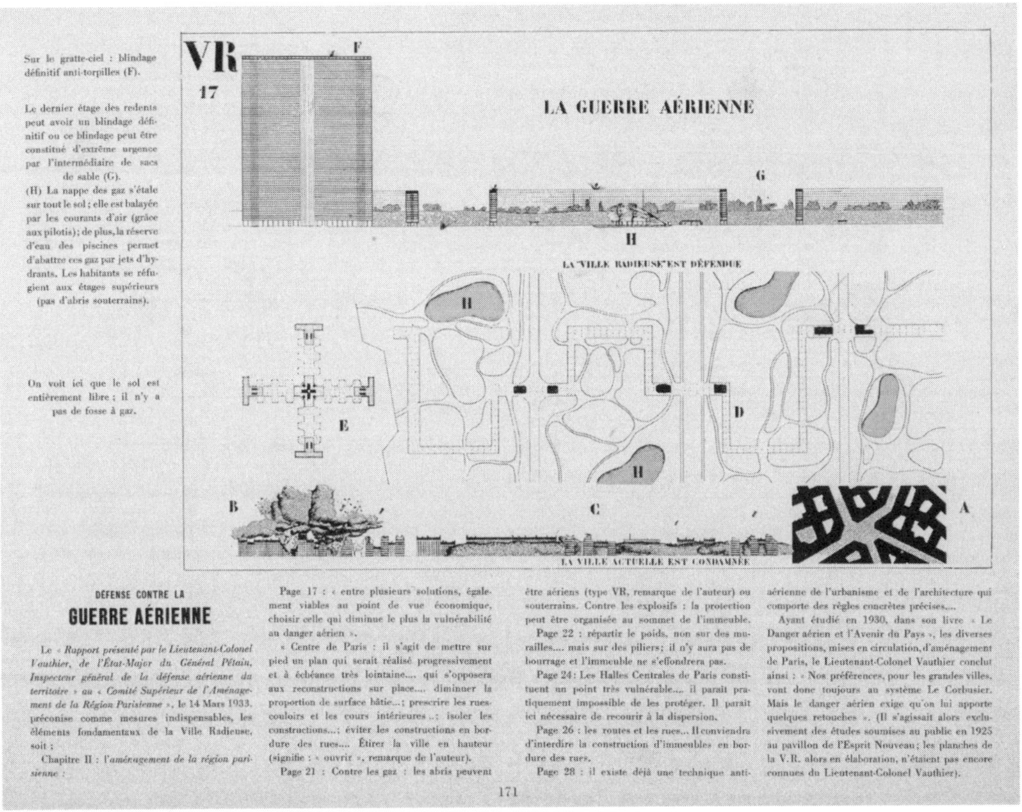

VR 17

LA GUERRE AÉRIENNE

Sur le gratte-ciel : blindage définitif anti-torpilles (F).

Le dernier étage des redents peut avoir un blindage définitif ou ce blindage peut être constitué d'extrême urgence par l'intermédiaire de sacs de sable (G).

(H) La nappe des gaz s'étale sur tout le sol ; elle est balayée par les courants d'air (grâce aux pilotis); de plus, la réserve d'eau des piscines permet d'abattre ces gaz par jets d'hydrants. Les habitants se réfugient aux étages supérieurs (pas d'abris souterrains).

LA "VILLE RADIEUSE" EST DÉFENDUE

On voit ici que le sol est entièrement libre ; il n'y a pas de fosse à gaz.

LA VILLE ACTUELLE EST CONDAMNÉE

DÉFENSE CONTRE LA

GUERRE AÉRIENNE

Le « *Rapport présenté par le Lieutenant-Colonel Vauthier, de l'État-Major du Général Pétain, Inspecteur général de la défense aérienne du territoire* » au « *Comité Supérieur de l'Aménagement de la Région Parisienne* », le 14 Mars 1933, préconise comme mesures indispensables, les éléments fondamentaux de la Ville Radieuse, soit :

Chapitre II : l'*aménagement de la région parisienne* :

Page 17 : « entre plusieurs solutions, également viables au point de vue économique, choisir celle qui diminue le plus la vulnérabilité au danger aérien ».

« Centre de Paris : il s'agit de mettre sur pied un plan qui serait réalisé progressivement et à échéance très lointaine.... qui s'opposera aux reconstructions sur place.... diminuer la proportion de surface bâtie...; prescrire les rues-couloirs et les cours intérieures ..; isoler les constructions...; éviter les constructions en bordure des rues.... Étirer la ville en hauteur (signifie : « ouvrir », remarque de l'auteur).

Page 21 : Contre les gaz : les abris peuvent être aériens (type VR, remarque de l'auteur) ou souterrains. Contre les explosifs : la protection peut être organisée au sommet de l'immeuble.

Page 22 : répartir le poids, non sur des murailles.... mais sur des piliers; il n'y aura pas de bourrage et l'immeuble ne s'effondrera pas.

Page 24 : Les Halles Centrales de Paris constituent un point très vulnérable.... il paraît pratiquement impossible de les protéger. Il paraît ici nécessaire de recourir à la dispersion.

Page 26 : les routes et les rues... Il conviendra d'interdire la construction d'immeubles en bordure des rues.

Page 28 : il existe déjà une technique anti-aérienne de l'urbanisme et de l'architecture qui comporte des règles concrètes précises....

Ayant étudié en 1930, dans son livre « Le Danger aérien et l'Avenir du Pays », les diverses propositions, mises en circulation, d'aménagement de Paris, le Lieutenant-Colonel Vauthier conclut ainsi : « Nos préférences, pour les grandes villes, vont donc toujours au système Le Corbusier. Mais le danger aérien exige qu'on lui apporte quelques retouches ». (Il s'agissait alors exclusivement des études soumises au public en 1925 au pavillon de l'Esprit Nouveau; les planches de la V.R. alors en élaboration, n'étaient pas encore connues du Lieutenant-Colonel Vauthier).

171

Figure 4.15. Le Corbusier's reaction to the threat of air warfare on an urban scale. Le Corbusier, *La ville radieuse* (Boulogne-sur-Seine: Éditions de l'architecture d'aujourd'hui, 1933), p. 171. © F.L.C./ Bildrecht, Wien 2025.

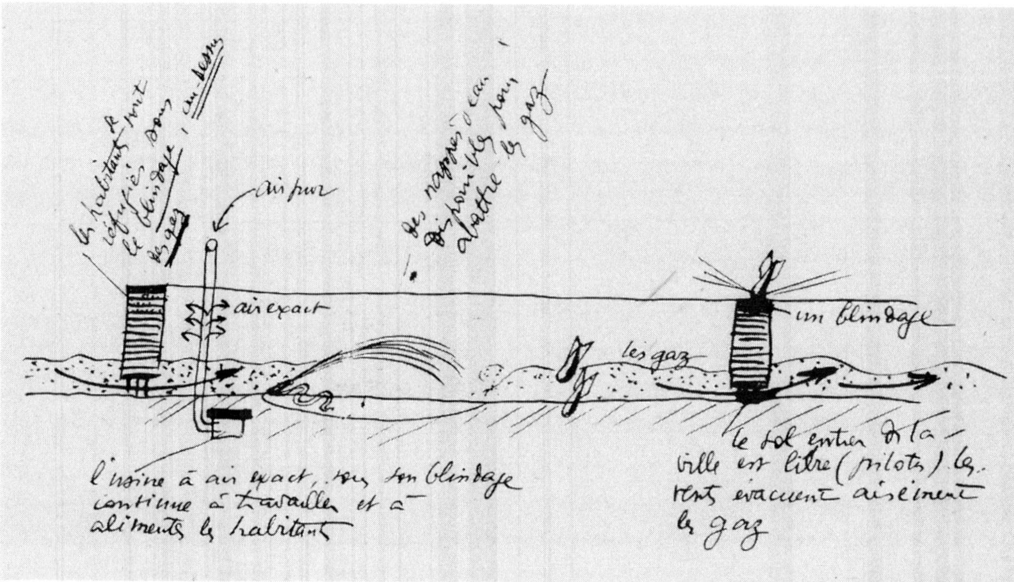

Figure 4.16. Countermeasures against the risks of future gas warfare by means of elevated housing blocks. Le Corbusier, *La ville radieuse* (Boulogne-sur-Seine: Éditions de l'architecture d'aujourd'hui, 1935), p. 65. © F.L.C./ Bildrecht, Wien 2025.

Where wind was seen as a nuisance in the context of TB management and late-nineteenth century health debates, here it appears as a welcome natural force to counteract the dangers of toxic fumes, setting the atmosphere in motion with the help of unobstructive buildings. In Le Corbusier's claim that we would need to elevate the building masses of future cities to maintain a continuous ground space, reduce the buildings' immediate footprint, and allow toxic fumes to dissipate swiftly (fig. 4.16), it becomes evident that the atmosphere was no longer seen merely as a remedy for unhygienic soil—as he describes in respect to the Villa Savoye—but rather as an element that could itself acquire a dreadful and dangerous agency. However, viewed more broadly, what we have seen is that the atmosphere—engulfing or immersive, invisible or visible, still or in motion—could serve as both a source of existential threat and a means of recovery, oscillating between danger and remedy.

Architecture operates between these two extremes.[86] Next, we'll focus in detail on the differing ways in which major actors in the domains of art history, architectural history and criticism, and architecture itself conceived of how buildings should do so.

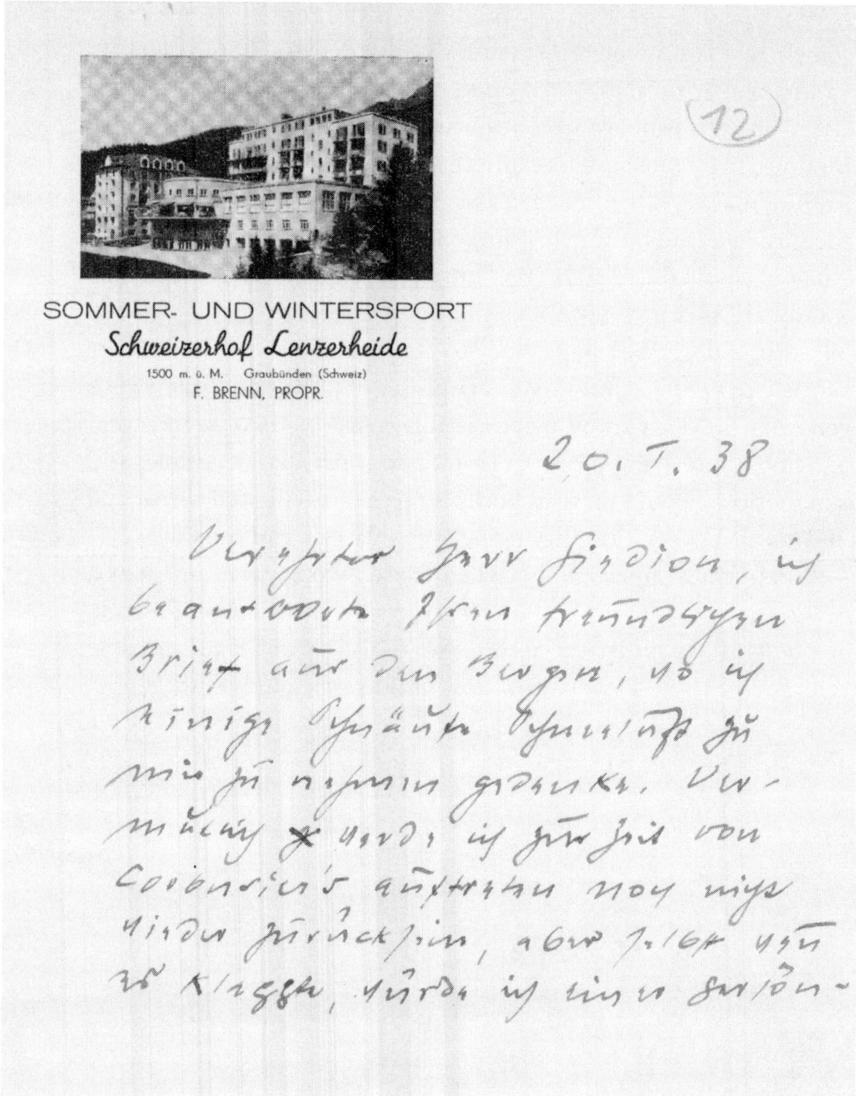

SOMMER- UND WINTERSPORT
Schweizerhof Lenzerheide
1500 m. ü. M. Graubünden (Schweiz)
F. BRENN, PROPR.

(12)

20. I. 38

Figure 5.1. Letter from Heinrich Wölfflin to Sigfried Giedion, written in Lenzerheide, January 20, 1938. In Ulrich Stucky, ed., *Hommage à Giedion: Profile seiner Persönlichkeit* (Basel: Birkhäuser, 1971), gta Archive ETH Zürich.

CHAPTER FIVE

Pneumatic Houses

It is widely held that Switzerland offers a particularly pristine setting for taking a breath of fresh air. Its alpine regions stand out for their often barren, yet scenic landscape, and numerous are the renderings and images of such renowned peaks as the Matterhorn or the Tinzenhorn. Situated in the canton of Graubünden, the Parpaner Rothorn is perhaps less known, but nevertheless rises up to a considerable height of 9,511 feet (2,899 meters). At the foot of the Parpaner Rothorn lies the small village of Lenzerheide, and it is here that Heinrich Wölfflin (1864–1945) found himself on a late January day in 1938. It may seem natural that a Swiss art historian of his caliber would spend time in this part of the world during the cold winter season, and yet he could just as well have visited Zurich, instead, where only five days before, Le Corbusier's exhibition *Oeuvre plastique 1919–1937* had opened at the Kunsthaus.[1] The exhibition, organized by his local friends, was anticipated with bated breath and planned as a grand, festive event.[2] Instead of making Le Corbusier's acquaintance, though, Wölfflin preferred to stay up in the mountains, intending "to catch a few sniffs of snowy air" (*einige Schnäufe Schneeluft zu mir zu nehmen*).[3] Breathing won over art.

Apparently, Wölfflin did not regret missing the opportunity to meet Le Corbusier in person, because he felt that the generational discrepancies between him and the artist-architect were too great to overcome. In a letter written from the Schweizerhof Hotel in Lenzerheide responding to a letter from Giedion, one of his former students and by then an eminent proponent of the modern movement, Wölfflin professed distant admiration for Le Corbusier's disposition in general, but declared that even though his works gleamed like the "Northern Lights" (or because they did), they didn't warm him up (fig. 5.1).[4]

Wölfflin's expression of even this limited admiration was met with distant skepticism. Where Wölfflin sensed an "irreconcilable generational discrepancy" (*unüberbrückbare Generationsunterschied*), his former doctoral student Giedion had long turned toward the present and had become a critic of modernist architecture, and an advocate to the work of Le Corbusier in particular. This unconsummated meeting, a moment of potential association and actual disconnection between three of the major figures in contemporary art, the history of art and architecture, and modernist architecture, points us toward the different ways in which the metaphoric, analogous, and actual relationship between architecture and breathing was conceived and actualized in the early twentieth century.

In the late 1880s, Wölfflin explored the building-body relationship within the framework of the empathy theory of aesthetics that was current at the time and ascribed breathing as an attribute to certain architectural forms. In Le Corbusier's case, the connection became even more explicit through patterns of analogy as he began incorporating actual lungs and physiological data into his publications from the late 1920s onward. For Giedion, the ideal house—most compellingly championed by Le Corbusier—was one that is permeated by air, a point he made abundantly clear in his first monograph from 1928. What follows next is a story about breathing told through the works of these three men, intended as a guide to rethinking the body-building correlation at the crossroads of discourse and construction.

The Proportions of Breathing

When breathing becomes a form of expression, its weight seems to tilt from physiology to psychology, redirecting the focus from bodily phenomena to the world of emotions. This shift, however, does not make breathing any less somatic and—perhaps unexpectedly—no less architectural. In 1886, Wölfflin evokes breathing for the first time in his dissertation, published as *Prolegomena zu einer Psychologie der Architektur* (Prolegomena to a psychology of architecture), a youthful meditation on architecture's affective power in which the physiological process retained a formative role as a mode of expression.[5] How is it possible, Wölfflin wonders, that an inanimate object such as a building transmits an impression one can feel as an expression? Between a blind alley and a foundational work, his thesis ponders the psychosomatic connection between bodies and buildings in which breathing serves as a kind of communication device between both realms. When Wölfflin analyzes the characteristics of proportions, he assumes buildings to have agency over the human body's inner workings by way of affect.

Every building has its encounters with breathing subjects, but this is only half the truth. After all, Wölfflin argues, the proportions of architectural structures, in other words, have the power to influence our way of breathing. "Powerful columns energetically stimulate us; our respiration harmonizes with the expansive or narrow nature of the space. In the former case we are stimulated as if we ourselves were the supporting columns; in the latter case we breathe as deeply and fully as if our chest were as wide as the hall."[6] Our respiration is affected by the architectural space in which we find ourselves.

We saw how the idea that people are psychosomatically touched by the atmosphere was to become central to early twentieth-century conceptions of the relation between architecture and the gaseous envelope in the work of the physician and psychologist Willy Hellpach and the architect Siegfried Ebeling, but it was with Wölfflin at the end of the nineteenth century that the idea of an effective influence of architecture on breathing was articulated within the broader framework of empathy theory in nineteenth-century German aesthetics.

German philosopher Robert Vischer (1847–1933) postulated that the human body (and with it, the soul) project themselves unwittingly "into the form of the object." *Einfühlung*, or empathy, quite literally means to feel into something. "In rooms with low ceilings," Vischer writes, "our whole body feels the sensation of weight and pressure."[7] Imagine the uplifting feeling induced by a Gothic spire or the firm stance one might sense in front of a baroque facade, with all its mass and symmetry. Vischer's work laid out a path Wölfflin would follow, reconciling mental and bodily stimulation, psychology and physiology. For the empathy theorists, every space directly speaks to our body, and Wölfflin elaborated that claim into a theory of psychophysical response. An analogy between the human body and the laws of proportion had been made since ancient Greek antiquity, but instead of focusing on the body's own structural organization — symmetry, proportion, directionality — Wölfflin foregrounds its capacity to empathize with other forms. The body's inner processes, especially breathing, he claimed, are susceptible to external impressions, and he finds great interest in "the relation of proportions to the *rate of breathing*" (his emphasis):[8] Gothic spaces, narrow and tall, inhibit a person from deep breathing and thus induce feelings of awe or devotion. The lateral expansion missing in the architectural space inflects the extension of the corporeal space, preventing the ribs from moving outward. The physical effect, however, is experienced as affect and not actually imposed by the walls and ceilings — the lack of physical cause and effect is offset by bodily empathy.

Among the many references Wölfflin parsed in developing this account was Wilhelm Wundt's *Grundzüge der Physiologischen Psychologie* (General description of physiological psychology, 1874), one of the foundational texts in the history of psychology.[9] Wundt (1832–1920) sought to connect physiology and psychology at the crossroads of inner and outer observation of the human body. Noting that "all affects have significant physical repercussions," he distinguishes between "sthenic" and "asthenic" affects, that is, between those that cause tension in the body and those that lead to relaxation. Sthenic affects—the cause of which could be anger or zeal—provoke a faster heartbeat as well as a "greatly increased respiratory rate."[10] Wölfflin took parts of this system and applied it to architecture.

The affective bonds between buildings and our physiology, between spatial proportions and a person's breathing rate, can occur in the experience of architecture because their occurrence is part of a more general psychophysiological process that also occurs between living bodies. As Wölfflin saw it, the synchrony of feeling and the respiratory rate is not coincidental, but represents the close ties between mental and physical acts inside the body. As a result, this transmission leads to a mutual reaction through which we can sympathize with another person, just as one tends to catch the yawn of someone else, a contagious reaction we nowadays link to empathy (and something to which psychopaths are said to be immune). The breath opens a portal to a world of emotions, forging bonds between two individuals. And it cuts both ways. "For the internal organs," Wölfflin remarks to highlight the two decisive aspects of his corporeal thinking,

> are sympathetically affected, and according to my observations it is respiration that is most susceptible to change. The rhythm of breathing that we perceive in others is what is most easily transferred to us. We may remain impassive when viewing the physical pain of another person, but we are horrified to see someone suffocating, for we vicariously feel the agony. This fact is important, for breathing is the most direct organ of expression.[11]

Wölfflin doesn't theorize how buildings can function affectively in the same way; he just notes that they do. For example, consider "the impression of two wavy lines of different wavelengths":

> Short undulations appear quick and lively, long undulations appear calm and often tired. The former suggests lively, rapid breathing; the latter, a dull, slow breathing. The length of the undulation gives the duration; the height of the wave gives the depth. Considering the importance of the rate

> of respiration for the expression of moods, this is a highly important aspect of historical character. It can even be observed that the older a nation is, the more rapidly its architecture begins to breathe; it becomes excited. How still and restful are the lines of the ancient Doric temple: everything is broad and slow-measured. With the Ionic there is already a quicker movement, a pursuit of slenderness and lightness. As antique culture approached its end, it ever more feverishly demanded faster movement. People who are by nature hot-blooded reach the highest emotional pitch. One need only think of the breathless haste of Arab decorative lines.[12]

"Unfortunately," he writes, while "a historical psychology, or better yet, a psychological history of art, must be able to track the growing speed of linear movement with great precision," at present, "I must satisfy myself with hints."[13]

Wölfflin's fixation for the breathing rate has to be seen in the context of the more pervasive fascination with all things respiratory, we have been exploring here, a cross-cultural awareness that permeated various disciplines, from art history to physiology, from experimental hygiene to philosophy. But Wölfflin's conjecture about the expressiveness of buildings by virtue of lines and proportions also has an antecedent in the sciences of music and evolution, where related assumptions had been put forward by the Austrian composer Friedrich von Hausegger (1837–1899) and by Charles Darwin (1809–1882).

In 1885, a year before Wölfflin published his thesis, Hausegger's *Die Musik als Ausdruck* (Music as expression) presented expressions as body movements, including vocal utterances, in which an emotional state becomes recognizable.[14] This is the reason why an expression conveys meaning someone else understands, regardless of whether it originates from the human body, music, or a building. Hausegger's account has striking parallels with the relationship between the human body and form the way Wölfflin sought to establish it, except that Hausegger's form was musical.

The physiological backbone of Hausegger's study was to a large extent shaped by Darwin's third major work of evolutionary theory,

The Expression of the Emotions in Man and Animals (1872), in which he explores the history and behavioral aspects of emotional life from a biological point of view.[15] Darwin pursues this work on interspecies comparisons with vivid descriptions of how certain emotions, from the low spirits to the high spirits, from grief and despair to love and devotion, elicit specific body responses irrespective of any conscious efforts to regulate them.[16] Such emotional responses are largely automatic and not the product of society or culture; they are inherited rather than learned. While postures and gestures can be cultivated, elementary expressions are the result of physiological processes beyond our control. They derive from elsewhere: emotions in animals prefigure the ones we experience.

While breathing for Darwin does not exhaust the full range of expressions and is but one step in a convoluted chain of actions that entails blood circulation, muscular contractions, arterial relaxation, as well as the heartbeat, it is an important element. In the concluding remarks one paragraph brings together both classes, humans and animals, and it specifies a set of behaviors according to their relevance. Darwin writes that

> actions of all kinds . . . may consist of movements of any part of the body, as the wagging of a dog's tail, the shrugging of a man's shoulders, the erection of the hair, the exudation of perspiration, the state of the capillary circulation, laboured breathing, and the use of the vocal or other sound-producing instruments. Even insects express anger, terror, jealousy, and love by their stridulation. With man the respiratory organs are of especial importance in expression, not only in a direct, but in a still higher degree in an indirect manner.[17]

On the margin of the manuscript for his *Prolegomena*, Wölfflin scribbled "Baroque: irregular breathing," as if the style as a whole was one of Darwin's animals suffering from grief or anxiety, an organism imbued with life.[18] Darwin had recognized the expressive power of breathing, but it was Wölfflin who saw an affective potential in architectural forms to arouse in us physiological reactions the way other human beings do.

Breathing Forms

Wölfflin would become engrossed with the problem of baroque art and architecture over the next couple of years after he completed the *Prolegomena*, a preoccupation that dominated much of his academic career, and thirty years later, he returned to his early intuition in *Kunstgeschichtliche Grundbegriffe* (Principles of art history, 1915), one of the most influential books in art history throughout the twentieth century and up until today.[19] Wölfflin wrote *Principles* in the months leading up to the outbreak of World War I with the aim of giving universal significance to his concept of form. The system he developed there employs ten categories ranked in five groups of polar opposites: linear and painterly, plane and recession, multiplicity and unity, clearness and unclearness, and especially closed form and open form, for which he coined the terms "tectonic" (a term that subsequently came to be used by Wölfflin to characterize architecture) and "a-tectonic."[20] Wölfflin observes that in the baroque era, the closed, "tectonic" form characteristic of Renaissance classicism (and inherent in the nature of built structures) began to take on a dynamic quality, as if they were beginning to "breathe":

> Classical taste consistently works with clear lines, tangible boundaries; every place has a clear edge, every cube speaks as an entirely tangible form, there is nothing that is not comprehensible in its pure corporeality. The baroque demotes line from its status as a boundary marker, it multiplies the edges, and as the form as such becomes more complicated and the order more convoluted, it becomes increasingly difficult for the individual parts to assert their plastic values: regardless of the specific view, a (purely optical) movement flares up over the totality of forms. The wall vibrates, every corner of the space twitches.[21]

Thus, "the forms have a generally different effect. . . . In the tectonic arts as with the other arts," Wölfflin argues, "the basic idea of the baroque" is that "there should no longer be anything that solidifies into tangible lines and planes; as with the other arts, the impression of permanence should be superseded by the impression of transformation; as with the other arts, form should breathe."[22]

But of course, walls don't really vibrate, space doesn't really twitch, and buildings don't really breathe for Wölfflin. He is talking about aesthetic responses to the blurring of boundaries produced by perceived differences of light and shadow that are engendered by architectural forms.[23] And now these responses are treated purely as an "impression of transformation," not as in the *Prolegomena* but as determinative of empathic physical changes on the part of the viewer. Thus, the respiratory being, conceived of as an emphatic subject attuned to space, was replaced by an architectural form itself metaphorically breathing.

Emil Kaufmann (1891–1953), whose slender 1933 book *Von Ledoux bis Le Corbusier* (From Ledoux to Le Corbusier), traces the origins of modernism to Claude-Nicolas Ledoux (1736–1806), whose neoclassical, revolutionary architecture of the late eighteenth century, he claims, with its emphasis on autonomy foreshadowed the work of Le Corbusier.[24] In one instance, Kaufmann examines the gradual staggering of the facade of Ledoux's Hôtel de Montmorency, a structure he considers transitional in terms of stylistic evolution and thus still rooted in the old baroque spirit.[25] The formal distinctions between the baroque and neoclassicist periods are captured in what Kaufmann calls "baroque union" (*Barocker Verband*) and "pavilion system" (*Pavillon-System)*, two principles reminiscent of Wölfflin's formal approach.[26] According to Kaufmann, Ledoux's work marked a fundamental break from the unifying system of the baroque, replacing it with an autonomous architecture that championed "a pavilionized and decentralized system of composition":

> The emergence of the autonomous floor plan may be illustrated by some of Ledoux's schemes. The simple classicism of its exterior gives little hint of the bold innovator that we encountered in the designs. In the house of Mézières at Eaubonne, the dining room is already off axis, but in such a way that it is still possible to see through from the vestibule. In the house

> of the Mademoiselle de Saint-Germain from 1772 or in the house that the architect built for himself in 1780 in the Rue Poissonière, the staircase is in the middle, interrupting the main artery of the building. This interruption to the circulation marks the end of the breathing baroque organism. The classical baroque tradition is dying before our eyes. It is replaced by a clearly purposeful interior design.[27]

Breathing, in this instance, no longer designates the ability to produce visual effects in viewers—Kaufmann associates it literally with the circulation of human inhabitants inside the structure (fig. 5.2). Where a central void would assert the spatial continuity between inside and outside in the interior of the house—a critical feature of the "classic-baroque tradition" in Kaufmann's view—Ledoux's scheme shows a small entry room (labeled as *I* in the drawing) wedged between the external portico and the internal staircase and thus compartmentalizing what used to be continuous. Unlike contemporary discussions of breathing, health, and hygiene, this account also has little to do with the ways in which a building's interior physically supports an inhabitant's body. Instead, it deals metaphorically with the form of a building as itself a "breathing . . . organism," a conception that is being replaced by the advent of architecture as exemplified by the work of Ledoux.

Giedion arrived at a similar conclusion about architecture's conceptualization of the form of a building as a body via a completely different genealogy of modern architecture. In contrast with Kaufmann's approach, his 1928 study, *Bauen in Frankreich, Bauen in Eisen, Bauen in Eisenbeton* (Building in France, building in iron, building in ferroconcrete), makes explicit references to both physical culture and air more generally, beginning his discussion by noting that "physiologists have shown that a person's body build and nature are inseparably connected. Science traces specific characters back to certain bodily types. The connection between respiration and mental balance has been discovered. The body takes its form internally through breathing, gymnastics, sport."[28]

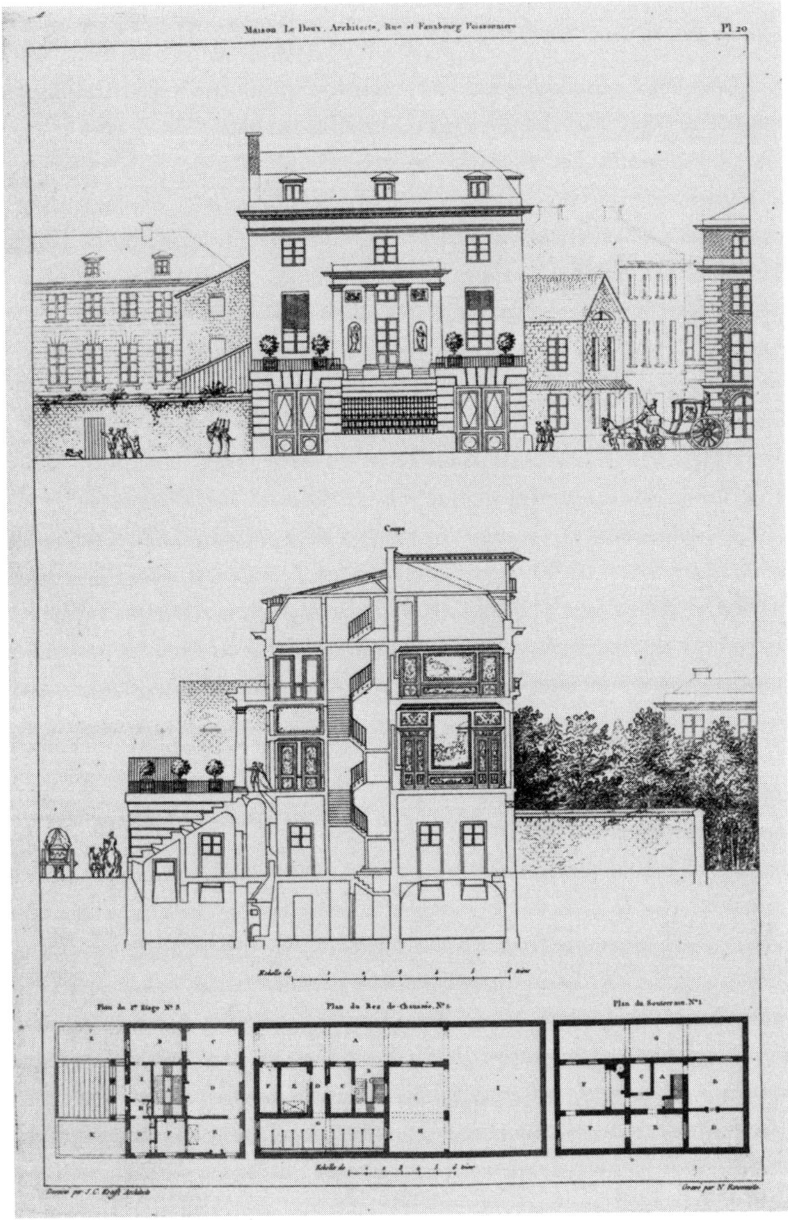

Figure 5.2. The end of the breathing baroque organism: elevation, longitudinal section, and floor plan of Ledoux's house at Rue Poissonière, 1801. Jean-Charles Krafft, *Plans, coupes, élévations des plus belles maisons et des hôtels construits à Paris et dans les environs, publiés* (Faubourg Germain: F. Benoist, 1802). BNF Paris, public domain.

Just as a body develops from within, a building evolves through construction, Giedion argued, and he evokes "the connection between respiration and mental balance" as an example of organic, corporeal integrity that overcomes the polarity between outer appearance and internal structure. This connection, he claimed, is precisely what nineteenth-century historicist buildings failed to achieve: though constructed with modern techniques, such as skeletal iron frameworks, they masked their true nature by dressing their exteriors behind stifling stone settings and in retrograde historical styles. Although new construction techniques had long been developed, early nineteenth-century society was unprepared for their systematic implementation.[29]

Prompted by Le Corbusier, and contrary to the historical argument put forth by Kaufmann, *Bauen in Frankreich*, Giedion's first architectural monograph, traces the lineage of modernist architecture and that of Le Corbusier specifically not to Ledoux but back to anonymous iron constructions and proposes a new genealogy of modern ferroconcrete architecture, the origins of which are to be found in nineteenth-century France.[30] An unofficial vernacular of French iron constructions — outside the traditional scope of architectural history — brought innovation and undermined the dominance of historicism, Giedion argues. *Bauen in Frankreich* seeks to connect anonymous engineering with known architecture and eventually connect figures such as Gustave Eiffel (1832–1923) and Le Corbusier. This connection was grounded in a "new constructional interpenetration of a building," a concept Giedion claims was central to understanding an evolutionary history in which the dormant tradition of iron constructions could be uncovered in contemporary ferroconcrete productions. Like the 1920s residential houses of Le Corbusier, these constructions (the Eiffel Tower and the Pont Transbordeur, a former transporter bridge spanning the industrial harbor of Marseille) were characterized by interpenetration (*Durchdringung*), a term he used throughout many of his texts to consolidate a set of spatial qualities into an epistemic framework.[31] Perhaps not coincidentally, the term also aptly captures the spatial dimension of our lungs, an organ that facilitates the interpenetration of a body's exterior with its interior through the medium of air.

Air, in turn, serves as the common link between French iron constructions and Le Corbusier's architecture: "The significance of the Eiffel Tower lies in its structure. By its silhouette undoubtedly a product of its age: monument, sculpture. But all flesh has been left off, everything is reduced to connective parts, and the air drawn into the interior of the piers now becomes, in an unprecedented way, a formative material."[32] Here, air is no longer a background medium in which structures are immersed. Instead, it becomes an integral part of the tower, a substance essential to its aesthetic and material existence.

In contrast to the passive air of Davos, however, this air is always in motion and never static, as is evinced by the many allusions to flow. It is drawn into the openwork of the Eiffel Towel and its "air-flooded stairs,"[33] and "cubes of air spill over" into Le Corbusier's houses of the 1920s. These cubes of air are "onrushing," and the houses in turn are "penetrated" or "flooded with air."[34] Air replaces solid volumes, as if space had previously not been empty. "The solid volume is opened up wherever possible by cubes of air, strip windows, immediate transition to the sky," writes Giedion. The invisible substance enters architecture not due to a flaw or lack of airtightness, but as an intentional aesthetic experience. "Corbusier's houses are neither spatial nor plastic: air flows through them! Air becomes a constituent factor!"[35] This air is more poetic than scientific, conceptual, rather than chemical, and not intended to oxygenate the human lung as nourishment for the body. Instead, it evokes the interpenetration of inside and outside. Like our bodies, the modern house is intimately connected to the air that surrounds it. Compare this flow of air that Giedion refers to in German as "Durchspültsein des Hauses von Luft" to an image often deployed in medical circles. As the contemporary physician and homeopathic healer Ludwig Schmitt put it in *Das Hohelied vom Atem* (The canticles of breath, 1933): "Breath floods the body like a wave."[36]

Pettenkofer had shown that walls mistakenly assumed to be airtight in the nineteenth-century house actually enabled the interior to communicate with the atmosphere, but Giedion celebrated Le Corbusier's houses of the 1920s for the way in which they dispensed entirely with the distinction between interior and exterior. They abolished the load-bearing exterior wall altogether, and the house as a whole was bathed in air.

Air is what makes Le Corbusier's architecture modern, as Giedion saw it. This air is less about the technical aspects of ventilation or the need to dissipate noxious fumes and carbon dioxide and more about air in motion as an architectural element itself. The architectural instantiation of this concept was the Maison Dom-Ino, with its open floor plan, reinforced concrete columns, and a stairway providing vertical access.[37] While Pettenkofer's bricks were permeable, Le Corbusier's Dom-Ino diagram dispensed with bricks entirely, creating, in the words of Giedion, "the eternally open house."[38] Thus exposed, it allowed "Cubes of air within, cubes of air without. Cubes of air down to the very smallest units at Pessac and the individual cells of a *cité universitaire*. Maximum of air, minimum of walls!"[39] Giedion advocates for such pneumatic qualities in the modern house *tout court*: "This flow of air through the house: inside, outside, below, above (the flat roof is but a partial problem in a larger unity): this is what we demand from the new house!"[40] Thus flooded with air, a modern structure in Giedion's account evokes a breathing body.

Giedion's concept of interpenetration and his treatment of air as an architectural element was not the only way describing the concept of an extensive, isotropic, homogeneous space evenly filled with air, a corporeal entity—whether human or architectural. When in 1965 sections of Robert Venturi's forthcoming book, *Complexity and Contradiction in Architecture* (1966), were released for the first time in *Perspecta: The Yale Architectural Journal*, he engaged with the modernist notion of seamless continuity between interior and exterior space. The formal mechanisms that previously defined the interior and exterior of a Renaissance church, Venturi argues, had been superseded by a new architectural approach, where corners were increasingly dematerialized. Venturi refers to this new paradigm as "flowing space," which he considers "the boldest contribution of orthodox modern architecture," fostering a seamless continuity between inside and outside by virtue of interrelated horizontal and vertical planes.[41] The visual autonomy of these continuous surfaces was achieved not only through new structural techniques that transformed the once load-bearing exterior wall into a mere screen, as Giedion had claimed, but also through the use of transparent plate glass in the connecting areas. In Venturi's formal reading, windows no longer appears as voids in the wall, but as interruptions within its surface—elements the eye was meant to overlook rather than register as distinct architectural features. The result was what he describes as "an ultimate continuity of space," a continuity however more perceived than actual and thus fundamentally paradoxical. "Its expressive and psychological emphasis on the oneness of interior and exterior space was permitted by the very technology which, for the first time, made the inside thermally independent of the outside by means of mechanical equipment."[42] In this view, it is precisely the climatic separation between inside and outside that makes their architectural unity intellectually possible. While the blurred boundaries between inside and outside had become a well-established modernist trope for Venturi and his contemporaries in the 1960s, Giedion envisioned the modernist house as something more radical: a pneumatic structure animated and almost constituted by airflow. Just as *pneuma* as a vital force was held to flow through an ancient body while also always being outside of it, Giedion saw Le Corbusier's houses as being flooded with air, an element that had become a formative material for modern architecture.

In this line of thinking, the modern house requires this dynamic interpenetration of air to be truly modern, depending on it much as a living body relies on breath. But while the "ghostwriter of modern architecture's dreams," as architectural historian Reinhold Martin called Giedion,[43] envisioned a paradigm of airy interpenetration, the concept of the house as a body and the role of the atmosphere and of breath in architecture could also lead to the opposite conclusion: the need for tightly managed and enclosed environments. And it led Le Corbusier in that direction, as well.

Exact Respiration

In *Précisions sur un état présent de l'architecture et de l'urbanisme* (Details of the current state of architecture and urban planning. 1930) and *La ville radieuse* five years later, Le Corbusier devoted the same care, precision, and control that physicians and educators demanded of breathing bodies in the name of health to the construction of enclosed interior space. In this conception of the building as a body, the interior spaces were seen as its lungs. In a 1934 letter to the Princess de Polignac written while Le Corbusier was working on the proofs of *La ville radieuse*, he confesses that "the fundamental chapter in the book, the keystone as you will, is precisely on the question of the lungs in dwelling spaces; that is to say, the quality of air to be introduced into buildings."[44] Le Corbusier not only included an illustration of the lungs there, as we have seen (figs. 2.2 and 2.3), but also one depicting the pulmonary alveoli, almost as if he were aware of the drawings featured in *The American Woman's Home* (fig. 5.3).

His *Précisions sur un état présent de l'architecture et de l'urbanisme* already had demonstrated his interest in forcing air into closed rooms. It features a sketch that illustrates his own version of an early air-conditioning system, aptly named "l'air exacte" and later transformed into "la respiration exacte," or exact respiration, to achieve architecture's autonomy from the untreated surrounding air. The Fondation Le Corbusier in Paris holds the original drawing (fig. 5.4). Orange vectors indicate the airflow emitted from machinery outside the building's perimeter—a diagram of his unrealized competition entry for the Palace of the League of Nations—which

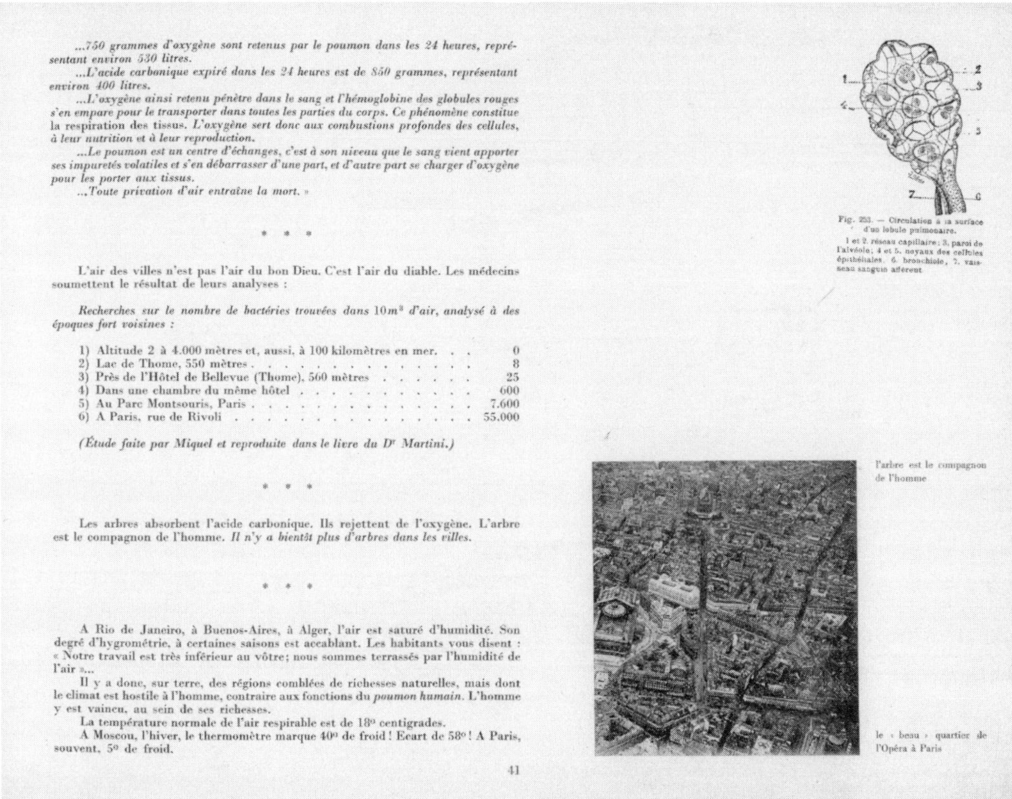

...750 grammes d'oxygène sont retenus par le poumon dans les 24 heures, représentant environ 530 litres.

...L'acide carbonique expiré dans les 24 heures est de 850 grammes, représentant environ 400 litres.

...L'oxygène ainsi retenu pénètre dans le sang et l'hémoglobine des globules rouges s'en empare pour le transporter dans toutes les parties du corps. Ce phénomène constitue la respiration des tissus. *L'oxygène sert donc aux combustions profondes des cellules, à leur nutrition et à leur reproduction.*

...Le poumon est un centre d'échanges, c'est à son niveau que le sang vient apporter ses impuretés volatiles et s'en débarrasser d'une part, et d'autre part se charger d'oxygène pour les porter aux tissus.

...Toute privation d'air entraîne la mort. »

* * *

L'air des villes n'est pas l'air du bon Dieu. C'est l'air du diable. Les médecins soumettent le résultat de leurs analyses :

Recherches sur le nombre de bactéries trouvées dans 10 m³ d'air, analysé à des époques fort voisines :

1) Altitude 2 à 4.000 mètres et, aussi, à 100 kilomètres en mer.	0
2) Lac de Thome, 550 mètres	8
3) Près de l'Hôtel de Bellevue (Thome), 560 mètres	25
4) Dans une chambre du même hôtel	600
5) Au Parc Montsouris, Paris	7.600
6) A Paris, rue de Rivoli	55.000

(Étude faite par Miquel et reproduite dans le livre du Dr Martini.)

* * *

Les arbres absorbent l'acide carbonique. Ils rejettent de l'oxygène. L'arbre est le compagnon de l'homme. *Il n'y a bientôt plus d'arbres dans les villes.*

* * *

A Rio de Janeiro, à Buenos-Aires, à Alger, l'air est saturé d'humidité. Son degré d'hygrométrie, à certaines saisons est accablant. Les habitants vous disent : « Notre travail est très inférieur au vôtre; nous sommes terrassés par l'humidité de l'air »...

Il y a donc, sur terre, des régions comblées de richesses naturelles, mais dont le climat est hostile à l'homme, contraire aux fonctions du *poumon humain*. L'homme y est vaincu, au sein de ses richesses.

La température normale de l'air respirable est de 18° centigrades.

A Moscou, l'hiver, le thermomètre marque 40° de froid ! Ecart de 58° ! A Paris, souvent, 5° de froid.

Fig. 253. — Circulation à la surface d'un lobule pulmonaire.

1 et 2. réseau capillaire; 3. paroi de l'alvéole; 4 et 5. noyaux des cellules épithéliales. 6. bronchiole, 7. vaisseau sanguin afférent

l'arbre est le compagnon de l'homme

le « beau » quartier de l'Opéra à Paris

41

Figure 5.3. Close-up of pulmonary alveoli. Le Corbusier, *La ville radieuse* (Boulogne-sur-Seine: Éditions de l'architecture d'aujourd'hui, 1935), p. 41.

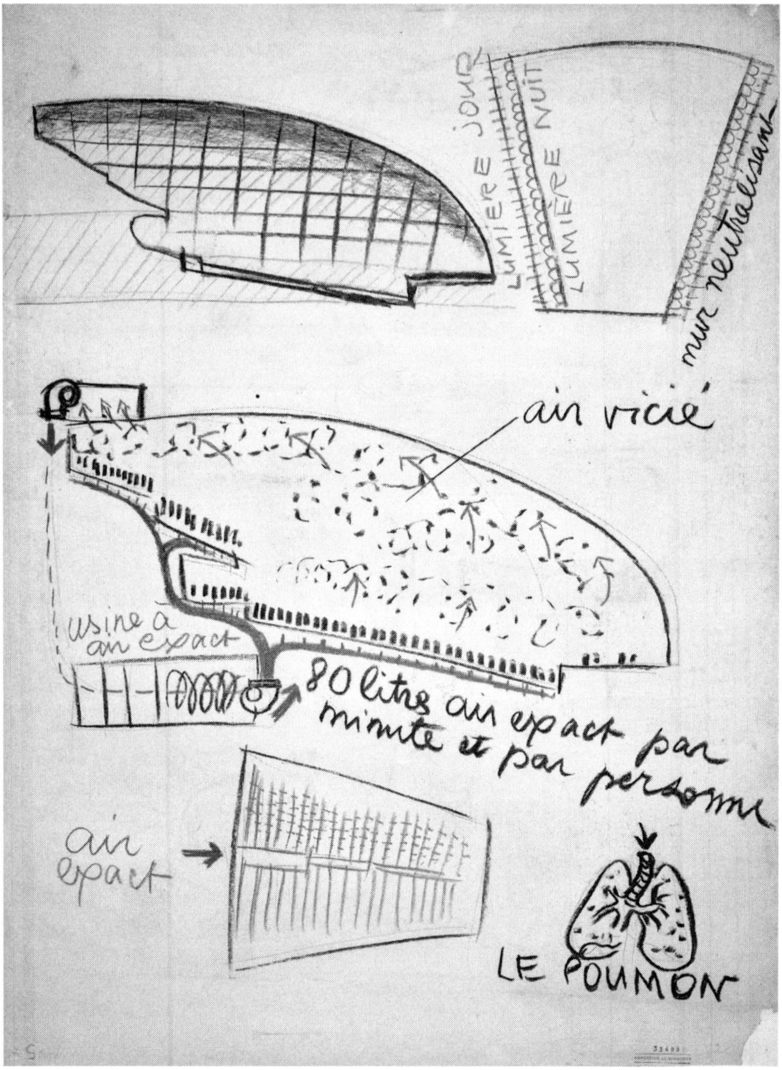

Figure 5.4. The analogy of anatomy and architecture as breathing and ventilation. Le Corbusier, *Precisions on the Present State of Architecture and City Planning*, trans. Edith Schreiber Aujame (Cambridge, MA: MIT Press, 1991), p. 167. Fondation Le Corbusier, Accession Number 33495B © F.L.C./ Bildrecht, Wien 2025.

then enters the structure, circulates to replace used air, and is subsequently conditioned again in a plant. Promising to inject the incredible amount of eighty liters of treated air per person per minute into the interior, the scheme would have supplied over thirteen times the ventilation rate typically required by an adult male based on the current state of research.[45] Adjacent to this setup, a pair of lungs looms large in the lower right corner, where another vector is suggestive of the same kind of principle, indicating the air entering the trachea. As if the illustration itself were not clear enough, Le Corbusier underscores its significance with a caption in all caps that reads "LE POUMON," or "THE LUNGS."[46] As "la respiration exacte," respiration is here again transposed into the realm of architecture, where the supply and extraction of air is more commonly referred to as "ventilation."

Giedion may have claimed the interpenetration of inside and outside in Le Corbusier's houses of the 1920s as the defining characteristic of modern architecture, but the Swiss-French architect also embarked on an effort to tame and domesticate this air by virtue of technology, striving to make it quantifiable, scientific, and precise. At a time when Giedion perceived Le Corbusier's private residences as being bathed in air, the architect was, in fact, working toward isolating his large-scale buildings from their surrounding atmosphere.

This endeavor, however, was doomed to fail. His approach to the total mechanization of air was conceptually rooted in the works of Gustave Lyon (1857–1936), a French engineer who patented an elementary form of closed-circuit air-conditioning that he called "l'air ponctuel," or "regulated-air."[47] In the late 1920s, Le Corbusier collaborated with Lyon on a number of projects aimed at implementing mechanical systems to control the interior atmosphere. Le Corbusier called this innovative heating and ventilation system "conditioned air."[48] In the words of architectural historian Kenneth Frampton, "this is the house as a 'machine for living' taken to its theoretical extreme."[49] The goal was to maintain a constant

Figure 5.5. The nearly hermetically sealed Salvation Army in Paris. © F.L.C./ Bildrecht, Wien 2025.

interior air flow at exactly 18 degrees Celsius (64.4 degrees Fahrenheit) — the exactitude refers to the temperature rather than the consistency of airflow. Le Corbusier had tested his theory of exact respiration earlier at the Palace of the League of Nations in Geneva in 1927 and later, in 1932, at the Cité de Refuge de l'Armée du Salut, a dormitory in Paris. Exact respiration, complemented by what he called a "mur neutralisant," a neutralizing wall — a sandwichlike building envelope consisting of two glass skins with circulating air in between to manage temperature fluctuations — were the two "master concepts" that Le Corbusier envisioned in the late 1920s as a way to produce conditioned air in sealed spaces.[50]

Except that they did not. The competition entry for the unbuilt Palace of the League of Nations in Geneva proposed both concepts, which Le Corbusier claimed previously to have united for the first time, at least conceptually, in the design of the Centrosoyus Palace in Moscow in the late 1920s. Although a double skin was finally implemented, the system for mechanical ventilation was essentially rejected, and for good reason. Neither of these two technologies would have prevented solar heat gain in the interior, a major shortcoming in a structure in which the provision of air through operable windows and porous materials was replaced by mechanical ventilation supporting a hermetically sealed building envelope.

The struggles involved in supplying mechanized, "conditioned" air to a hermetically sealed building appear nowhere better than in the Cité de Refuge (1932–1933), an ambitious, yet arduous endeavor in terms of environmental control, widely regarded as a failure in Le Corbusier's œuvre, his own enthusiasm notwithstanding (fig. 5.5).[51] He later recalls in *Quand les cathédrales étaient blanches* (When the cathedrals were white) that "the sheet of glass was hermetic, since warmed and cleaned air circulated abundantly inside, regulated by the heating plant and the blowers."[52] The issue was this: wrapping the structure with an all-glass envelope, known as the "pan de verre," led to overheating, especially on the side facing south.[53] The resulting glass house required technologies to make the interior habitable. Due to financial constraints, the Cité de Refuge was equipped with a pan de verre instead of the double-layered glass *mur neutralisant* and rather than implementing *respiration exacte*, the building relied on basic heating technology. To fence off Parisian air pollution, the structure, in theory, was hermetically sealed, though not entirely leak free. Pleasant when it first opened, in the winter, the Salvation Army Hostel (as it is referred to in English) turned out to be a disaster during the summer, leading to intense debates between the architect and the planning authorities and forcing Le Corbusier to retrofit the single-glazed facade with "fenêtres d'illusion," or "false windows"—essentially, operable vents.[54] Instead of achieving exact respiration, the building ultimately relied on conventional ventilation. And instead of improving the air quality inside, it caused carbon dioxide levels to rise above standard.[55] While he later added the solar shading system known as a "brise soleil" to mitigate solar heat gain, the air quality remained unregulated beyond its temperature, and exact respiration was concerned not only with thermal comfort, but also with ensuring the purity of the air.

In spite of these countermeasures, as he caustically commented, it was the authorities of the City of Paris who "repudiated the most decisive kind of progress: pure air for the lungs of the city dwellers."[56] For Le Corbusier, this air was to be delivered through mechanical breathing machinery, functioning as the lungs of a building, a conviction resting on his unswerving devotion to high-tech solutions during the short period in which he sought to overcome the shortcomings of the tenuous relationship between the respiratory system and the urban atmosphere through technological innovation.[57]

Le Corbusier may not have successfully resolved the notion of architectural respiration during this phase of his career, but he was clearly conversant with the latest physiological knowledge that began to surface in the first quarter of the twentieth century. His plans for implementing exact respiration emerged from the widespread breathing culture prevalent during that era. A concept perfectly attuned to the machine metaphor Le Corbusier employed for architecture in the 1920s, as a mechanical approach to ventilation in large buildings, exact respiration is the desire to manage breathing applied to the building seen as body. From this perspective, what is illuminating is not the term "respiration," with its distinctly physiological and organic connotations evoking lungs, cells, oxygen supply to the bloodstream, and the exchange of gases at the level of pulmonary alveoli, but the notion of *exactness*, which turns respiration into something mechanical, machinelike, and ultimately regulated. Le Corbusier thus asks in one of his lectures included in *Précisions*: "What is the basis of life? *Breathing*." "Breathing what?" he continues, "hot, cold, dry, damp?" "Breathing pure air at a constant temperature and a regular degree of humidity."[58]

As we saw, during this period, breathing was seen as a physiological activity that needed to be trained, mastered, disciplined, and controlled to counteract the side effects of modernity, including the perceived disconnect between body and mind, with ramifications resulting in unhygienic living conditions brought about by overcrowding, industrialization, and air pollution. Despite its imperfections and utopian aspirations, exact respiration was a system through which Le Corbusier reaffirmed that architecture revolves around the human body, emphasizing that the house is pneumatic in precisely the way on which the lungs are connected to the surrounding atmosphere—even when conceived as hermetically sealed.

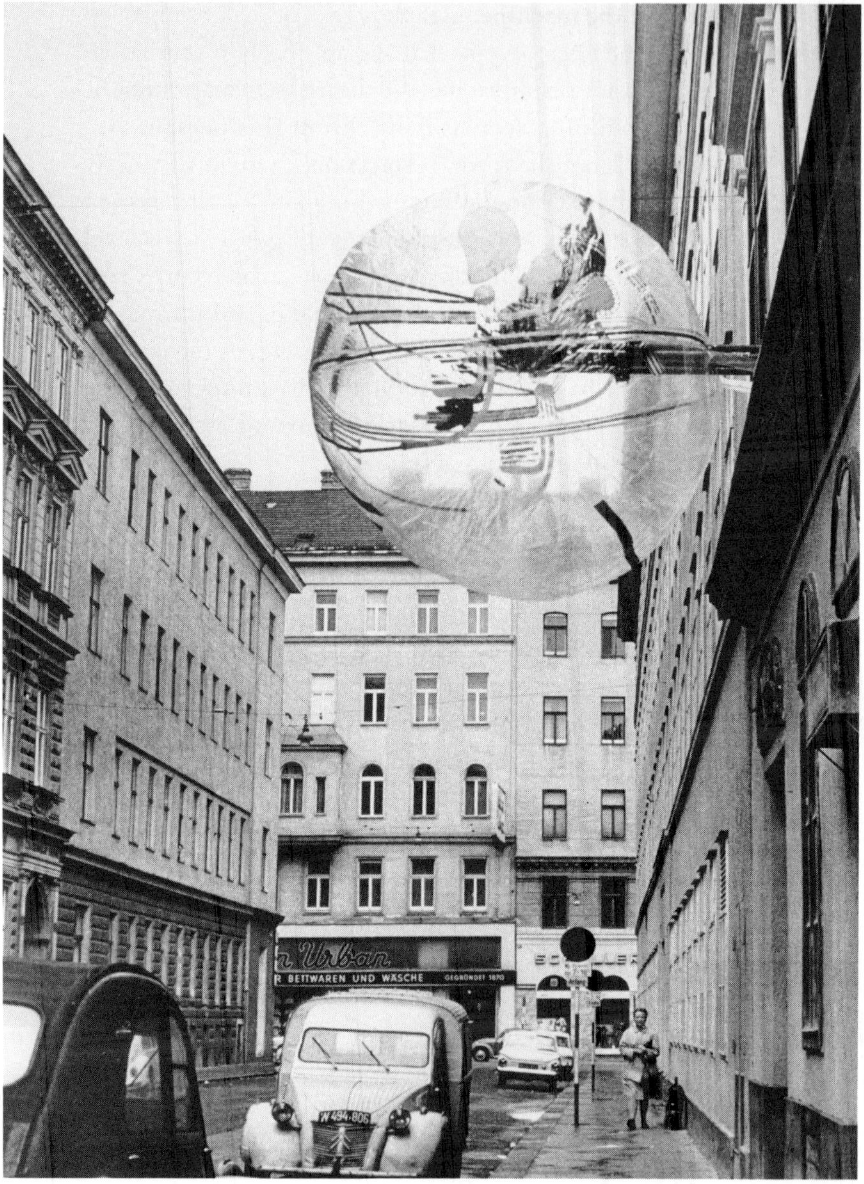

Figure C.1. Haus-Rucker-Co's *Ballon für Zwei*, Apollogasse, Vienna, 1967, as a metaphoric soap bubble trapping a single breath. Image © Haus-Rucker-Co, Gerald Zugmann.

CODA

Sealed Bubbles

From the works of Wölfflin to those of Giedion and Le Corbusier we can trace a gradual transition in the focus of architecture from the breathing body to the breathing structure and back again within the paradigm of respiratory modernism. In 1967, Reyner Banham spent an entire day inside an inflatable dome designed by Peter Murray and Tony Gwilliam set up on a floor of the BBC television studio. What he saw and experienced there and how he responded to and conceptualized it are one way to mark the end of that paradigm in modern architecture.

Banham was so delighted by the experience that he concluded his 1968 article "Monumental Wind-Bags" with a verdict at once succinct and refreshingly colloquial: "I *like* that."[1] Prior to this first in-depth experience with air-inflated environments, his relationship with such structures since around 1961 was nothing more than a "fleeting acquaintance," too shallow to share his insights in a meaningful way. But now, he was unequivocal in his admiration. What he found captivating about this experience was that it was responsive to the environment to an extent that was unheard of within the spectrum of "conventional architecture," which merely "stands rigidly to attention and deteriorates," whereas "inflatables (and tents, to a lesser extent) move and are so nearly living and breathing that it is no surprise that they have to be fed (with amps, if not oats)."[2]

Banham calls this "active homeostasis," the ability or tendency—usually of an organism—to maintain internal stability in response to the external environment through coordinated reactions of bodily processes. While inflatables appeared to Banham to be almost breathing, traditional buildings did not. The inflatable low-pressure dome's enclosure is a "largely self-regulating membrane" that is "more truly like the skin of a living creature," compared with "the metaphorical 'skin' of . . . a glass-walled office block."[3] Thus, "Quite unlike the relationship with the static shell of a traditional building where you can beat your fists on the walls and scream and get no more than an echo for response; here a blow directed at the enclosing skin would produce a flurry of reproachful quivering and creaking, quickly dying away as the even tenor of its normal breathing ways was resumed."[4]

The buoyant air structures of the 1960s thus mark a departure from traditional rigid forms and embody a new approach toward space and its cultural manifestations during the space-age era, characterized by a fascination with eccentric plastic forms, as opposed to the attempts to make the rigid "skins" of traditional structures "breathe" that were characteristic of the era from the mid-nineteenth century to the early twentieth. But more radically, the pneumatic project of the 1960s and 1970s also marks the end of respiratory modernism as an understanding of architectural space as air—architectural space as an integral part of the atmosphere, animated by airflow and conceived both pneumatically and in relation to pneumatic beings. Architecture in the modern period had been defined by awareness of the atmosphere as the primary realm for habitation, an alternative envelope for the building body. It was fundamentally predicated on the concept of breathing space, with all the connotations of literal breath and of space that both metaphorically and literally breathes—spaces inhabited by and designed for pneumatic beings, creatures of the air. The radical postwar expressions of the inflatable movement suppressed the continuous, life-sustaining process of breathing in favor of a single breath trapped within a hermetically sealed membrane. While modern architecture's ability to breathe was both metaphorical and literal, that of the pneumatic movement was mimetic and symbolic, virtually encapsulating one exhalation held within a plastic membrane.

An air-supported structure evokes notions of encapsulation and withdrawal. While natural breathing allows for a constant exchange of gases, breaching the boundary between inside and outside, these bubbles do the opposite: they reinforce the separation between the inner and outer environments, offering a space filled with air, yet disconnected from the life-giving atmosphere. Breathing space, once the result of a collective, open-ended, and capacious process, was now confined to the actions of a select few individuals, sometimes just a single person. These inflatables are typically described by their instability—as temporary structures, or countercultural objects—and the utopian visions of pneumatics in the 1960s may have stemmed from a unique mix of political, economic, social, and environmental concerns, but they primarily convey a sense of seclusion. Continuous breathing was replaced by cocooned air; interpenetration gave way to containment.

While it is true that the various inflatables of that era should not be lumped together, a number of structures illustrate the change that occurred in the avant-garde culture during the late 1960s and early 1970s. In 1972, the architectural collective Haus-Rucker-Co, an experimental group from Vienna, installed a pneumatic oasis, *Oase Nr. 7* (Oasis no. 7), at Kassel's Fridericianum to expand one of the first public museums in Europe by means of an air bubble. An intervention for Documenta 5, it was grafted onto the existing museum facade, coexisting with and relying on the "host structure" for both support and atmosphere, upon which the bubble was also dependent.[5] Similarly, an earlier project from 1967, *Ballon für Zwei* (Balloon for two), protruded from an existing Viennese building (fig. c.1). The air-supported bubble encapsulated two palm trees in the case of *Oase Nr. 7* and two revolving seats in *Ballon für Zwei*.

Another example of breath-trapping spaces can be found in Graham Stevens's artistic explorations into pneumatic microenvironments from the late 1960s, which led him to develop several methods of walking on water. One such solution consisted of an inflatable bubble made out of "fine plastic film" and "a marginal difference in air pressure."[6] Like many others during this period, Stevens understood "the inexpensive power and potential of air" as a way to reconsider the human relationship with architecture and the environment.[7] Similarly, the English architecture group Archigram turned toward inflatable structures as a radical means to subvert prevailing cultural standards. One of its members, the British architect Michael Webb, proposed the so-called *Suitaloon* for the 1968 Milan Triennale, a hybrid of suit and balloon to challenge traditional notions of buildings and clothing. Here, domesticity was produced by an inflated plastic pod, radically questioning architecture's common understanding of interiority.

While these interventions can be read as both environmental and countercultural endeavors, they rest on a history that has its technological origins in 1917, the year when ideas for air structures had first been patented.[8] After gradually and covertly developing within the military sphere, these technologies began slowly to gain broader acceptance from the late 1950s onward, though they continued to be viewed as a novelty during the 1960s.[9] Segregating a small group of individuals within technologically mediated ecosystems, the capaciousness of modernism's breathing space becomes subverted and compartmentalized, trapping in its iconography a small bulk of air symbolically reduced to a single breath within a cocooning membrane.

This perspective stands in stark contrast to Banham's in his 1968 article, in which such structures are perceived as breathing and, being made from supple, pliable plastics, seem alive. But these air-based structures do *not* breathe. They inhibit air flow and isolate us from the outside environment, epitomizing not the interpenetration of outside and inside, but rather what the late Marc Dessauce called "asylum."[10] By replacing the atmosphere as an engulfing envelope with a sealed membrane of Mylar, plastic, or vinyl, they symbolize a desire for safety, seclusion, and separation, mirroring the rise of HVAC systems in the 1960s — a suite of technologies that collectively disconnects our buildings from their aerial surroundings in favor of increased comfort and climatic confinement.[11] Thus, the pneumatic projects of the 1960s and 1970s, often viewed as a countercultural movement or a new model challenging entrenched notions of architecture as a static container for program, is more usefully understood as a series of discontinuous spaces that sever a truly pneumatic connection with the atmosphere. As avant-garde practices, they express a much deeper propensity for disconnection actualized in our numerous closed worlds that can affect our well-being.[12] After all, we are creatures of the air.

In a blistering 1965 polemic against North American houses and their inadequate thermal insulation, Banham endorsed a synthesis between nature and technology, reified in what he termed the "un-house" — a subversive, countermonumental device designed to fulfill "the dream of the good life in the clean countryside."[13] In his view, the shells that enclosed the traditional American home had always been such an "inefficient heat barrier" that they required additional mechanical services to compensate for a lack of comfort in the interior.[14] Why not pack the necessary services together and provide a shell that allows the house to be not only mobile, but also more energy efficient?

His proposal sought to do away with the permanent elements of shelter, replacing them with a sealed interior housed in a mobile plastic bubble. This structure would enclose a "standard-of-living-package," essentially a cluster of air conditioning, heating, and lighting devices that reimagined the archaic fire pit as a modern technological service station (fig. C.2).[15] As a sealed interior, the sheltering membrane could be inflated by conditioned air expelled by the package itself or supported "on a column or two, here and there, or even on a brick-built bathroom unit," achieving what, in

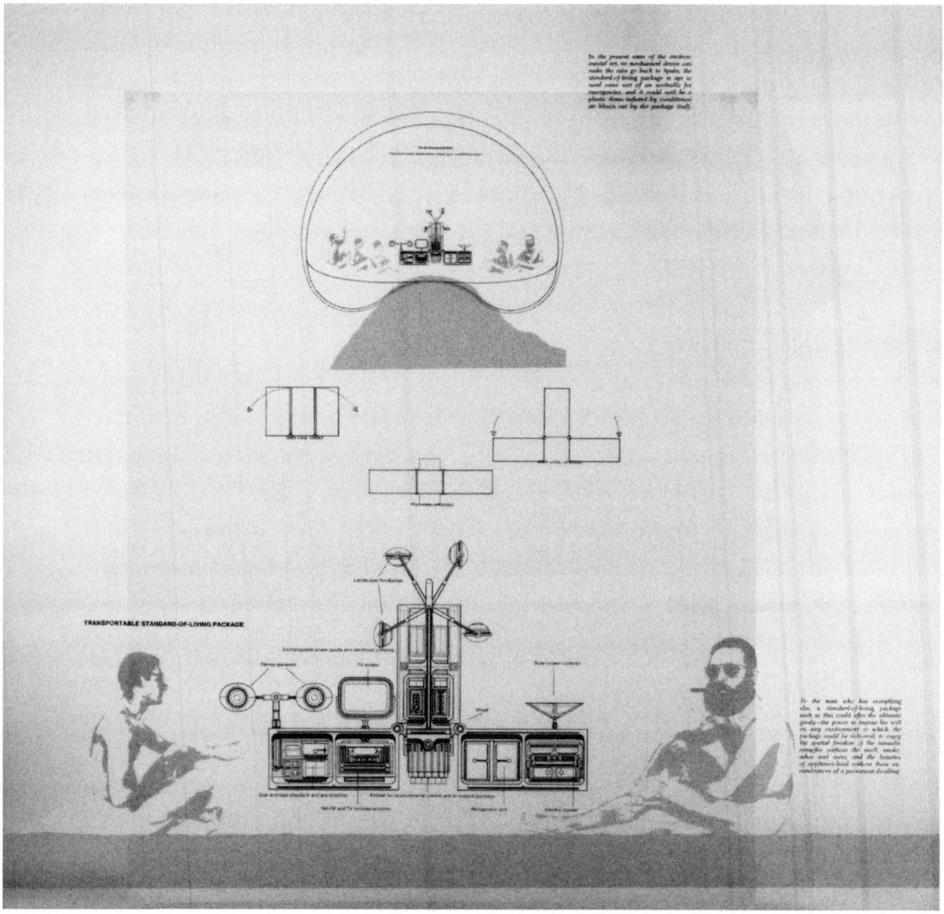

Figure C.2. A home is not a house, but a bubble. Reyner Banham, "A Home Is Not a House," *Art in America* 2 (1965), p. 77. Illustration by François Dallegret, 1960.

Banham's view, the conventional architectural shell specifically in North America had failed to deliver.[16]

Replace the brick-built bathroom with vertical circulation, set aside Banham's reliance on a centralized service station and you are left with Le Corbusier's Maison Dom-Ino — a house "like a soap bubble," as he described it in his famous manifesto.[17] Or perhaps more accurately, a soap bubble yet to come, for the Dom-Ino diagram lacks precisely the filmlike membrane that Francois Dallegret would later suggest with two not quite parallel lines in his illustration of Banham's "un-house." In this sense, unlike Banham's concept, the Dom-Ino remains ambiguous, oscillating between an eternally open house and a structure imagined as eventually sealed by a future membrane.

A well-known painting by the Prussian architect Karl Friedrich Schinkel (1781–1841) sums up the relations between these two paradigms of modern architecture's attempt to conceptualize buildings as habitations for pneumatic beings: Schinkel's *Weibliche Figur auf Pegasus reitend über einer Industriestadt* (Female figure riding on Pegasus above an industrial city, 1837) (fig. C.3). On the one hand, the painting captures the act of breathing through the symbolic gesture of blowing soap bubbles. On the other, it stages a fictionalized conquest of the atmosphere. This image thus seduces because it can conjure up our two extreme relationships with air and the atmosphere: the stark contrast between radical exposure and complete enclosure.

In this watercolor, the atmosphere appears both as an immersive medium and as a vessel carrying sealed bubbles, each encapsulating a single breath. An allegory of and birthday present for Christian Peter Wilhelm Beuth (1781–1853), a nineteenth-century politician and close friend of Schinkel's, known for his contributions to the Prussian "transformation of a basically agricultural state into a haven of industry and education," and the industrial city above which the female figure is riding Pegasus,[18] set against the backdrop of a distant mountain ridge, is replete with puffing chimneys, their

Figure C.3. *Weibliche Figur (Seifenbläserin), auf dem Pegasus über einer Industriestadt reitend.* Watercolor by Karl Friedrich Schinkel, 1837. Kupferstichkabinett, Staatliche Museen zu Berlin Inv.-Nr.: SM 54.12 = KdZ 28498.

thick white and black smoke wafting into the atmosphere, much like the scenes that could be observed across London at the time when Engels made his astute observations about air pollution.[19] As the composition emphasizes, the city here incarnated had promised progress, prosperity, and cultural transformation.

At the bottom of the painting, however, smoke accumulates to form a frame allowing us to glimpse into Beuth's office, a superimposition of different scales consistent with the painting's allegorical character that simultaneously presents interior and exterior space. The nude figure ascends on the back of Pegasus toward the clouds whose white substance forms the counterpart to the industrial smoke billowing up from below. In fact, they fly over Beuth's office as much as over the city.[20] In her left hand, she holds a golden jug, while with the right, she blows air bubbles through a long white straw. Each bubble, produced from a single puff trapped inside a delicate soap film, is on the verge of bursting, rejoining the atmosphere, like our own exhalations. Indeed, these spheres *are* our exhalations. With a bubble just beginning to form at the end of the straw, Schinkel captures the essence of breathing, giving tangible shape to the moment of exhalation. At the same time, he ironically symbolizes Beuth's shattered dreams: the existing bubbles, each labeled, include one marked "Ischia," the Italian island where Beuth fancied building a summer house, which never happened.[21] This imagery reflects us as pneumatic beings, creatures of the air who consume the same atmosphere we inhabit.[22] It also reflects the two extreme poles of architecture: permeable dwellings that embrace life in the atmosphere and hermetically sealed containers engineered to trap us within a metaphorical membrane, skin, or envelope—often in the name of energy efficiency or protection against unwieldy environmental forces in the atmosphere and to control an indoor climate for reasons of comfort.

The term "breathing space" commonly refers to a moment of rest, a chance to recover or time to reflect on what to do next. When stripped of this idiomatic meaning, the present participle makes this phrase an equivocal conjunction divulging its ambiguities. It is no longer clear whether space itself is breathing or if it is being breathed. The distinction between subject and object begins to dissolve. If space is the object, then who — or what — is the subject? Around the turn of the twentieth century, it was no doubt a consciously breathing being, intricately connected with its surroundings by virtue of permeable architecture, the pervasive presence of intrusive air, and an engulfing atmosphere. Breathing space seems a normal thing, a commonplace, but it is distinct. It arises where pneumatic beings envision the architecture they wish to inhabit, consciously attuned to the act of breathing. Breathing space is not a closed environment; it is neither sealed nor sustained by machinery. Rather, it is a form engaged with the larger atmosphere. Breathing space is neither interior nor exterior. Instead, it is both, connecting our respiratory systems to a vast network of flows and particles. This is the aerial matrix Schinkel encapsulated in his watercolor. Riding above the city together with this female figure on the back of Pegasus, we fly off into the clouds, just as light and ephemeral as the bubbles emerging from her straw.

Acknowledgments

I have long been thinking about the vulnerability and power of our lungs, both within the context of architecture and beyond. A concomitant curiosity about breathing may have been sparked as much by countless laps in the pool as by the practice of advanced Ashtanga yoga. Unconsciously, it might have been sparked, too, by my time inside Rudolph Hall—the Yale School of Architecture building—where none of the windows are actually operable. This book is based on my doctoral thesis completed at Yale in May 2018. Neither its core ideas nor its title have changed, and yet the manuscript has since been substantially revised, expanded, but also condensed so as to appeal to a broader audience. It speaks to those whose curiosity in matters of air and breathing has long existed—or has been spurred by the COVID-19 pandemic; to those who now approach air with heightened sensitivity, wondering in what ways it might affect architecture and the production of space; and to those who like to conceive of the atmosphere as a subject with broader cultural implications.

I was living in New York City when I rewrote the first chapter, and I left the city when the COVID-19 pandemic hit in March 2020. In the preceding weeks, the atmosphere felt eerily normal and calm, as if nothing was amiss—university campuses were still operating, museums remained open, and store shelves were still stocked with toilet paper. Yet, when connecting with friends in Europe, most conversations revolved excessively around rising case numbers, test kits, and all things respiratory. Soon, it seemed that really everyone was preoccupied with breathing and the mechanics of our lungs—it had become a daily focus in the media. Despite the project's topical relevance to these dramatic events, I was determined that the manuscript should not be inflected by the pandemic but remain a historical study, no matter how contemporary or pertinent its subject matter may be. In that sense, its outlines were drawn long before this respiratory disease emerged, and it appears in book form long after the WHO declared an end to the public health emergency, which was marked by widespread shortness of breath. If the recent pandemic brought breathing to the forefront of public consciousness, this book seeks to do the same within architectural discourse by examining material from around the turn of the twentieth century. Yet one of its core premises—that breathing is typically a background activity—must now be reconsidered in a new light: the pandemic has fundamentally altered this condition. For how long, however, remains an altogether different question. So much for history.

Writing is an act of solitude. And yet, a book of this scope would be impossible to conceive without the witty minds and helping hands of a great many friends and scholars with whom I had the pleasure of engaging in scintillating conversations. Exchanging ideas in ways at once profound and casual often opened new avenues to follow, introduced different perspectives on well-known texts and objects, and brought to light voices and episodes I had not previously considered. I am incredibly grateful to those who contributed to the development of this project from its embryonic stages to its culmination as a PhD, especially my exceptional doctoral committee members: Kurt W. Forster, Nicola Suthor, Anthony Vidler, and Christopher S. Wood. Their sustained support and mentorship profoundly shaped the cultural and multidisciplinary latitude this investigation ultimately embraced. It is with deep sadness that a number of mentors and companions involved at various stages in the genesis of this project, as well as friends who played important roles in my life, will no longer experience the publication of this book. I wish I could gift a copy to Kurt W. Forster, Anthony Vidler, Alice Hadler, Thomas Duffy, and Jörg Trempler. You guys are dearly missed. What brings me some comfort is the thought that you all would have appreciated the final outcome of this book. The generous atmosphere at Yale, and particularly at the School of Architecture, the Department of the History of Art, as well as the Department of Germanic Languages and Literatures, has been instrumental in shaping the beginnings of this work. At the School of Architecture, it was thanks to the stewardship of Bob Stern and Deborah Berke that my intellectual curiosity was met with a broad, critical understanding of architecture—one that propelled this endeavor forward, particularly beyond traditional disciplinary boundaries. Nary a colleague should go unmentioned, yet over the years, many voices offered insights on aspects of this work or words of encouragement in ways that may not be fully reflected here. At Yale, I would like to thank in particular Paul North, Francesco Casetti, Rüdiger Campe, John Durham Peters, and Alan Plattus. Over the years, I have received illuminating suggestions from Stanislaus von Moos, Spyros Papapetros, Mary McLeod, Jörg Gleiter, Maristella Casciato, Elisabetta Terragni, Philip Ursprung, Jörg Trempler, Regina Stephan, Laurent Stalder, Reto Geiser, Enrique Ramirez, Michael Levine, Scott Wolf, Louisa Hutton, Peter Eisenman, Eeva-Liisa Pelkonen, Bruno Maurer, Caitlin Woolsey, Surry Schlabs, Kyle Dugdale, Hinnerk Utermann, Chris Gramer, Rembert Hüser, and other colleagues on both sides of the Atlantic. The transformation from PhD to book manuscript benefited from a series of conversations I have had with Thomas Weaver. The idea of entering this book through the chimney while leaving it by virtue of Schinkel's Pegasus I owe to him.

I was able to present aspects of this work at various international venues and institutions and am thankful for the comments I received at the ETH Zurich, the International Walter Benjamin Society Conference, the SAH International Conference, the TU Wien, the TU Darmstadt, the Technion Haifa, ICOMOS Deutschland and from my peers at the Yale School of Architecture and the University of

Innsbruck. An international fellowship at the Institute for Advanced Study in the Humanities (KWI) Essen gave me additional time to refine the manuscript in an environment inherently interdisciplinary, and I am indebted to my cohort and the members of the institute, especially to Hanna Engelmeier and Kris Decker, whose reactions to this material provided a fresh perspective. I feel much obliged as well to those who supported my research in various libraries and archives, all of whom provided information and resources that proved far more relevant than I can fully acknowledge, including the staff at Beinecke Library, the gta Archive at the ETH Zurich, the Kunstbibliothek Berlin, the Bauhaus Archiv in Berlin, the Staatsarchiv Thurgau, the Fondation Le Corbusier in Paris, as well as the Dokumentationsbibliothek Davos. Staying at Peter Haimerl's Denkerhaus Schedlberg provided the quiet and focus essential for finishing the last two chapters of this manuscript. At Innsbruck, Laura-Marie Glas helped procure the necessary image rights while Bettina Schlorhaufer's encouragement for this publication never abated, and it is thanks to her and Gülten Kaddar that I had the funds to cover the necessary image rights. I am incredibly happy to have found a home with Zone Books, the very press I had always hoped would bring this kind of work to life. My heartfelt thanks to the extraordinary team, who have been a joy to work with — Meighan Gale, Kyra Simone, and Julie Fry — and especially to Jonathan Crary for his enthusiasm in taking a breath of fresh air with me. Bud Bynack's deft edits helped streamline the manuscript and eliminated redundancies that might have tried your patience as readers.

Above all, I am immensely grateful for my mother, Hannelore, for her infinite optimism and unquestioned support for everything I do. Thanks to her, I developed the kind of inquisitiveness that drives one to seek a doctoral degree far from home. Finally, I want to thank Regina who has been a tower of strength for me. I am much indebted to her thoughts, her endurance to climb this mountain with me, and to her *quoi qu'il arrive, en tous temps* — usually somewhere between Berlin, New York City, and Innsbruck.

Notes

CHAPTER ONE: EXHALING CHIMNEYS

1. A good overview of the topic of fireplaces can be found in the book by Sébastien Marot as part of Rem Koolhaas, et al., eds., *Elements: A Series of 15 Books Accompanying the Exhibition Elements of Architecture at the 2014 Venice Architecture Biennale* (Venice: Marsilio Editori Spa, 2014).

2. Herman Melville, "I and My Chimney," in *Pierre, Israel Potter, The Confidence-Man, Tales, and Billy Budd* (New York: Library of America, 1984), pp. 1298–1327.

3. To learn more about the consequences of this shift, see Anthony Vidler, *The Architectural Uncanny: Essays in the Modern Unhomely* (Cambridge, MA: MIT Press, 1992).

4. Melville, "I and My Chimney," p. 1304.

5. In contrast to Melville's dominant cohabitant, the rise of smaller fireplaces and chimneys as heating technology in medieval England had significant social implications because they led to the compartmentalization of domestic space, allowing for smaller individual rooms due to the flexible distribution of multiple heat sources. This shift toward more private heat and away from the communal central hearth, in turn, changed the ways in which labor was perceived and divided within the household. Individually heated rooms also had an effect on love life in the Middle Ages. On the sociopolitical aspects of chimneys, see LeRoy Dresbeck, "The Chimney and Social Change in Medieval England," *Albion: A Quarterly Journal Concerned with British Studies* 3.1 (Spring 1971), pp. 21–32, https://doi.org/10.2307/4048469.

6. The chimney could be seen as a special portal into the world of witchcraft and the home, mediating between the natural world and the spiritual world. See Holly Tucker,

Pregnant Fictions: Childbirth and the Fairy Tale in Early-Modern France (Detroit: Wayne State University Press, 2003), p. 68.

7. Jeffrey Burton Russell, *Witchcraft in the Middle Ages* (Ithaca: Cornell University Press, 1972), p. 236. For recent discussion of witchcraft and a witch hunt to which thousands of women fell victim to, see Silvia Beatriz Federici, *Caliban and the Witch*, 2nd rev. ed. (New York: Autonomedia, 2014).

8. Jean-Henri Fabre, *L'air, nécessaire à la vie*, ed. Christopher Middleton, in *Po&sie*, no. 26 (1983), p. 124, https://po-et-sie.fr/texte/lair-necessaire-a-la-vie/. My translation. On the role of fire in architecture, see Luis Fernández-Galiano, *Fire and Memory: On Architecture and Energy*, trans. Gina Cariño (Cambridge, MA: MIT Press, 2000).

9. Leon Battista Alberti, *On the Art of Building in Ten Books*, trans. Joseph Rykwert, Neil Leach, and Robert Tavernor (Cambridge, MA: MIT Press, 1988), p. 148.

10. Ibid.

11. Ibid., p. 355.

12. Detlef Mertins, *Modernity Unbound* (London: Architectural Association Publications, 2011), p. 5.

13. Benjamin Franklin, *Observations on Smoky Chimneys, Their Causes and Cure; with Considerations on Fuel and Stoves*, 3rd ed. (London: I. and J. Tayler, 1793).

14. Ibid., p. 8. For a recent discussion on Franklin in the context of climate, air, and heating methods, see the chapter on "Chimney Effects," in Moritz Gleich, *Inhabited Machines: Genealogy of an Architectural Concept*, 1st ed., Exploring Architecture 1 (Boston: Birkhäuser, 2022), pp. 44–57. As Lisa Heschong notes in her study on thermal qualities, the shift from radiation to convection, brought about by the Franklin stove, led to a reconceptualization of architecture in its relation to air. "For the first time people began to understand a building as an enclosure for a bubble of warmed air and realized that attention had to be paid to making the building more airtight." Lisa Heschong, *Thermal Delight in Architecture* (Cambridge, MA: The MIT Press, 1979), p. 14.

15. Reyner Banham, *The Architecture of the Well-Tempered Environment* (London: Architectural Press, 1969). This book is one of the pioneering studies exploring the interplay between architecture and technical media in the creation of spatial environments.

16. Cited throughout from the second edition. Reyner Banham, *The Architecture of the Well-Tempered Environment*, 2nd ed. (Chicago: University of Chicago Press, 1984), p. 30.

17. Ludwig Hilberseimer, "Bauten in Eisenbeton und ihre architektonische Gestaltung," in Julius Vischer and Ludwig Hilberseimer, *Beton als Gestalter: Bauten in Eisenbeton*

und ihre architektonische Gestaltung, Ausgeführte Eisenbetonbauten (Stuttgart: Julius Hoffmann, 1928), p. 15. My translation.

18. Emil Fader, *Auf dem Wege zum neuen Baustil* (Berlin: Wilhelm Ernst & Sohn, 1927), p. 20. My translation.

19. On the history of Luckenwalde after World War I, see Thomas Drachenberg, *Die Baugeschichte der Stadt Luckenwalde von 1918–1933: Siedlungen, Industriebau, Verwaltungs-, Wohlfahrts- und Privatbauten (Beiträge zur Denkmalpflege im Land Brandenburg)* (Worms: Wernersche, 1999).

20. Adolf Behne, *Der Moderne Zweckbau* (Berlin: Gebrüder Mann, 1998), p. 40.

21. Erich Mendelsohn to Luise Mendelsohn, August 11, 1925, Staatliche Museen zu Berlin Kunstbibliothek, Erich Mendelsohn Archiv, Der Briefwechsel von Erich und Luise Mendelsohn 1910–1953, http://ema.smb.museum/959.

22. Erich Mendelsohn to Luise Mendelsohn, August 19, 1925, http://ema.smb.museum/961.

23. Luise Mendelsohn, "My Life in a Changing World," typescript, Getty Research Collections, Erich and Luise Mendelsohn Papers 1894–1992, series 7, Luise Mendelsohn travel diaries, biography of Erich Mendelsohn, and autobiography, Luise Mendelsohn autobiography, ca. 1974–1976, pp. 79 and 74–75.

24. Ibid., pp. 155–56.

25. Erich Mendelsohn to Luise Mendelsohn, July 16, 1926, http://ema.smb.museum/971.

26. Erich Mendelsohn to Luise Mendelsohn, July 31, 1926, http://ema.smb.museum/975.

27. Erich Mendelsohn, "Erich Mendelsohn: Bauten und Skizzen," *Wasmuths Monatshefte für Baukunst und Städtebau*, no. 8 (1924), pp. 1–68. Adolf Behne, *Der Moderne Zweckbau* (Berlin: Gebrüder Mann, 1998). For an English edition see Adolf Behne, *The Modern Functional Building*, trans. Michael Robinson (Santa Monica: Getty Center for the History of Art and the Humanities, 1996). Kathleen James has pointed out the extent to which the structure had been published at the time. Kathleen James, *Erich Mendelsohn and the Architecture of German Modernism* (Cambridge: Cambridge University Press, 1997), pp. 79–80.

28. Peter M., Bode, "Unter einem hutförmigen Dach wurde der Filz getrocknet," *art: Das Kunstmagazin*, no. 10 (1994), p. 131.

29. Eventually, these louvers fell victim to the numerous alterations that took place over the decades. Traces were still visible in 1992, when a German architecture practice was

commissioned to do a structural survey. See Gerald Kühn-von Kaehne, Christoph Lebek, and Mathias Noell, "Luckenwalde: Die ehemalige Hutfabrik Friedrich Steinberg, Herrmann & Co. von Erich Mendelsohn," *Brandenburgische Denkmalpflege* 1.1 (1992), pp. 75–84.

30. John Berlowitz, "Die Lösung des Entnebelungsproblems," *Technische Rundschau: Wochenschrift des Berliner Tageblatts* July 2, 1924, p. 1.

31. Ibid. My translation.

32. Ibid.

33. The Luckenwalde hood was taken down in 1935 as soon as the factory was "Aryanized." Of Jewish origin, Luise and Erich Mendelsohn were not the only ones associated with Luckenwalde who left Germany in the wake of National Socialism's rise: Herrmann's family also departed in 1933 to escape the looming anti-Jewish pogroms. Gustav Herrmann died in 1932, and his death set in motion the company's shutdown in 1934. See Detlef Karg, "Pflegefälle: Anmerkungen zur Denkmalpflege," in Regina Stephan, ed., *Erich Mendelsohn: Wesen Werk Wirkung* (Ostfildern: Hatje Cantz, 2006), pp. 99–103. Shortly afterward, the factory grounds were taken over by a machine-building company largely controlled by the German Air Force and Herrmann Göring. See Drachenberg, *Die Baugeschichte der Stadt Luckenwalde von 1918–1933*, p. 95. When transforming the factory into a war plant, those responsible removed its most prominent component for reasons of air raid protection. With its unique outline, the roof could have been too easily targeted during Allied aerial bombings. In hindsight, the roof's dismantling may indeed have spared the complex from air strike demolition. Restoration attempts following German reunification resulted in the successful reconstruction of the roof, and after several years of dormancy, the facility may soon be reactivated.

For the history of the factory until 1990, see Drachenberg, *Die Baugeschichte der Stadt Luckenwalde von 1918–1933*, p. 95. A good impression of the years after the German reunification is offered in Bode, "Unter einem hutförmigen Dach wurde der Filz getrocknet," p. 131. Work by students from the Architectural Association in London resulted in the publication Frank Barkow and Charles Tashima, eds., *Ruins of Modernity: Erich Mendelsohn's Hat Factory in Luckenwalde* (London: Architectural Association, 1998). For information addressing the years after 2000, see Susanne Altmann, "Sanierung ohne Hut," *art: Das Kunstmagazin*, no. 2 (2002), p. 115; Frank Peter Jäger, "Den Hut aufsetzen: Mendelsohns berühmte Fabrik in Luckenwalde wird saniert," *Der Tagesspiegel*, September 30, 2003; Tim Altenhof, "Mendelsohn's Rudderless Ship," *Ra: Revista de Arquitectura*, no. 25 (2023), pp. 92–103, https://doi.org/10.15581/014.25.92-103. After first attempts to reconstruct the complex, the initial enthusiasm waned. In October 2000, the factory wound up in the hands of a Lebanese investor. In 2024, it seems as if there is a more positive outlook toward a possible reuse of the structure.

34. See Arnold Whittick, *Eric Mendelsohn* (New York: F. W. Dodge Corporation, 1956), p. 56. He describes the dye works as "an entirely new type, which Mendelsohn invented." Bruno Zevi alludes to a "special ventilation system" that Mendelsohn "invented." Bruno Zevi, *Erich Mendelsohn: The Complete Works* (Basel: Birkhäuser, 1999), p. 74. Kathleen James sees in the dye works "a significant technical innovation." Kathleen James, *Erich Mendelsohn and the Architecture of German Modernism*, p. 80. Art historian Sigrid Achenbach notes "a novel ventilation system." Sigrid Achenbach, *Erich Mendelsohn 1887–1953: Ideen—Bauten—Projekte* (Berlin: Staatliche Museen Preussischer Kulturbesitz, 1987), p. 64.

35. See John F. Fitchen, "The Problem of Ventilation Through the Ages," *Technology and Culture* 22.3 (July 1981), pp. 485–511, especially p. 491.

36. For a comparison, see illustration 62 in Julius Vischer and Ludwig Hilberseimer, *Beton als Gestalter* (Stuttgart: Julius Hoffmann, 1928).

37. See E. Mörsch, *Der Eisenbetonbau: Seine Theorie und Anwendung*, 4th ed. (Stuttgart: Konrad Wittwer, 1912), p. 427.

38. Zevi, *Erich Mendelsohn*, p. xv.

39. Philibert de L'Orme, *Le premier tome de l'architecture* (Paris: Federic Morel, 1567), p. 276.

40. For a brief discussion on air in architectural treatises, see Paul Emmons and Marco Frascari, "Making Visible the Invisible: Signs of Air in Architectural Treatises," in Barbara Kenda, ed. *Aeolian Winds and the Spirit in Renaissance Architecture* (London: Routledge, 2006), pp. 87–102. An attempt toward a more comprehensive understanding of air's role in architecture was undertaken by Cyrille Simonnet, *Brève histoire de l'air* (Versailles: Quae, 2014). The book offers a wide range of perspectives on air as a material entity, with various ramifications for architecture.

41. Lewis W. Leeds, *Lectures on Ventilation* (New York: John Wiley & Son, 1869), p. 45.

42. Catherine E. Beecher and Harriet Beecher Stowe, *The American Woman's Home: Or, Principles of Domestic Science* (New York: J. B. Ford, 1869), p. 43.

43. Reyner Banham might have been the first to focus on their work. See especially chapter 3 in *The Architecture of the Well-Tempered Environment.*

44. Leeds, *Lectures on Ventilation*, p. 18.

45. See, for instance, John H. Griscom, *The Uses and Abuses of Air* (New York: Redfield, 1854), p. 227, and Beecher and Beecher Stowe, *The American Woman's Home*, p. 60.

46. Conversely, air understood as a medium can also carry heat. See Moritz Gleich, "From Storage to Transmission: Architecture and the Communication of Heat," *Perspecta*, no. 51 (2018), pp. 199–213.

47. This is one of the main reasons for the success of mechanical ventilation, the second major type of forced ventilation. For a sweeping account, see Robert Bruegmann, "Central Heating and Forced Ventilation: Origins and Effects on Architectural Design," *Journal of the Society of Architectural Historians* 37.3 (1978), pp. 143–60.

48. Griscom, *The Uses and Abuses of Air*, p. 226.

49. Bruegmann, "Central Heating and Forced Ventilation," p. 143. Gleich, "From Storage to Transmission," p. 211.

50. David Boswell Reid, *Illustrations of the Theory and Practice of Ventilation: With Remarks on Warming, Exclusive Lighting, and the Communication of Sound* (London: Longman, Brown, Green & Longmans, 1844), p. 71.

51. Ibid., p. 81.

52. Ibid., p. 229.

53. Daly César, "Du chauffage et de la ventilation," *Revue générale de l'architecture et des travaux publics* 5 (1844), p. 118. My translation.

54. For a comprehensive historical overview of the pneumatic revolution in the seventeenth century and its impact on architecture, see Jeanne Kisacky, "Breathing Room: Calculating an Architecture of Air," in Anthony Gerbino, ed., *Geometrical Objects: Architecture and the Mathematical Sciences 1400–1800* (Cham: Springer, 2014), pp. 247–79, https://doi.org/10.1007/978-3-319-05998-3.

55. Leeds, *Lectures on Ventilation*, title page, table of contents, and p. 7.

56. Ibid., p. 7.

57. See Alfred S. Evans, "Pettenkofer Revisited: The Life and Contributions of Max von Pettenkofer (1818–1901)," *Yale Journal of Biology and Medicine*, no. 46 (1973), pp. 161–76.

58. Max Pettenkofer, *Über den Luftwechsel in Wohngebäuden* (Munich: Literarisch-Artistische Anstalt der J. G. Cotta'schen Buchhandlung, 1858), pp. 76–77. Most of his key beliefs are already nascent in this early article.

59. For a recent account on the proximity between architecture and physiology in nineteenth-century Germany, see Didem Ekici, "The Physiology of the House: Modern Architecture and the Science of Hygiene," in Sarah Schrank and Didem Ekici, eds., *Healing Spaces, Modern Architecture, and the Body* (Oxford: Routledge, 2017), pp. 47–64.

60. Max Pettenkofer, "Ueber einen neuen Respirations-Apparat," *Abhandlungen der*

Mathemat.-Physikalischen Classe der Königlich Bayerischen Akademie der Wissenschaften 9 (1863), pp. 229–76.

61. Ibid., p. 233. As far as dogs were concerned, see Max Pettenkofer and Carl von Voit, "Respirationsversuche am Hunde bei Hunger und ausschliesslicher Fettzufuhr," *Zeitschrift für Biologie* 5 (1869), pp. 369–92.

62. Pettenkofer, "Über einen neuen Respirations-Apparat," p. 233. See also Max Pettenkofer, "Über die Respiration," *Annalen der Chemie und Pharmacie* 2 (1963).

63. Pettenkofer, "Über einen neuen Respirations-Apparat," p. 240. My translation.

64. Max von Pettenkofer, *Beziehungen der Luft zu Kleidung, Wohnung und Boden: Drei Populäre Vorlesungen* (Braunschweig: Druck und Verlag von Friedrich Vieweg und Sohn, 1872), p. 71. The book was published in English as Max von Pettenkofer, *The Relations of the Air to the Clothes We Wear, the House We Live in, and the Soil We Dwell On: Three Popular Lectures*, trans. Augustus Hess (London: N. Trübner, 1873), p. 39. Citations of the English are in parentheses (p. 36).

65. For a recent reassessment of the notion of skin in modernist architecture, see Didem Ekici, "Skin, Clothing, and Dwelling: Max von Pettenkofer, the Science of Hygiene, and Breathing Walls," *Journal of the Society of Architectural Historians* 75.3 (September 2016), pp. 281–98.

66. Pettenkofer, *Beziehungen der Luft zu Kleidung, Wohnung und Boden*, p. 55 (p. 52).

67. Carl Breiting, "Luft in Schulzimmern," *Deutsche Vierteljahrsschrift für öffentliche Gesundheitspflege* 1.2 (1870), p. 17.

68. Richard Haimann, "Wenn Gebäude Atemnot haben," *Berliner Morgenpost*, June 8, 2016, https://www.morgenpost.de/incoming/article207655477/Wenn-Gebaeude-Atemnot-haben.html.

69. Josef von Fodor, *Das gesunde Haus und die gesunde Wohnung* (Braunschweig: Druck und Verlag von Friedrich Vieweg und Sohn, 1878), p. 63. My translation.

70. Ibid., p. 15. My translation.

71. Ibid., p. 79. My translation.

72. Fodor's assumptions about outside air quality are relative. Indeed, he acknowledges that "the atmosphere in cities is usually so foul, especially in summer and fall that we will hardly have the necessary good air even in the healthiest homes." Ibid., p. 86. My translation. Yet with regard to the stoves, he refers to a somewhat idealized notion of "pure alley air" (*reine Gassenluft*) entering the room. Ibid., p. 74. My translation.

73. Ibid., p. 56. My translation.

74. Although it was not immediately accepted among medical experts, the English physician John Snow had rebutted the hypothesis of the infected ground as early as 1859. Cholera is chiefly transmitted through polluted water. Stephen Halliday, "Death and Miasma in Victorian London: An Obstinate Belief," *British Medical Journal* 323 (December 2001), pp. 1469–71.

75. The phrase he uses is "auf die Bodenluft aufsaugend wirken." Fodor, *Das gesunde Haus und die gesunde Wohnung*, p. 24.

76. To prevent further air drafts, Fodor suggested a ventilation grate invented by Douglas Strutt Galton, a British engineer engaged in dealing with issues ranging from submarine telegraphy to sanitary science. In his grate, the outside air required to replace the rising warm air is drawn inside next to the chimney funnel, warming it en route to the interior. Galton treats the fireplace as a breathing engine with properties valuable for modern living conditions. In his *Observations on the Construction of Healthy Dwellings* (1880), Galton notes with apprehension that this engine "is thus powerful enough to draw into the room all the air it wants; and for this purpose will use indiscriminately all other openings, whether inlets or outlets if necessary." Douglas Galton, *Observations on the Construction of Healthy Dwellings: Namely Houses, Hospitals, Barracks, Asylums, Etc.* 2nd ed. (Oxford: Clarendon Press of Oxford University Press, 1896), pp. 124–26. The book was first published in 1880. He contrasts the power of this engine with the kind of stagnation occurring in the middle of the room in a hospital ward above the patients' beds. Although warmed air enters the interior right below the windows, its horizontal velocity soon vanishes, and the upward movement fails to warm the space evenly. As a countermeasure, he suggests additional elevated apertures at the sides to help extract the stale air, but he also reminds his readers about the effect of extraction shafts, which could mimic the workings of a fireplace in terms of the circulation of air. Ibid., p. 140.

77. de L'Orme, *Le premier tome de l'architecture*, p. 276.

78. Wilhelm Flam, "Wie Du atmest, so lebst Du!," *Der Querschnitt* 7.9 (1927), p. 657. My translation.

79. Ibid.

80. For a recent discussion of *pneuma* in the context of air's manipulation and its place in Western thought, see Marijn Nieuwenhuis, "The Politics of Breathing: Knowledge on Air and Respiration," in Lenart Škof and Petri Berndtson, eds., *Atmospheres of Breathing* (Albany: State University of New York Press, 2019), pp. 199–218.

81. See Silvia Benso, "The Breathing of the Air: Presocratic Echoes in Levinas," in Brian Schroeder and Silvia Benso, eds., *Levinas and the Ancients* (Bloomington: Indiana University Press, 2008), p. 14: "As handed down to the tradition by Aetius, the words commonly accepted as a direct quotation from Anaximenes are: 'Just as,' he says, 'our soul [*psuche*], being air [*aer*], holds us together, so do breath [*pneuma*] and air [*aer*] encompass the whole world.'"

82. Because the Stoics' understanding of the body's vital functions served as a template to interpret all other natural processes, the classic scholar Anthony Arthur Long characterized Stoic cosmology as essentially biological. The Stoics ultimately envisioned the world as a temporal, living organism. A. A. Long, "The Stoics on World-Conflagration and Everlasting Recurrence," in *From Epicurus to Epictetus: Studies in Hellenistic and Roman Philosophy* (Oxford: Clarendon Press of Oxford University Press, 2006), p. 259.

83. See Peter Barker, "Stoic Contributions to Early Modern Science," in Margaret J. Osler, ed., *Atoms, Pneuma, and Tranquility: Epicurean and Stoic Themes in European Thought* (Cambridge: Cambridge University Press, 1991), p. 138.

84. Jürgen Ebach, *Weltentstehung und Kulturentwicklung bei Philo von Byblos: Ein Beitrag zur Überlieferung der biblischen Urgeschichte im Rahmen des altorientalischen und antiken Schöpfungsglaubens* (Stuttgart: Kohlhammer, 1979), pp. 36–37. My translation.

85. Berthold Hub, "Material Gazes and Flying Images in Marsilio Ficino and Michelangelo," in Christine Gottler and Wolfgang Neuber, eds., *Spirits Unseen: The Representation of Subtle Bodies in Early Modern European Culture* (Leiden: Brill, 2008), p. 93.

86. Andrea Palladio, *The Four Books on Architecture*, trans. Robert Tavernor and Richard Schofield (Cambridge, MA: MIT Press, 1997), p. 64.

87. For further reading, see Barbara Kenda, ed., *Aeolian Winds and the Spirit in Renaissance Architecture* (London: Routledge, 2006).

CHAPTER TWO: INHALING LUNGS

1. Johann Jakob Scheuchzer, *Kupfer-Bibel, In welcher Die Physica Sacra, Oder Geheiligte Natur-Wissenschaft Derer in Heil. Schrift vorkommenden Natürlichen Sachen, Deutlich erklärt und bewährt*, 4 vols. (Augspurg und Ulm: Christian Ulrich Wagner, 1731–1735), vol. 3, p. 415. My translation.

2. The correlation between pneumatic knowledge and architectural designs, between air and form, can be traced to the eighteenth century, as demonstrated by Jeanne Kisacky's "Breathing Room: Calculating an Architecture of Air." My point in

this book is to emphasize the close-knit ties between architecture, science, and a broad-based popular culture in Europe attuned to breathing.

3. An understanding of air as nourishment is a common theme in many books on air and breathing. See, for instance, Jean-Henri Fabre, *L'air, nécessaire à la vie*, ed. Christopher Middleton, in *Po&sie*, no. 26 (1983), https://po-et-sie.fr/wp-content/uploads/2018/08/26_1983_p123_127.pdf.

4. John Durham Peters, "The Media of Breathing," in Lenart Škof and Petri Berndtson, eds., *Atmospheres of Breathing* (Albany: State University of New York Press, 2018), pp. 179–95.

5. They include but are not limited to Alfred Jones's body-enclosing ventilator, patented in 1864, and Dr. E. J. Woillez's artificial respirator resembling an iron lung. See Arthur S. Slutsky, "Ventilator-Induced Lung Injury: From Barotrauma to Biotrauma," *Respiratory Care* 50.5 (2005), pp. 646–59. Another was the suction mask: see E. Kuhn, *Die Lungenmaske in Theorie und Praxis* (Berlin: Springer, 1911). The so-called Kirchberg-Drägersche Druck- und Saugapparat is discussed in Franz Kirchberg, *Atemgymnastik und Atmungstherapie von Dr. Franz Kirchberg* (Berlin: Springer, 1913), pp. 139–40. Illustrations of patents on other devices can also be found in Karoline von Steinaecker, *Luftsprünge: Anfänge moderner Körpertherapien* (Munich: Urban & Fischer, 2000).

6. Its visual representation can be found in the many X-ray images of lungs produced to provide evidence of the disease. Beatriz Colomina analyzes the parallel histories of transparency in medical and architectural contexts in the modern period. Beatriz Colomina, *X-Ray Architecture* (Zürich: Lars Müller Publishers, 2019).

7. Maurice Merleau-Ponty, *The Primacy of Perception*, trans. James M. Edie (Evanston: Northwestern University Press, 1971), p. 122.

8. Ibid.

9. John Durham Peters, "Spirometer, Whale, Slave: Breathing Emergencies c. 1850," *SubStance* 52.1 (2023), pp. 85 and 86.

10. The proximity between life and breath is not always appreciated by experts. The German physician Karl Amersbach noted that an overly loose understanding of the term "breathing" as life devalues its meaning, necessitating new terminology for effective communication among physicians. Breathing properly speaking implies the supply of oxygen and the removal of carbon dioxide. See Karl Amersbach, *Atmung: Aufnahme und Abgabe gasförmiger Stoffe*, vol. 2 of *Handbuch der normalen und pathologischen Physiologie* (Berlin: Julius Springer, 1925), p. 4.

11. Heinrich Johannes Boruttau, "Versuch einer kritischen Geschichte der Atmungstheorien," *Archiv für Geschichte der Medizin* 2.5 (February 1909), pp. 301–50.

12. Stanislaus von Moos, *Le Corbusier: Elements of a Synthesis* (Rotterdam: 010 Publishers, 2009), p. 183.

13. Le Corbusier, *La ville radieuse* (Boulogne-sur-Seine: Éditions de l'architecture d'aujourd'hui, 1935). First published in 1933. Throughout, I cite the English edition, Le Corbusier, *The Radiant City: Elements of a Doctrine of Urbanism to Be Used as the Basis of Our Machine-Age Civilization* (New York: Orion Press, 1967).

14. My translation.

15. Le Corbusier, *The Radiant City*, p. 40.

16. Le Corbusier, *Une Maison — Un Palais* (Paris: G. Crès, 1928), p. 33.

17. John Durham Peters focuses on medical instruments, the whaling industry, and struggles for the abolition of slavery in his study on breathing around 1850, the year that for him brought cultural interest in lungs to the fore. Peters, "Spirometer, Whale, Slave."

18. See Moritz Alsberg, *Die gesunde Wohnung* (Berlin: Habel, 1883), p. 22. My translation.

19. For a brief discussion of the instrument's evolution, see H. Beigel, "On Spirometry," *The Lancet* 83.2109 (January 30, 1864), pp. 119–20.

20. Standards are often contaminated by ideology, and "there is no swampier region of medical history than anthropometry." Peters, "Spirometer, Whale, Slave," p. 87. Lundy Braun has shown in her work on the spirometer that the idea of racial difference in lung capacity has been deeply entrenched in mainstream culture and thus normalized to the extent that these biases have significantly influenced spirometric standards, leading to the normalization of racial adjustments in the instrument itself. Informed by cultural notions of race, as well as categories such as ethnicity and geographic regions, what was meant to provide robust scientific measurements served to reinforce existing preconceptions. See Lundy Braun, *Breathing Race into the Machine: The Surprising Career of the Spirometer from Plantation to Genetics* (Minneapolis: University of Minnesota Press, 2014).

21. John Hutchinson, "On the Capacity of the Lungs, and on the Respiratory Functions, with a View of Establishing a Precise and Easy Method of Detecting Disease by the Spirometer," *Medico-Chirurgical Transactions* 29 (1846), pp. 137–252.

22. Ibid., p. 143.

23. Marey had a keen curiosity about the vital functions of both human and animal bodies. In addition to studying the respiratory process, which he represented

graphically, he also explored the circulatory system and the mechanics of speech. See, for instance, Étienne-Jules Marey, *Physiologie expérimentale: Travaux du laboratoire de M. Marey*, 4 vols. (Paris: G. Masson, 1875). In 1894, he anticipated the potential of chronophotography for documenting the ways in which "different parts of the thorax play in respiratory movements." Étienne-Jules Marey, *Le mouvement* (G. Masson: Paris, 1894), p. 270. My translation.

24. The best historic overview on this issue is Jeanne Kisacky, "Breathing Room: Calculating an Architecture of Air," in Anthony Gerbino, ed., *Geometrical Objects: Architecture and the Mathematical Sciences 1400–1800* (Cham: Springer, 2014), pp. 247–79.

25. Heinrich Albrecht, *Die Wohnungsnot in den Großstädten und die Mittel zu Ihrer Abhülfe* (Munich: R. Oldenbourg, 1891), p. 88. See Hans Wiegand, *Die Deutsche Stadt: Die Stadtplanung, der Städtebau* (Mannheim: Reinhard Welz Vermittler, 2007), p. 405.

26. Albrecht, *Die Wohnungsnot in den Großstädten und die Mittel zu Ihrer Abhülfe*, p. 88. See Nicholas Bullock and James Read, *The Movement for Housing Reform in Germany and France 1840–1914* (Cambridge: Cambridge University Press, 1985), p. 101.

27. "Entwurf zu gesetzlichen Vorschriften zum Schutze des gesunden Wohnens," *Illustrierte Kunstgewerbliche Zeitschrift für Innendekoration* 1.10 (n.d.), p. 81.

28. Ibid.

29. Catherine E. Beecher and Harriet Beecher Stowe, *The American Woman's Home: Or, Principles of Domestic Science* (New York: J. B. Ford, 1869), p. 59.

30. "Bilder vom Menschen," *Berliner Morgenpost*, postcard set, 1931. The caption for figure 30 reads: "The 300 million alveoli would cover a carpet 75 square meters in size if unfolded." My translation. For a reprint of the image, see Uta von Debschitz, Thilo von Debschitz, and Stephen Heller, *Fritz Kahn: Infographics Pioneer* (Cologne: Taschen, 2017), p. 121. For information on the role of Fritz Schüler in his collaboration with Fritz Kahn, see Patrick Rössler, "'Das Buch über Dich': Zur Editionsgeschichte von Fritz Kahns *Das Leben des Menschen*," *Aus dem Antiquariat* 16.1 (2018), pp. 2–20.

31. In 1911, Swiss physician Adolf Keller-Hoerschelmann (discussed later in this chapter), suggested an extension of approximately 500 square feet and in the event of deep breathing of more than 1200 square feet. Adolf Keller-Hoerschelmann, *Mein Atmungssystem: Bestes Buch praktischer Gesundheitspflege!*, 2nd ed. (Olten: Hambrecht, 1911), p. 37.

32. Le Corbusier, *The Radiant City*, p. 40.

33. Cover designs based on the illustration are used, for instance, for Walead Beshty, ed., *Picture Industry: A Provisional History of the Technical Image 1844–2018* (Zurich: JRP

Ringier, 2018); Gilles Deleuze and Félix Guattari, *Anti-Oedipus: Capitalism and Schizophrenia* (New York: Penguin Books, 2009); and von Debschitz and von Debschitz, eds., *Fritz Kahn: Infographics Pioneer*. For a monograph on Kahn's works, see Michael Sappol, *Body Modern: Fritz Kahn, Scientific Illustration, and the Homuncular Subject* (Minneapolis: University of Minnesota Press, 2017).

34. For more information on the image and Kahn's illustrations, see Miriam Eilers, "Fritz Kahns *Das Leben des Menschen*: Zur Produktion und Transkription eines populären Werks," *NTM Zeitschrift für Geschichte der Wissenschaften, Technik und Medizin* 23.1–2 (September 2015), pp. 1–31, and Cornelius Borck, "Communicating the Modern Body: Fritz Kahn's Popular Images of Human Physiology as an Industrialized World," *Canadian Journal of Communication* 32.3–4 (2007), pp. 495–520.

35. Friedrich-Beda Stubenvoll, *Die Heilung durch den Atem: Gemeinverständliche "Pneumopaedie" oder Unterweisung im richtigen Atem für Kranke und Gesunde* (Bad Reichenhall: E. Thiele, 1914), pp. 31–32.

36. Ibid. My translation.

37. The idea of breath as a form of nutriment can be already found in Aristotle's attempts to inquire the function of breathing. See Aristotle, *On the Soul. Parva Naturalia. On Breath*, trans. W. S. Hett (Cambridge, MA: Harvard University Press, 1957), p. 487.

38. Lewis Mumford, *The Culture of Cities* (New York: Harcourt, Brace, 1938), p. 393. As Mumford points out, it was often "sheer necessity" that "caused the industrialist to build houses for his workers, when his plant was situated in the open country."

39. On Lux, see Mark Jarzombek, "Josef August Lux: Werkbund Promoter, Historian of a Lost Modernity," *Journal of the Society of Architectural Historians* 63.2 (2004), p. 204.

40. "Gesundheitskodex des Arbeiterdorfes Bournville," *Hohe Warte* 1.9 (1905), p. 192. My translation.

41. Émile Jaques-Dalcroze, et al., *The Eurythmics of Jaques-Dalcroze* (London: Constable, 1912), p. 27.

42. Gartenstadt Hellerau bei Dresden G.m.b.H., *Gartenstadt Hellerau: Ein Bericht über den Zweck, die Organisation, die Ansiedelungs-Bedingungen, die bisherigen Erfolge und die Ziele* (Dresden: Gartenstadt Hellerau, 1911).

43. Jaques-Dalcroze, *The Eurythmics of Jaques-Dalcroze*, pp. 21 and 27.

44. For a critique on rhythm in relation to modern working conditions see Karl Bücher, *Arbeit und Rhythmus* (Leipzig: S. Hirzel, 1896), an author known to the Hellerau circle.

45. Émile Jaques-Dalcroze, *Le rythme, la musique et l'éducation* (Paris: Rouart, Lerolle,

1920). Cited throughout from Émile Jaques-Dalcroze, *Rhythm, Music and Education*, trans. Harold F. Rubinstein (New York: G. P. Putnam's Sons, 1921), p. 311.

46. Jaques-Dalcroze, *Rhythm, Music and Education*, p. 313.

47. Jaques-Dalcroze, *The Eurythmics of Jaques-Dalcroze*, p. 25.

48. Jaques-Dalcroze, *Rhythm, Music and Education*, p. 82.

49. See Peter Kühnst, *Sport: Eine Kulturgeschichte im Spiegel der Kunst* (Dresden: Kunst Dresden, 1996), p. 303; Günter Witt, "Das Bauhaus, seine Künstler und der Sport," in Winfried Simmat, ed., *Weimarer Vorträge über Beziehungen des Sports zu Kunst und Kultur* (Weimar: Bauhaus-Universität Weimar Universitätsverlag, 2000), p. 77.

50. Johannes Itten, *Design and Form: The Basic Course at the Bauhaus and Later*, rev. ed. (New York: Van Nostrand Reinhold, 1975), p. 9.

51. Paul Citroen, "Mazdaznan at the Bauhaus," in Eckhard Neumann, ed., *Bauhaus and Bauhaus People: Personal Opinions and Recollections of Former Bauhaus Members and Their Contemporaries*, trans. Eva Richter and Alba Lorman, rev. ed. (New York: Van Nostrand Reinhold, 1992), pp. 46–47.

52. George Adams, "Memories of a Bauhaus Student," *Architectural Review* 144.858 (September 1968), p. 192.

53. Itten showed a general interest in East Asia. For a discussion on Itten and Zen, see Kaneko Yoshima, "Johannes Itten and Zen," in Christoph Wagner, ed., *Esoterik am Bauhaus: Eine Revision der Moderne?* (Regensburg: Schnell & Steiner, 2009), pp. 150–73. On Itten's "patchwork identity," see also Swantje Scharenberg, "Johannes Itten: Ein Kunst-Turner prägt das Bauhaus," in Arnd Krüger and Bernd Wedemeyer, eds., *Aus Biographien Sportgeschichte lernen: Festschrift zum 90. Geburtstag von Prof. Dr. Wilhelm Henze* (Hoya: Niedersächsisches Institut für Sportgeschichte Hoya e.V., 2000), pp. 134–48. A more recent discussion can be found in Elizabeth Otto, *Haunted Bauhaus: Occult Spirituality, Gender Fluidity, Queer Identities, and Radical Politics* (Cambridge, MA: MIT Press, 2019), pp. 26–32.

54. Itten learned about Mazdaznan for the first time in 1912 through Hermann Röthlisberger's mother-in-law, who alerted Itten to the doctrine's vegetarian diet. See Eva Badura-Triska, *Johannes Itten: Tagebücher. Stuttgart 1913–1916. Wien 1916–1919*, 2 vols. (Vienna: Löcker 1990), vol. 1, p. 116. Hanish is first mentioned in Itten's diary in the fall of 1918. On a double-page spread written between September 3 and 5, 1918 (pp. 81–82), Itten jotted down a few notes under the caption "2.Vortrag." As Badura-Triska conjectures, these thoughts served as cues for the seminar Itten gave for art historians (p. 116). The diary entry reads as follows: "2nd Lecture: Unleashing the body and mind. Development

of the body, mind, and emotions. Their enhancement through reason (form and color) (mental), through the eye (sensory), and through nourishment (physical). Z. Hanish. 3. *Form and Color.* Forms in organic nature. Perfection in crystals, the material recognized as pure laws. Representation of basic forms in *proportion*, *rhythm* (surfaces and cubes), and the polarities of forms and colors. *Physical Training*: Z. Hanish, *Rhythm*, Breath, and Nutrition. *Sensual*, Eye: Goethe's Theory of Colors (Nature), Old Masters. Develop the other senses as far as possible through nature, since we have no theory of tones (Bach) or taste analogous to Goethe's theory of colors. Spiritual: the thoughts of great thinkers" (p. 335).

55. Its racial theory was advanced through the theosophic ideas of Russian occultist Helena Blavatsky (1831–1891). See Christoph Wagner, "Johannes Itten und die Esoterik: Ein Schlüssel zum frühen Esoteriker?," in Wagner, ed., *Esoterik am Bauhaus*, p. 119. The racial underpinnings, its emphasis on eugenics, and the alleged supremacy of the Aryan race as the climax of evolution had little in common with beliefs of the soon-to-emerge National Socialism. In fact, Mazdaznan and other esoteric associations were outlawed by the Nazis around 1935 with an SS remark claiming that "it must be destroyed." See Otoman Zar-Adusht Ha'nish, *Mazdaznan Health and Breath Culture: The First Six Exercises*, ed. Ian Whittlesea (London: Open Editions, 2012), p. 65.

56. Otoman Zar-Adusht Ha'nish, *Mazdaznan Health and Breath Culture* (Chicago: Sun Worshiper, 1902), p. 5.

57. Ibid., p. 17.

58. Ibid., p. 7.

59. His breathing system in German was published as O. Z. Hanish, *Masdasnan Atemlehre*, ed. David Ammann (Herrliberg: Masdasnan, 1919).

60. On Mazdaznan's body system, see Bernd Wedemeyer-Kolwe, "*Der Neue Mensch*": Körperkultur im Kaiserreich und in der Weimarer Republik (Würzburg: Königshausen & Neumann, 2004), p. 162.

61. Ha'nish, *Mazdaznan Health and Breath Culture*, p. 18.

62. Ludger Busch, "Das Bauhaus und Mazdaznan," in Rolf Bothe, Peter Hahn, and Hans Christoph von Tavel, eds., *Das frühe Bauhaus und Johannes Itten* (Ostfildern-Ruit: Gerd Hatje, 1994), pp. 83–90.

63. Ibid., pp. 83–90.

64. With his progressive, rational ideas, it seems as if Gropius first acquiesced but later increasingly rejected the curious Mazdaznan culture embraced by Itten. However, Christoph Wagner cautions against drawing such hasty conclusions in his study of

Johannes Itten and the role of esotericism. For the extent to which Gropius might have been an esoteric, too, see Wagner's meticulous discussion in "Johannes Itten und die Esoterik,“ pp. 108–49. After Itten's departure from the Bauhaus and before he founded his own school in Berlin, he spent the intermittent years from 1923 to 1926 at the international Mazdaznan temple community in Herrliberg on Lake Zurich. See Badura-Triska, *Johannes Itten: Tagebücher*, vol. 2, p. 116. On the relationship between Itten and Gropius, see also Karin Wilhelm, "Auf der Suche nach dem neuen Menschen: Zum Verhältnis von Walter Gropius und Johannes Itten," in *Das frühe Bauhaus und Johannes Itten*, pp. 59–71.

65. Citroen, "Mazdaznan at the Bauhaus," p. 50.

66. Ibid., p. 49.

67. Adams, "Memories of a Bauhaus Student," pp. 192–93.

68. Citroen, "Mazdaznan at the Bauhaus," p. 47.

69. Adams, "Memories of a Bauhaus Student," pp. 192–93.

70. Itten, *Design and Form*, p. 9.

71. Ibid.

72. As Harry Francis Mallgrave notes, "the point of these activities was to tap into the body's natural biological rhythm." Harry Francis Mallgrave, *Architecture and Embodiment: The Implications of the New Sciences and Humanities for Design* (London: Routledge, 2013), p. 128.

73. Titles include, but are not limited to, A. K. Neumann, *Die Atmungskunst des Menschen* (Leipzig: C. F. Amelang, 1859); Leo Kofler, *The Art of Breathing as the Basis of Tone-Production*, 2nd ed. (London: Trübner, 1890); Henry Hughes, *Atemkuren, mit 115 Rezepten* (Würzburg: Curt Kabitsch, 1909), which provided a lot of data about respiration patterns under different conditions; Franz Kirchberg, *Atemgymnastik und Atmungstherapie von Dr. Franz Kirchberg* (Berlin: Springer, 1913); Ludwig Hofbauer, *Atmungs-Pathologie und-Therapie* (Berlin: Springer, 1921); Johannes Ludwig Schmitt, *Das Hohelied vom Atem*, 1st ed. (Munich: Dorn, 1927).

74. "Review: Rules for Respiration—Atemkuren by Henry Hughes," *British Medical Journal* 2. 2535 (1909), p. 271.

75. On this, see Bernd Wedemeyer-Kolwe, *Aufbruch: Die Lebensreform in Deutschland* (Darmstadt: Philipp von Zabern, 2017).

76. While this technique was featured in numerous books on breathing, there also were entire publications dedicated solely to this subject. See S. Otabe, *Tiefatmen für unsere Gesundheit* (Berlin: Hirschwald, 1914).

77. Daniel Gottlob Moritz Schreber, *Aerztliche Zimmer-Gymnastik* (Leipzig: Friedrich Fleischer, 1855), p. 31.

78. On this aspect of gender, see the comprehensive survey by Karoline von Steinaecker, *Luftsprünge: Anfänge moderner Körpertherapien* (Munich: Urban & Fischer, 2000).

79. After Müller became internationally successful, he dropped the umlaut in his name, changing it to Muller.

80. J. P. Muller, *My System: 15 Minutes Exercise a Day for Health's Sake*, New Edition Revised by Capt. L. P. Mueller (London: Link House Athletic Publications, n.d.), p. 59.

81. Ibid.

82. Ibid.

83. When Müller adapted his system specifically to women, Kafka sent a copy of this book to his fiancée Felice Bauer, urging her to follow the exercises meticulously. Mark Anderson, *Kafka's Clothes: Ornament and Aestheticism in the Habsburg Fin de Siècle* (Oxford: Clarendon Press of Oxford University Press, 1992), pp. 79–80.

84. Susan Sontag, *Illness as Metaphor and AIDS and Its Metaphors* (New York: Farrar, Straus, and Giroux, 1977), p. 19.

85. J. P. Muller, *My Breathing System* (London: Link House Athletic Publications, 1921), p. 34.

86. Ibid., preface to the first edition.

87. Ibid., p. 9.

88. *Wege zu Kraft und Schönheit: Ein Film über moderne Körperkultur*, documentary (UFA-Kulturfilmabteilung, 1925).

89. Ibid. My translation.

90. Peter-André Alt, *Franz Kafka: Der ewige Sohn. Eine Biographie* (Munich: C. H. Beck, 2005), p. 209.

91. Keller-Hoerschelmann, *Mein Atmungssystem*, p. 5.

92. Hans Surén, *Atemgymnastik*, 42nd ed. (Stuttgart: Franck'sche Verlagshandlung, 1935). The conflation of health and race and how National Socialism harnessed these breathing systems is not my focus here and is discussed elsewhere. See, for instance, Matthew Jefferies, "'For a Genuine and Noble Nakedness'? German Naturism in the Third Reich," *German History* 24.1 (2006), pp. 62–84. On Hans Surén, see Nina J. Morris, "Naked in Nature: Naturism, Nature and the Senses in the Early 20th Century Britain," *Cultural Geographies* 16.3 (2009), pp. 283–308.

93. Surén, *Atemgymnastik*, p. 33. My translation.

94. Susanne Hauser thinks of skin as an in-between space. Susanne Hauser, "Die Haut als Zwischenraum," in Mechthild Cramer von Laue, ed., *Topos RAUM: Die Aktualität des Raumes in den Künsten der Gegenwart* (Nuremberg: Verlag für moderne Kunst, 2005), pp. 308–19.

CHAPTER THREE: BREATHING WALLS

1. Max Pettenkofer, *Über den Luftwechsel in Wohngebäuden* (Munich: Literarisch-Artistische Anstalt der J. G. Cotta'schen Buchhandlung, 1858), p. 82.

2. Max Pettenkofer, "Über den Unterschied zwischen Luftheizung und Ofenheizung hinsichtlich der Zusammensetzung der Luft," *Dinglers Polytechnisches Journal* 119 (1851), pp. 40–51, and Max Pettenkofer, "Über den Unterschied zwischen Luftheizung und Ofenheizung hinsichtlich der Zusammensetzung der Luft," *Dinglers Polytechnisches Journal* 120 (1851), pp. 418–23.

3. Pettenkofer, "Über den Unterschied zwischen Luftheizung und Ofenheizung hinsichtlich der Zusammensetzung der Luft," p. 420. My translation. On sealed buildings, see Lydia Kallipoliti, *The Architecture of Closed Worlds, Or, What Is the Power of Shit?* (Zurich: Lars Müller, 2018). For an example of a sealed building envelope see, for instance, the discussion in Reinhold Martin, "Risk: Excerpts from the Environmental Division of Labor," in James Graham, ed., *Climates: Architecture and the Planetary Imaginary* (New York Columbia Books on Architecture and the City, 2016). See also Alejandro Zaera and Jeffrey S. Anderson, *The Ecologies of the Building Envelope: A Material History and Theory of Architectural Surfaces* (New York, Barcelona: Actar, 2021).

4. Ibid. My translation.

5. Ibid., p. 422. My translation.

6. These experiments were based on Thomas Graham's earlier explorations into the diffusion of gas. Graham demonstrated the permeability of plaster. Thomas Graham, *Lehrbuch der Chemie*, ed. Dr. Friedrich Julius Otto, 2 vols. (Braunschweig: Druck und Verlag von Friedrich Vieweg und Sohn, 1840), vol. 1, p. 86. The book was published in English as *Elements of Chemistry: Including the Applications of the Science in the Arts* (London: Hippolyte Bailliere, 1842).

7. Pettenkofer, *Über den Luftwechsel in Wohngebäuden*, p. 96.

8. Max von Pettenkofer, *Beziehungen der Luft zu Kleidung, Wohnung und Boden: Drei Populäre Vorlesungen* (Braunschweig: Druck und Verlag von Friedrich Vieweg und Sohn, 1872), p. 42.

9. Ibid. Performed under ideal conditions, the result was obviously deceptive due to the significantly higher ratio of surface area to applied air pressure compared with natural wind conditions affecting the brick of a building.

10. Josef von Fodor, *Das gesunde Haus und die gesunde Wohnung* (Braunschweig: Druck und Verlag von Friedrich Vieweg und Sohn, 1878), p. 33. My translation.

11. Ibid., p. 55. My translation.

12. For a succinct discussion see Mirko Zardini, "Pelle, Muro, Facciata = Skin, Wall, Facade," *Lotus International*, no. 82 (1994), pp. 38–51.

13. Walter Curt Behrendt, *The Victory of the New Building Style*, ed. Detlef Mertins, trans. Harry Francis Mallgrave (Los Angeles: Getty Center for the History of Art and the Humanities, 2000), p. 121. First published in German as Walter Curt Behrendt, *Der Sieg des neuen Baustils* (Stuttgart: Fr. Wedekind, 1927).

14. Mies evoked this image in one of his lectures with regard to an "Eskimo's" summer tent (unclear if Inuit or Yupik). See the text of Mies's lecture for the Association of German Architects in Berlin on December 12, 1923, titled "Solved Tasks: A Challenge for our Building Industry," reprinted in Fritz Neumeyer, *The Artless Word: Mies van Der Rohe on the Building Art*, trans. Mark Jarzombek (Cambridge, MA: MIT Press, 1991), p. 245.

15. Adrian Forty unpacks the use of "circulation" as a notable example of a physiological metaphor in architecture, asserting that he found its first use in its current meaning, implying the movement of humans inside a building, in a lecture by Eugène Viollet-le-Duc in 1872. See Adrian Forty, *Words and Buildings: A Vocabulary of Modern Architecture* (London: Thames & Hudson, 2000), p. 87.

16. Leon Battista Alberti, *On the Art of Building in Ten Books*, trans. Joseph Rykwert, Neil Leach, and Robert Tavernor (Cambridge, MA: MIT Press, 1988), p. 72.

17. Ibid.

18. Heinrich Johannes Boruttau, "Versuch einer kritischen Geschichte der Atmungstheorien," *Archiv für Geschichte der Medizin* 2.5 (February 1909), p. 304.

19. Plato, *Timaeus* 78d–e, trans. Benjamin Jowett, The Internet Classics Archive, http://classics.mit.edu/Plato/timaeus.html.

20. Ibid., 79b.

21. Claudia Benthien, *Haut: Literaturgeschichte–Körperbilder–Grenzerfahrungen* (Reinbeck bei Hamburg: Rowohlt Taschenbuch, 1999). Cited here from Claudia Benthien, *Skin: On the Cultural Border Between Self and the World*, trans. Thomas Dunlap (New York: Columbia University Press, 2002) p. 24.

22. Benthien identifies two metaphorical levels: as part of the skin, the orifices act as a sensory organ and allow external stimuli to enter only selectively. On another level, the process of circulation in the body, involving the intake and removal of metabolic substances, is likened to the movement of entering and exiting a house, with the bodily openings associated with this process understood as doors or portals.

23. Benthien, *Skin*, 28.

24. Ibid., p. 40.

25. Pettenkofer, "Über den Unterschied zwischen Luftheizung und Ofenheizung," p. 420. My translation.

26. Joseph von Gerlach, "Über das Hautathmen," *Archiv für Anatomie, Physiologie und wissenschaftliche Medicin* (1851), pp. 431–79.

27. "Suppression of lung breathing, the most important part of the entire respiratory process, results in immediate death by asphyxiation; prolonged and complete suppression of skin breathing results in slow death by asphyxiation." Gerlach, "Über das Hautathmen," p. 473. My translation. A book on horses published in 1888 would reiterate his hypothesis in a chapter on skin. Graf Carl Gustav Wrangel, *Das Buch vom Pferde* (Stuttgart: Schickhardt & Ebner, 1888), p. 524.

28. Gerlach, "Über das Hautathmen," pp. 459–60. The hypothesis is partially reiterated in more recent studies. See M. Stücker, et al., "The Cutaneous Uptake of Atmospheric Oxygen Contributes Significantly to the Oxygen Supply of Human Dermis and Epidermis," *Journal of Physiology* 538.3 (February 2002), pp. 985–94.

29. Ibid., pp. 431 and 433. My translation.

30. David Boswell Reid, *Illustrations of the Theory and Practice of Ventilation: With Remarks on Warming, Exclusive Lighting, and the Communication of Sound* (London: Longman, Brown, Green & Longmans, Paternoster Row, 1844), p. 172.

31. Catherine E. Beecher and Harriet Beecher Stowe, *The American Woman's Home: Or, Principles of Domestic Science* (New York: J. B. Ford, 1869), p. 48.

32. Gottfried Semper, *Die vier Elemente der Baukunst* (Braunschweig: Druck und Verlag von Friedrich Vieweg und Sohn, 1851).

33. Ibid., p. 57.

34. Ákos Moravánszky, *Stoffwechsel* (Basel: Birkhäuser, 2018), pp. 100–101.

35. Again, these equations are discussed in Benthien. The skin has been compared to both a wall and a layer of clothing.

36. See Benthien, *Skin*, p. 245 n. 8.

37. On the environmental history of the building, see Henrik Schoenefeldt, "The Crystal Palace, Environmentally Considered," *Architectural Research Quarterly* 12.3–4, pp. 283–94, https://doi.org/10.1017/S1359135508001218.

38. As Eva Horn notes, rather than shielding visitors from outside, the Crystal Palace

was a space that offered the experience of being "outside"—without the accompanying discomforts typically associated with exposure to the elements. Eva Horn, "Air Conditioning: Taming the Climate as a Dream of Civilization," in *Climates: Architecture and the Planetary Imaginary* (Zürich: Lars Müller, 2016), pp. 239–40.

39. Joseph Paxton, *What Is to Become of the Crystal Palace?* (London: Bradbury & Evans, 1851), pp. 6–7.

40. Friedrich Engels, *Die Lage der arbeitenden Klasse in England*, 2nd ed. (Stuttgart: J. H. W. Dietz, 1892). Quoted throughout from Frederick Engels, *The Condition of the Working Class in England in 1844 with Appendix Written 1886, and Preface 1887*, trans. Florence Kelly Wischnewetsky (New York: John W. Lovell Company, 1887), here, p. 64. London has had a long history of smog and air pollution, prompting one of the first critical contributions to the issue, the so-called *Fumifugium*, published by the English diarist John Evelyn in 1661. One day that year, he sauntered through the Palace of Whitehall, its interior so obscured with smoke that people barely recognized each other. Evelyn set out to persuade England's King Charles II, to take countermeasures against the debilitating atmospheric conditions in London by relocating the kilns and coal-mining industries to the outskirts and by planting plots with fragrant flowers so as to imbue London's atmosphere with pleasant scents. Originally published in 1661, the *Fumifugium* was reprinted as John Evelyn, *Fumifugium: Or, the Inconveniencie of the Aer and Smoak of London Dissipated Together with Some Remedies Humbly Proposed by J. E. Esq. to His Sacred Majestie, and to the Parliament Now Assembled* (Exeter: The Rota at the University of Exeter, 1976).

41. Engels, *The Condition of the Working Class*, p. 65. Pettenkofer also noted the detrimental effects of overcrowding among the poor, who, lacking firewood in winter, were not only cold, but also unable to create the temperature differential needed to induce proper air exchange between the interior and exterior. See Pettenkofer, *Über den Luftwechsel in Wohngebäuden*, pp. 91–92.

42. Schoenefeldt, "The Crystal Palace, Environmentally Considered," p. 292.

43. Paxton, *What Is to Become of the Crystal Palace?*, p. 9.

44. Although Paxton does not use terms such as "skin" or "envelope," he refers to the building as a "roof," "glass structure," or "sky-roof." Paxton, *What Is to Become of the Crystal Palace?*, pp. 1, 6, 12.

45. Walter Gropius, *The New Architecture and the Bauhaus* (Cambridge, MA: MIT Press, 1937), p. 26. Originally conceived by the architect Eduard Werner, the initial scheme for the

Fagus Factory failed to satisfy company owner Carl Benscheidt, whose foresight demanded a distinctly modern appearance. Contrary to popular belief, the construction of the Fagus Factory was not particularly innovative. Much of the structure followed Werner's initial plans, using traditional brickwork with iron beams connecting the battered piers to the back wall. The real innovation lay in the soon-to-be-famous facade, which wrapped around the corner at a right angle without visible support. This was a novel approach, inverting conventional design principles. While Behrens had emphasized the heavy presence of the corner in his AEG turbine factory, Gropius and Meyer introduced weightlessness precisely where it was least expected, turning their mentor's lesson on its head. See Annemarie Jaeggi, *Fagus: Industrial Culture from Werkbund to Bauhaus*, trans. Elizabeth M. Schwaiger (New York: Princeton Architectural Press, 2000), p. 29. Displeased with Werner's proposals, Benscheidt relieved him of further design tasks but kept him involved as a local consultant. This was the moment for the then-twenty-six-year-old Gropius to continue under favorable conditions what he and Meyer had learned at Behrens's office.

46. Jürgen Götz, "Maintaining Fagus," in Jaeggi, *Fagus*, p. 137.

47. Ibid., p. 138.

48. Sigfried Giedion, *Space, Time and Architecture: The Growth of a New Tradition* (Cambridge, MA: Harvard University Press, 2008), pp. 494–95.

49. Walter Gropius, *Bauhausbauten Dessau* (Munich: A. Langen, 1930), p. 47. My translation.

50. A quick glance at one of the numerous publications on the Dessau Bauhaus illustrates what I have in mind: "the glass façade . . . spans the building like an external skin. The glass façade, also known as a curtain wall, was actually only connected to the individual floors at a few points. . . . The glass façade resembles a membrane which connects the internal and external spaces." Christian Irrgang and Ingolf Kern, *The Bauhaus Building in Dessau* (Leipzig: Spector Books, 2014), pp. 35–36.

51. Gropius, *Bauhausbauten Dessau*, 1930, pp. 15, 23, 47, 60.

52. Ibid., p. 25.

53. Ibid., pp. 23, 25, 47. My translation.

54. Daniel A. Barber, "Heating the Bauhaus: Understanding the History of Architecture in the Context of Energy Policy and Energy Transition," Kleinman Center for Energy Policy, October 2019, p. 7, Knowledge Common Works. The article was later included in Daniel Barber, "Heating the Bauhaus," *Perspecta*, no. 53 (2020), pp. 234–48.

55. Many of the aperture systems widely deployed at the Bauhaus echo those exhibited in publications from the same decade, such as *Stahlfenster für Wohnhäuser und Profanbauten* (Steel windows for residential and civil buildings), by Fenestra Critall A.G., a merger of the Düsseldorf based Fenestra G.m.b.h. and Crittall Manufacturing Co. Ltd., from Braintree, England. The first photograph shown in a section of the book dedicated to built works with window systems from the company is one of the Törten Estate, a project tackled by Gropius soon after the Bauhaus building was finished. A diligent observer could reasonably infer that both projects are outfitted with Fenestra Crittall windows, and historically, this connection suggests itself. The windows utilized in the Bauhaus building were, in fact, delivered and installed by a German company called Nordische Eisen- u. Drahtindustrie, commonly known as Norddraht. Although Gropius made no mention of preexisting window solutions in his recommendation, he praised the partially novel designs with such enthusiasm that the manufacturing company featured his endorsement in an advertisement published in *Bauwelt Katalog* (Berlin: Bauwelt, 1929). Gropius emphasized the precision and quality of the preliminary drawings and the execution of the closing mechanisms, which were indeed cleverly designed. The chain pulley and hand-wheel systems, described by Gropius as "novel, partially complicated, and difficult," stood out as distinctive features in stark contrast to conventional, standardized mechanisms. These complexities are noteworthy, especially since simpler alternatives were available. Fenestra, for instance, also provided the windows for the second construction phase of the Fagus Factory, so Gropius had already set up points of contact much earlier. See Jaeggi, *Fagus*, p. 136.

56. Peter Blundell Jones writes that Gropius "evidently wanted the steel cage and the machinery of the opening lights to have a strong physical presence." Peter Blundell Jones, *Modern Architecture Through Case Studies* (Oxford: Architectural Press, 2002), p. 69. Similarly, Julius Posner commented on the dense mesh of steel mullions holding each glass pane in place. He noted that framings of similar sizes were used in much smaller parts of the building, suggesting that they were intended as a distinct architectural element. See Julius Posener, "Ein Besuch im Bauhaus Dessau," in *Was Architektur sein kann: Neuere Aufsätze* (Basel: Birkhäuser, 1995).

57. Walter Gropius, "Glasbau," *Die Bauzeitung vereinigt mit "Süddeutsche Bauzeitung" München* 23.20 (May 25, 1926), p. 161. My translation.

58. I discuss the claim that this was Gropius's strategy for the Bauhaus at large in Tim Altenhof, "The Aesthetics of Blurred Boundaries: From Wölfflin's Baroque to

Giedion's Interpenetration," *21 Inquiries into Art, History, and the Visual* 3.4 (December 2022), pp. 817–61, https://doi.org/10.1588/xxi.2022.4.91462.

59. Gropius, *Bauhausbauten Dessau*, p. 53. My translation.

60. See, for example, Gropius, "Glasbau," p. 160: "The sense of space is changing, while the old days of completed cultural developments embodied the heavy earthboundness in solid, monolithic-looking structures and individualized interiors, the works of modern, trend-setting architects demonstrate a changed sense of space that reflects the principle of movement, the traffic of our time, in a loosening of structures and spaces, that denies the enclosing wall and seeks to maintain the connection between the interior and the surrounding space [*Allraum*]. Something floating, light, rhythmically moving lies above these buildings; the heavy weight, the earth's inertia, is overcome in effect and appearance. The horizontal, the symbol of movement, overcomes the vertical, the earth's gravity." My translation.

61. Ebeling, a short-term Bauhaus student, arrived in Weimar in 1922 after military service and being released from British captivity during World War I. A polymath, he had studied philology and theology before the war and archaeology and art history afterward. When the Bauhaus moved from Weimar to Dessau, Ebeling's life followed a similar trajectory; he relocated to Dessau in 1925. Despite the geographical proximity, Ebeling's relationship with the Bauhaus was strained. See Walter Scheiffele, *Das leichte Haus: Utopie und Realität der Membran-Architektur* (Leipzig: Spector Books, 2015). That he still wrote within the intellectual ambit of the Bauhaus in 1926 was for Fritz Neumeyer "recognizable by its unmistakable idiom," melding the philosophies of Friedrich Nietzsche and Raoul Francé into a "theory of architecture that was as prophetic as it was idiosyncratic." Neumeyer, *The Artless Word,* p. 171. As Ebeling grew increasingly distant from the school's core tenets, he developed strong ties with the Junkers company, a Dessau-based firm founded in 1895 by the German aircraft engineer Hugo Junkers (1859–1935) known for specializing in metal aircraft. As early as 1922, Ebeling began to write for the advertising unit of the company, but that does not mean his writings remained influenced with broader Bauhaus attitudes.

62. Siegfried Ebeling, *Der Raum als Membran* (Dessau: C. Dünnhaupt, 1926). Cited throughout from Siegfried Ebeling, *Space as Membrane*, ed. Spyros Papapetros, trans. Pamela Johnston (London: Architectural Association, 2010), pp. 9–10.

63. Ebeling, *Space as Membrane*, p. 6. Spyros Papapetros describes Ebeling's polemic as "a point-by-point attack on Gropius's politics and more specifically his 'one-sided' and

'rationalistic' attitude towards design." See Spyros Papapetros, "Future Skins," in *Space as Membrane*, p. xiv.

64. In a footnote, Ebeling amends his discussion on energy efficiency by stating that "up to now the tubular flue (as in a chimney) has been the only device in the house which transforms the physical conditions of exterior space into an immediate-dynamic function of the house-organism." Ebeling, *Space as Membrane*, p. 13.

65. Siegfried Ebeling, "Kosmologe Raumzellen: Ideen zur Kritik des konstruktiven Denkens," *Junge Menschen* 5.8 (November 1924), p. 173. My translation.

66. Ibid.

67. Ebeling, *Space as Membrane*, p. 13

68. Ibid., pp. 9–10.

69. Raoul Heinrich Francé, *Plasmatik: Die Wissenschaft der Zukunft* (Stuttgart Heilbronn: Walter Seifert, 1923). See the brief discussion in Walter Scheiffele, "Membran und Moderne," in a recent edition of *Der Raum als Membran* (Dessau: Spector Books, 2016), pp. 43–47.

70. Francé, *Plasmatik*, p. 13. My translation.

71. Raoul Heinrich Francé, *Die technischen Leistungen der Pflanzen* (Leipzig: Veit, 1919). Francé presents the plant as a "study subject for architects and mechanics," ushering in a new perspective on cells: "Of all cell constituents, neither the living content, nor the retained substances will be any longer of interest to us, but exclusively their membrane, because all the mechanical and static performances of the entire plant world are based on the plant's membrane qualities." Ibid., p. 152. My translation.

72. "Where Architecture Meets Biology: An Interview with Detlef Mertins," in Joke Brouwer and Arjen Mulder, eds., *Interact or Die!* (Rotterdam: V2, 2007), p. 111.

73. Francé, *Die technischen Leistungen der Pflanzen*, p. 9. My translation.

74. Ibid. My translation.

75. See Ebeling, *Space as Membrane*, p. 20.

76. Ibid., p. 29.

77. Ibid., pp. 32–33.

78. Ebeling, *Space as Membrane*, p. 21.

79. See the extensive discussion in Fritz Neumeyer, *The Artless Word: Mies van der Rohe on the Building Art*, trans. Mark Jarzombek (Cambridge, MA: MIT Press, 1991), pp. 171–77.

80. Ebeling, *Space as Membrane*, p. 34.

81. Papapetros, "Future Skins," in *Space as Membrane*, pp. xiii–xxiii.

82. Ibid., p. xvi.

CHAPTER FOUR: IMMERSIVE ATMOSPHERE

1. The first footnote in Ebeling's, *Space as Membrane* is dedicated to Hellpach.

2. Willy Hellpach, *Die geopsychischen Erscheinungen: Wetter, Klima und Landschaft in ihrem Einfluss auf das Seelenleben* (Leipzig: Wilhelm Engelmann, 1911), p. 2. My translation.

3. Craig Martin, "The Invention of Atmosphere," *Studies in History and Philosophy Science*, no. 52 (2015), p. 52. The terms "climate," "weather," "air," and "atmosphere" often are used interchangeably, but weather and climate both reflect conditions in the atmosphere, distinguished primarily by their duration. Weather refers to short-term atmospheric conditions at a specific location, whereas climate encompasses the long-term cumulative effect of these conditions. Air, the mixture of gases we breathe, primarily is composed of nitrogen, oxygen, and small amounts of other gases, while the atmosphere is the encompassing layer of gases surrounding the earth, which extends to various layers such as the stratosphere and ionosphere, playing a crucial role in climate and weather patterns. The atmosphere also acts as a protective shield around the earth, preventing excessive radiation.

4. Saint-Preux, the commoner, writes to Julie d'Étanges: "I find the countryside more cheerful, the greenery more fresh and lively, the air more pure, the Sky more serene." Jean-Jacques Rousseau, *Julie, or the New Heloise*, trans. Philip Stewart and Jean Vaché, in *The Collected Writings of Rousseau*, ed. Roger D. Masters and Christopher Kelly, 13 vols. (Hanover: Dartmouth College Press, 1997), vol. 6, p. 95. See Anthony Vidler, *The Scenes of the Street and Other Essays* (New York: Monacelli Press, 2011), p. 39.

5. Rafael Beneytez-Duran, "The Materiality of Air: From Oxidation to Carbon Accumulation," *Log*, no. 60 (Winter–Spring 2024), pp. 29–40. As Beneytez-Duran argues, the technosphere — a sweeping material network that has modified the planet — has only two options to maintain a livable atmosphere, either by recycling excess amounts of CO_2 or by adapting "biologically to metabolize air containing excessive amounts of CO_2."

6. Hellpach, *Die geopsychischen Erscheinungen*, p. 3.

7. John Durham Peters, "The Media of Breathing," in Lenart Škof and Petri Berndtson, eds., *Atmospheres of Breathing* (Albany: State University of New York Press, 2018), pp. 179–95.

8. Ibid., p. 191. Just as architecture could create its own atmosphere, so could clothing.

Swiss physician Adolf Keller-Hoerschelmann, for instance, urges readers to "just ask your nose once when taking off your clothes, in which atmosphere the skin was coffined." Adolf Keller-Hoerschelmann, *Mein Atmungssystem: Bestes Buch praktischer Gesundheitspflege!*, 2nd ed. (Olten: Herm. Hambrecht, 1911), p. 26. My translation.

9. Willy Hellpach, *Die Geopsychischen Erscheinungen: Wetter und Klima, Boden und Landschaft in ihrem Einfluss auf das Seelenleben*, 3rd ed. (Leipzig: Verlag von Wilhelm Engelmann, 1923), p. 338. My translation.

10. On the tension between conventional medicine (*Schulmedizin*), represented by regular physicians, and alternative life reform approaches, see especially chapter 6 in Michael Hau, *The Cult of Health and Beauty in Germany: A Social History, 1890–1930* (Chicago: University of Chicago Press, 2003).

11. Christoph Wilhelm Hufeland, *Enchiridion medicum oder Anleitung zur medizinischen Praxis*, 3rd ed. (Herisau: Im Litteratur-Comptoir, 1837). Hufeland (1762–1836) was an eminent German physician from Langensalza who counted prominent figures such as Johann Wolfgang von Goethe and Friedrich Schiller among his patients.

12. Sigfried Giedion, *Mechanization Takes Command: A Contribution to Anonymous History* (Minneapolis: University of Minnesota Press, 2013), p. 671.

13. Arnold Rikli, *Die Grundlehren der Naturheilkunde einschliesslich die atmosphärische Cur "Es werde Licht"* (Leipzig: L. Fernau, 1895). Rikli cites Hufeland as a source.

14. As we've seen and will continue to explore, the paradigm of walls as skins has persistently influenced theoretical discourses in the history of modern architecture, from Gottfried Semper and Otto Wagner to Adolf Loos. Adolf Loos, "Das Prinzip der Bekleidung," in *Adolf Loos: Sämtliche Schriften*, 2 vols. (Vienna: Herold, 1962), vol. 1, pp. 105–12. Recent scholarship has emphasized the analogy between the ideas of clothing and dwelling as systems of shells encasing the body in the domain of *Körperkultur* and the notion of the house as an extended form of dress among modernist architects. In this context, Didem Ekici highlights the overlooked history of the light-and-air hut, a simple wooden structure that emerged in the context of the naturopathy movement from the mid-nineteenth century onward, "designed as the minimum permeable shelter." Didem Ekici, "From Rikli's Light-and-Air Hut to Tessenow's Patenthaus: Körperkultur and the Modern Dwelling in Germany, 1890–1914," *Journal of Architecture* 13.4, pp. 379–406.

15. Giedion, *Mechanization Takes Command*, p. 672.

16. Ibid., p. 676.

17. See Ryan Kurt Johnson, "The Re-Enchanted Body in Fin-de-Siècle German

Culture," PhD diss. Vanderbilt University, 2010. Chapter 4 analyzes the "anatomy of an icon" and discusses *Lichtgebet* in depth.

18. The motive was later reenacted by a female actor in Leni Riefenstahl's 1938 film *Olympia.*

19. See, for instance, O. R. McCarthy, "The Key to the Sanatoria," *Journal of the Royal Society of Medicine* 94.8 (2001), pp. 413–17.

20. Thomas Dormandy, *The White Death: A History of Tuberculosis* (New York: New York University Press, 2000), p. 147. Dormandy's observation notwithstanding, a number of contributions to the scholarship provide a good overview. See, for instance, Jean-Bernard Cremnitzer, *Architecture et santé: Le temps du sanatorium en France et en Europe* (Paris: Éditions A. et J. Picard, 2005); Bernard Toulier and Jean-Bernard Cremnitzer, *Histoire et réhabilitation des sanatoriums en Europe: Actes du colloque* (Paris: Docomo International, 2008); and Miller Quintus, *Das Sanatorium: Entstehung eines Prototyps der Modernen Architektur* (Lausanne: École Polytechnique Fédérale de Lausanne Départment d'Architecture, 1992).

21. Most notably, Beatriz Colomina's study on the impact of X-ray technology on modern architecture outlines a parallel history she has explored for years. See Beatriz Colomina, "X-Ray Architecture: Illness as Metaphor," *Positions*, no. 0 (2008), pp. 30–35; Beatriz Colomina, "X-Ray Architecture: The Tuberculosis Effect," *Harvard Design Magazine*, no. 40 (2015), pp. 71–91; and Beatriz Colomina, *X-Ray Architecture* (Zürich: Lars Müller Publishers, 2019). In this context see also Margaret Campbell, "What Tuberculosis Did for Modernism: The Influence of a Curative Environment on Modernist Design and Architecture," *Medical History* 49.4 (2005), pp. 463–88.

22. Sigfried Giedion, *Befreites Wohnen* (Zurich: Orell Füssli, 1929); Richard Döcker, *Terrassen Typ* (Stuttgart: Julius Hoffmann, 1929). The sanatorium also appears in Sigfried Giedion, *Space, Time and Architecture: The Growth of a New Tradition* (Cambridge, MA: Harvard University Press, 1941); Stanislaus von Moos, *Le Corbusier: Elements of a Synthesis* (Rotterdam: 010 Publishers, 2009); Paul Overy, *Light, Air and Openness: Modern Architecture Between the Wars* (London: Thames and Hudson, 2007); Colomina, *X-Ray Architecture.* More recently the building is discussed in great detail in Daniel Korwan, *Queen Alexandra Sanatorium: Discovering Early Modernism in Switzerland*, 1st ed. (Boston: Birkhäuser, 2023) and also in light of its atmospheric relation in Tim Altenhof, "Inhabiting the Atmosphere: The Architecture of the Queen Alexandra Sanatorium," *Journal of the Society of Architectural Historians* 82.3 (September 2023), pp. 314–34.

23. Susan Sontag, *Illness as Metaphor and AIDS and Its Metaphors* (New York: Doubleday, 1989), p. 73.

24. Peter Warren, "The Evolution of the Sanatorium: The First Half-Century, 1854–1904," *Canadian Journal of Health History* 23.2 (2006), p. 458.

25. Ibid.

26. Hermann Werner, "Climate and Sea Voyages in the Treatment of Tuberculosis," *Boston Medical and Surgical Journal* 140, no. 23 (1899), p. 553.

27. Eva Horn, "Air as Medium," *Grey Room*, no. 73 (2018), p. 17.

28. The German chemist Carl Dorno established the observatory in 1907 to study atmospheric radiation, and his work later proved influential for Ebeling, following his visit to Dorno's institution. See Walter Scheiffele, "Membrane and Ecological Architecture," introduction to Siegfried Ebeling, *Space as Membrane*, ed. Spyros Papapetros, trans. Pamela Johnston (London: Architectural Association Publications, 2010), p. vii.

29. Werner, "Climate and Sea Voyages," p. 553.

30. Ibid.

31. Hugo Bach, *Das Klima von Davos nach dem Beobachtungsmaterial der eidgenössischen meteorologischen Station in Davos* (Zurich: Druck von Zürcher & Furrer, 1907), p. 87.

32. Günter Riedel, *Singularitäten des Davoser Klimas* (Berlin: Julius Springer, 1936), p. 4.

33. Vitruvius believed that wind results from a reaction between heat and moisture. He mentions a so-called *aeolipile*, a kind of steam engine that already existed in his time. Vitruvius, *The Ten Books on Architecture*, trans. Morris Hicky Morgan (Cambridge, MA: Harvard University Press, 1914), p. 25.

34. Ibid., pp. 25–26.

35. Leon Battista Alberti, *On the Art of Building in Ten Books*, trans. Joseph Rykwert, Neil Leach, and Robert Tavernor (Cambridge, MA: MIT Press, 1988), p. 9.

36. Ibid.

37. Anthony Vidler, *The Writing of the Walls* (New York, N.Y: Princeton Architectural Press, 1987), p. 64.

38. Thomas Mann, *The Magic Mountain*, trans. John E. Woods (New York: Vintage Books, 1995), pp. 8–9.

39. Tony Garnier, *Une cité industrielle: Étude pour la construction des villes*, 2 vols. (Paris: C. Massin & Cie, 1932), vol. 1.

40. Karl Turban, "Normalien für die Erstellung von Heilstätten für Lungenkranke

in der Schweiz," in *Tuberkulose-Arbeiten 1890–1909: Aus Dr. Turbans Sanatorium, Davos* (Davos: Buchdruckerei Davos, 1909), pp. 234–43.

41. Ibid., p. 238.

42. Ibid., pp. 237–38.

43. See Christof Kübler, "Davos, die Sonnenstadt im Hochgebirge wider den 'hermetischen Zauber,'" *Bündner Monatsblatt: Zeitschrift für Bündner Geschichte, Landeskunde und Baukultur*, no. 4 (1989), pp. 237–61.

44. For the history of the Queen Alexandra Sanatorium, especially with regard to its construction methods, see Korwan, *Discovering Early Modernism in Switzerland.*

45. For a history of medical institutions in the United States, see Jeanne Kisacky, *Rise of the Modern Hospital: An Architectural History of Health and Healing, 1870–1940* (Pittsburgh: University of Pittsburgh Press, 2017).

46. *The Queen Alexandra Sanatorium, Davos: A Short Account of the Building Reprinted from the Annual Report of 1909–10* (London: Waterlow and Sons, 1910), pp. 21–22. See also "The Queen Alexandra Sanatorium, Davos Platz, Switzerland," *Hospital* 47, no. 1231 (1910), pp. 668–69.

47. K. Mühle, "The Davos Climate," in *Davos as Health-Resort: A Handbook* (Davos: Davos Printing Company, 1907), pp. 107, 110, 123.

48. H. J. A. van Voornveld, "The Physiology of the Davos Climate," trans. W. G. Lockett, in *Davos as Health-Resort: A Handbook* (Davos: Davos Printing Company, 1907), pp. 160–61.

49. On the importance of pine scent at the intersection of medical and environmental histories around the beginning of the twentieth century, see Clare Hickman, "Pine Fresh: The Cultural and Medical Context of Pine Scent in Relation to Health—from the Forest to the Home," *Medical Humanities* 48.1 (2021), pp. 104–13.

50. Werner, "Climate and Sea Voyages," p. 554. That pine trees were more than incidental to the therapeutics of atmosphere is further corroborated by the fact that in 1899, Dr. Simon von Unterberger, surgeon and director of the military hospital in Zarskoje-Selo, advocated for what he called the Haus Sanatorium, which integrated "domesticated pine trees" as part of a finely calibrated interior environment resembling an alpine resort. See Eva Eylers, "Planning the Nation: The Sanatorium Movement in Germany," *Journal of Architecture* 19.5 (2014), pp. 667–92.

51. H. H. C., "Life in a Sanatorium," letter to the editor, *The Spectator*, August 23, 1913, p. 18.

52. Turban, "Normalien für die Erstellung von Heilstätten für Lungenkranke in der Schweiz," p. 237.

53. For the passage describing Hans Castorp's first approach toward the Schatzalp Sanatorium, see Mann, *The Magic Mountain*, p. 8. Dave Lüthi evokes the image of a hive in a paragraph about the Queen Alexandra Sanatorium in "The Influence of Good Air on Architecture: A 'Formal Cure'? The Appearance of the Alpine Sanatorium in Switzerland, 1880–1914," *Revue de géographie alpine* 93.1 (March 2005), p. 56.

54. In contemporary architectural discourse, this zone is also called "mid-doors." See, for instance, Erik Olsen, "Mid-Doors: The Zone Between Inside and Outside That Could Change Building Design," *Fast Company*, November 17, 2020, https://www.fastcompany.com/90575944/mid-doors-the-zone-between-inside-and-outside-that-could-change-building-design.

55. "The Queen Alexandra Sanatorium, Davos Platz, Switzerland," p. 668.

56. Sigfried Giedion, "Bauen in der Schweiz 1929," *Das neue Frankfurt: Internationale Monatsschrift für die Probleme kultureller Neugestaltung* 3.6 (1929), p. 106.

57. Sigfried Giedion, *Befreites Wohnen / Liberated Dwelling*, ed. Reto Geiser, trans. Reto Geiser and Rachel Julia Engler (Zurich: Lars Müller, 2018), p. 87. For the German original, see ibid., p. 65.

58. Colomina, *X-Ray Architecture*, p. 71.

59. Emanuele Coccia, *The Life of Plants: A Metaphysics of Mixture* (Cambridge: Polity Press, 2019), p. 35. Recently, Coccia's ideas have become vested in architectural discourse. See, for instance, Emanuele Coccia, "In Open Air: Ontology of the Atmosphere," *Log*, no. 60 (Winter–Spring 2024), pp. 51–66.

60. This conception contrasts with Gernot Böhme's influential notion of atmosphere as something that operates within the realm of aesthetics, rather than ontology: it is viewed as sensory, rather than scientific and exists in the plural, rather than the singular. Where Böhme sees various atmospheres that affect human perception in their immediate experience of a surrounding space, Coccia views the atmosphere of the earth as a physical environment. See Gernot Böhme, *Atmosphäre: Essays zur neueren Ästhetik* (Berlin: Suhrkamp, 2013). For an English edition see Gernot Böhme, *The Aesthetics of Atmospheres*, ed. Jean-Paul Thibaud (London: Routledge, Taylor & Francis, 2017).

61. Coccia, *The Life of Plants*, p. 49.

62. On the complex nature of air see Nerea Calvillo, *Aeropolis: Queering Air in Toxic-polluted Worlds* (New York: Columbia Books on Architecture and the City, 2023).

63. Luce Irigaray, *The Forgetting of Air in Martin Heidegger*, trans. Mary Beth Mader

(Austin: University of Texas Press, 1999), p. 8. The book was first published as Luce Irigaray, *L'oubli de l'air chez Martin Heidegger* (Paris: Éditions de Minuit, 1983).

64. Irigaray, *The Forgetting of Air in Martin Heidegger*, p. 8.

65. Peter Sloterdijk, *Terror from the Air*, trans. Amy Patton and Steve Corcoran (Cambridge, MA: MIT Press, 2009). The book was first published in German as Peter Sloterdijk, *Luftbeben: An den Quellen des Terrors* (Frankfurt: Suhrkamp, 2002).

66. See Marijn Nieuwenhuis, "The Politics of Breathing: Knowledge on Air and Respiration," in *Atmospheres of Breathing*, p. 200.

67. Sloterdijk has to mute the preceding atmospheric practices and breathing techniques for his narrative to achieve its full impact. For him, "the atmosphere" made a sudden, poignant appearance on a single day in history, the same day "the 20th century dawned," marking a paradigm shift in modern warfare—from direct attacks on the body to the deadly manipulation of the enemy's environment. *Terror from the Air*, p. 10. As others have demonstrated, Ypres did not signify a radical departure from established norms or practices, but rather an escalation of a previously employed battle tactic, albeit one that had been only partially effective in the past. See, for instance, Ulrich Trumpener, "The Road to Ypres: The Beginnings of Gas Warfare in World War I," *Journal of Modern History* 47.3 (1975), pp. 460–80.

68. See Margit Szöllösi-Janze, *Fritz Haber 1868–1934: Eine Biographie* (Munich: C. H. Beck, 1998), p. 327.

69. Initially, the Germans hoped to drive soldiers out of their trenches, not to kill them directly. See Gerard J. Fitzgerald, "Chemical Warfare and Medical Response during World War I," *American Journal of Public Health* 98.4 (2008), pp. 611–25, https://doi.org/10.2105/AJPH.2007.11930.

70. See Trumpener, "Road to Ypres," pp. 476–78.

71. Sloterdijk, *Terror from the Air*, p. 11.

72. For a brief contextualization, see Laurent Stalder, "Air, Light, and Air-Conditioning," trans. Jill Denton, *Grey Room* 40 (2010), pp. 84–99.

73. These masks often caused claustrophobic feelings, rather than relief.

74. Rudolf Hanslian, *Der Chemische Krieg* (Berlin: E. S.Mittler & Sohn, 1927), p. 153.

75. The first prototypes of rebreathers were designed by the German physiologist Theodor Schwann (1810–1882) in 1853. For more information about Schwann, see Rudolf Vierhaus, ed., *Deutsche Biographische Enzyklopädie (DBE)*, 2nd ed. (Munich: K. G. Saur, 2008), s.v. "Theodor Schwann."

76. On the role of Haber, see Szöllösi-Janze, *Fritz Haber.*

77. The world of architecture still recognized that sealing inhabitants in airtight spaces presented dangers to them. In 1933, Hermann Stelzner (1884–1942), the chief design engineer of the so-called Dräger-Tauchretter, a diving lung for German submariners during World War II, took up the problem of ventilation for air-raid shelters in "Grundsätzliches zur Belüftungsfrage von Sammelschutzräumen" (Fundamentals of the ventilation of collective shelters). What intrigued Stelzner was how long a human being would be able to survive in a hermetic space one cubic meter (35.3 cubic feet) without adding a further air supply. Based on the human's temper, he concluded a phlegmatic person might reach a critical point after six hours, whereas a choleric one might "tumble over" after one and a half hours due to an increased discharge of carbon dioxide. Stelzner assumed a minimum volume of air of one cubic meter per person and hour without mechanical ventilation. Hermann Stelzner, "Grundsätzliches zur Belüftungsfrage von Sammelschutzräumen," *Gasschutz und Luftschutz* 3.3 (March 1933), pp. 74–78.

78. Hanslian, *Der Chemische Krieg*, p. 294. My translation.

79. Ibid. My translation.

80. Ibid., p. 290. My translation.

81. Kenneth Frampton describes the residential zones as the "lungs" framing the cultural center on both sides. See Kenneth Frampton, "The Rise and Fall of the Radiant City: Le Corbusier 1928–1960," *Oppositions*, nos. 19–20 (Winter 1980), p. 2. In this article, Frampton also traces the influence of the Radiant City on European postwar urban developments.

82. Le Corbusier, *La ville radieuse* (Boulogne-sur-Seine: Éditions de l'architecture d'aujourd'hui, 1933), p. 60. For the English see *The Radiant City: Elements of a Doctrine of Urbanism to Be Used as the Basis of Our Machine-Age Civilization* (New York: Orion Press, 1967), p. 60: "What about air war?"

83. "1926: Une villa sur pilotis, à Poissy. Pourquoi ne pas aérer la maison et la dégager du sol humide?" Still from the film *L'architecture d'aujourd'hui* (1930), directed by Pierre Chenal.

84. Le Corbusier, *The Radiant City*, p. 60.

85. Ibid.

86. The spectrum unfolding between these two extremes has been addressed in architectural historian Cyrille Simonnet's short, yet sweeping history of air in which

he concludes that air is not for our eyes, but for our noses, stressing the existential ties with our bodies. Cyrille Simonnet, *Brève histoire de l'air* (Versailles: Quae, 2014), p. 201.

CHAPTER FIVE: PNEUMATIC HOUSES

1. The *Oeuvre plastique* exhibition in 1938 was the first to present Le Corbusier's paintings in Switzerland.

2. Peter Meyer, "Moderne Kunst in der Schweiz: Le Corbusier als Maler," *Das Werk: Architektur und Kunst* 25.3 (March 1938), pp. 74–78.

3. Letter from Heinrich Wölfflin to Sigfried Giedion, January 20, 1938, reproduced in Ulrich Stucky, ed., *Hommage à Giedion: Profile seiner Persönlichkeit* (Basel: Birkhäuser, 1971), pp. 46–47.

4. Ibid. The letter was written on hotel stationary shortly before Giedion's pending departure to Harvard, where he was soon to deliver the prestigious Charles Elliot Norton Lectures during the academic year 1938–1939, and only because of this we can assume that Wölfflin was staying at the Schweizerhof.

5. Heinrich Wölfflin, *Prolegomena zu einer Psychologie der Architektur* (Munich: Kgl. Hof- und universitätsbuchdruckerei Dr. C. Wolf & Sohn, 1886). Cited throughout from Heinrich Wölfflin, "Prolegomena to a Psychology of Architecture," in *Empathy, Form, and Space: Problems in German Aesthetics 1873–1893*, trans. Harry Francis Mallgrave and Eleftherios Ikonomou (Santa Monica: Getty Center for the History of Art and the Humanities, 1994), pp. 149–90.

6. Wölfflin, "Prolegomena to a Psychology of Architecture," pp. 154–55.

7. Robert Vischer, "On the Optical Sense of Form: A Contribution to Aesthetics," in *Empathy, Form, and Space*, p. 98.

8. Wölfflin, "Prolegomena to a Psychology of Architecture," p. 169.

9. Wilhelm Wundt, *Grundzüge der Physiologischen Psychologie* (Leipzig: Verlag von Wilhelm Engelmann, 1874).

10. Ibid., p. 803. My translation.

11. Wölfflin, "Prolegomena to a Psychology of Architecture," p. 156.

12. Ibid., p. 170.

13. Ibid.

14. Friedrich von Hausegger, *Die Musik als Ausdruck* (Vienna: Carl Konegen, 1887).

15. Charles Darwin, *The Expression of the Emotions in Man and Animals* (London: John Murray, 1872).

16. Darwin assumed certain actions to be unchangeable by will, while in fact there is a respiratory feedback in the formation of emotions. Just as emotions impact our breathing pattern we can act upon them through breathing.

17. Darwin, *The Expression of the Emotions in Man and Animals*, p. 350.

18. Wölfflin, "Prolegomena to a Psychology of Architecture," p. 170.

19. Heinrich Wölfflin, *Kunstgeschichtliche Grundbegriffe: Das Problem der Stilentwicklung in der neueren Kunst* (Munich: F. Bruckmann, 1915). Cited throughout from the most recent English edition, Heinrich Wölfflin, *Principles of Art History: The Problem of the Development of Style in Early Modern Art*, ed. Evonne Levy and Tristan Weddigen, trans. Jonathan Blower (Santa Monica: Getty Publications, 2015).

20. For recent discussion, see Evonne Levy, *Baroque and the Political Language of Formalism (1845–1945): Burckhardt, Wölfflin, Gurlitt, Brinckmann, Sedlmayr* (Basel: Schwabe, 2015); the introduction to Wölfflin, *Principles of Art History*; and Christopher S. Wood, *A History of Art History* (Princeton: Princeton University Press, 2019).

21. Wölfflin, *Principles of Art History*, p. 147.

22. Ibid.

23. See Tim Altenhof, "The Aesthetics of Blurred Boundaries: From Wölfflin's Baroque to Giedion's Interpenetration," *21: Inquiries into Art, History, and the Visual*, no. 4 (December 2022), pp. 817–61, https://doi.org/10.11588/xxi.2022.4.91462.

24. Emil Kaufmann, *Von Ledoux bis Le Corbusier: Ursprung und Entwicklung der Autonomen Architektur* (Vienna: Rolf Passer, 1933). For a critical examination of Kaufmann and the genealogy of modern architecture see Anthony Vidler, *Histories of the Immediate Present: Inventing Architectural Modernism* (Cambridge, MA: MIT Press, 2008). More specifically, with a focus on autonomy, see Hubert Damisch, "Ledoux with Kant," *Perspecta*, no. 33 (2002), pp. 10–15; see also Anthony Vidler, "The Ledoux Effect: Emil Kaufmann and the Claims of Kantian Autonomy," *Perspecta*, no. 33 (2002), pp. 16–29. On autonomy, see also Christopher S. Wood, "Why Autonomy?," *Perspecta* 33 (2002), pp. 48–53.

25. Kaufmann, *Von Ledoux bis Le Corbusier*, p. 19.

26. Ibid., pp. 13, 54.

27. Ibid., p. 47. My translation.

28. Sigfried Giedion, *Bauen in Frankreich, Bauen in Eisen, Bauen in Eisenbeton* (Leipzig: Klinkhardt & Biermann, 1928). Cited throughout from Sigfried Giedion, *Building in France, Building in Iron, Building in Ferroconcrete*, ed. Sokratis Georgiadis, trans. J. Duncan

Berry (Los Angeles: Getty Center for the History of Art and the Humanities, 1995), here, p. 87.

29. For a critical discussion see the introduction by Sokratis Georgiadis in Giedion, *Building in France, Building in Iron, Building in Ferroconcrete.*

30. The book is essentially organized in two parts: the first discusses iron construction, the second ferroconcrete.

31. For an analysis of the concept, see Altenhof, "The Aesthetics of Blurred Boundaries," and Hilde Heynen, *Architecture and Modernity: A Critique* (Cambridge, MA: MIT Press, 1999), pp. 29–42.

32. Giedion, *Building in France, Building in Iron, Building in Ferroconcrete*, p. 143.

33. Ibid., p. 91.

34. Ibid., pp. 168, 176, 176, 183.

35. Ibid., p. 169.

36. Johannes Ludwig Schmitt, *Das Hohelied vom Atem*, 3rd ed. (Munich: Dorn, 1933), p. 37. My translation.

37. For a recent discussion on the Dom-Ino see Daniel A. Barber, *Modern Architecture and Climate: Design Before Air Conditioning* (Princeton: Princeton University Press, 2020), pp. 32–36.

38. Giedion, *Building in France, Building in Iron, Building in Ferroconcrete*, p. 168.

39. Ibid.

40. Ibid., pp. 168–69.

41. Robert Venturi, "Complexity and Contradiction in Architecture: Selections from a Forthcoming Book," *Perspecta* 9–10 (1965), p. 21. Subsequently published as Robert Venturi, *Complexity and Contradiction in Architecture* (New York: Museum of Modern Art, 1966).

42. Ibid.

43. Reinhold Martin, *The Organizational Complex: Architecture, Media, and Corporate Space* (Cambridge, MA: MIT Press, 2005), p. 20.

44. Parts of the letter are included in Brian Brace Taylor, *Le Corbusier: The City of Refuge, Paris 1929/33* (Chicago: University of Chicago Press, 1988), p. 112.

45. Joachim D. Pleil et al., "The Physics of Human Breathing: Flow, Timing, Volume, and Pressure Parameters for Normal, On-Demand, and Ventilator Respiration," *Journal of Breath Research* 15.4 (September 27, 2021), p. 2, https://doi.org/10.1088/1752-7163/ac2589. The authors assume a ventilation rate of six liters per minute and person.

46. Le Corbusier, *Precisions on the Present State of Architecture and City Planning*, trans. Edith Schreiber Aujame (Cambridge, MA: MIT Press, 1991), p. 167. The book first appeared as Le Corbusier, *Précisions sur un état présent de l'architecture et de l'urbanisme* (Paris: G. Crès, 1930). In describing it as "la respiration exacte," or exact respiration, Le Corbusier was intent on ensuring that its physiological identity be easily understood, in contrast to other mechanical ventilation systems of the time such as "air-conditioning," or what Willis Carrier dubbed "Man-made weather." His descriptions are laced with physiological terms, for instance, when he mentions an "arterial system" and a "system of veins" for the provision and extraction of air, as well as when "air that has been breathed in and out" returns to the ventilating plant to be conditioned again. Le Corbusier, *Precisions*, p. 64. See the discussion in Banham, *The Architecture of the Well-Tempered Environment*, especially chapters eight and nine, pp. 143–94. Le Corbusier's collaboration with Gustave Lyon is a key moment in the history of building construction. Through exact respiration, Le Corbusier envisioned a universal interior climate independent of local conditions.

47. Le Corbusier, *When the Cathedrals Were White*, trans. Francis E. Hyslop (New York: McGraw-Hill, 1947), p. 17.

48. Ibid., p. 18.

49. Taylor, *Le Corbusier*, p. xi.

50. Reyner Banham, *The Architecture of the Well-Tempered Environment*, 2nd ed. (Chicago: University of Chicago Press, 1984), p. 156.

51. For a detailed account see ibid., pp. 111–12.

52. Le Corbusier, *When the Cathedrals Were White*, p. 18. For the French, see Le Corbusier, *Quand les cathédrales étaient blanches: Voyage au pays des timides* (Paris: Plon, 1937), p. 39.

53. For a critical discussion on this see Banham, *The Architecture of the Well-Tempered Environment*, pp. 153–58, and more recently Barber, *Modern Architecture and Climate*.

54. Le Corbusier, *When the Cathedrals Were White*, p. 20.

55. See Taylor, *Le Corbusier*, p. 113.

56. Le Corbusier, *When the Cathedrals Were White*, p. 20.

57. For a critical account of his different approaches to ventilation, see Harris Sobin, "From *l'Air Exact* to *l'Aérateur*: Ventilation and Its Evolution in the Architectural Work of Le Corbusier," in Association of Collegiate Schools of Architect, *84th ACSA Annual Meeting and Technology Conference Proceedings* (Washington, DC: ACSA Press, 1996), pp. 220–27.

58. Le Corbusier, *Precisions*, p. 64.

CODA: SEALED BUBBLES

1. Reyner Banham, "Monumental Wind-Bags," *New Society* 11.290 (1968), pp. 569–70.

2. Ibid., p. 570. The feeding apparatus to which he refers is necessary to sustain life inside a pneumatic structure supported by low air pressure. Low-pressure air-supported structures are maintained by a constant flow, while high-pressure structures, once inflated, enclose a single breath inside, sealed by an impervious membrane. Banham was in a low-pressure dome.

3. Ibid.

4. Ibid.

5. See Esther Choi, "Atmospheres of Institutional Critique: Haus-Rucker-Co's Pneumatic Temporality," in Andrew Blauvelt, ed., *Hippie Modernism: The Struggle for Utopia* (Minneapolis: Walker Art Center, 2015), pp. 31–43.

6. Will McLean, "Atmospheric Industries," *AA Files,* no. 70 (2015), p. 139.

7. Will McLean and Pete Silver, *Air Structures, Form + Technique* (London: Laurence King Publishing, 2015), p. 11.

8. Frederick William Lanchester conceived and patented an air-supported field hospital in 1917, which was never realized. See Roger Dent, *Principles of Pneumatic Architecture* (New York: Halsted Press, John Wiley & Sons, 1972), pp. 27–30.

9. Whitney Moon, "Environmental Wind-Baggery," in Daniel A. Barber and Eduardo Regae, eds. "Structural Instability," *e-flux Architecture*, August 1, 2018, https://www.e-flux.com/architecture/structural-instability/208703/environmental-wind-baggery. Pneumatics find their precedent in balloons, sharing not only air as a constitutive material, but also a revolutionary spirit. On this aspect in particular, see Marc Dessauce, "On Pneumatic Apparitions," in Marc Dessauce, ed., *The Inflatable Moment: Pneumatics and Protest in '68* (New York: Princeton Architectural Press, 1999), pp 13–25.

10. Dessauce, "On Pneumatic Apparitions," p. 15.

11. Daniel A. Barber, "After Comfort," *Log*, no. 47 (Fall 2019), pp. 45–50.

12. On the ramification of such closed worlds, see Michelle Murphy, *Sick Building Syndrome and the Problem of Uncertainty: Environmental Politics, Technoscience, and Women Workers* (Durham: Duke University Press, 2006). Murphy traces the consequences of airtight office buildings and the concomitant chemical exposures that occurred inside. For a genealogy of closed worlds see Lydia Kallipoliti, *The Architecture of Closed Worlds, Or, What Is the Power of Shit?* (Zurich: Lars Müller, 2018).

13. Reyner Banham, "A Home Is Not a House," *Art in America* 2 (1965), p. 78.

14. Ibid., p. 73

15. Ibid., p. 76.

16. Ibid. For a recent discussion of Banham's essay in the context of climate design, see Lydia Kallipoliti, *Histories of Ecological Design: An Unfinished Cyclopedia* (Barcelona: Actar, 2024), pp. 152–56. Whitney Moon discusses the "un-house" in relation to the contemporary resurgence of pneumatics in "Environmental Wind-Baggery."

17. Le Corbusier, *Toward an Architecture*, trans. John Goodman, Texts & Documents (The Getty Research Institute, 2007), p. 216.

18. Kurt W. Forster, *Schinkel: A Meander Through His Life and Work* (Boston: Birkhäuser, 2018), pp. 120–21.

19. Schinkel witnessed firsthand the impact of industrialization in Manchester and traveled together with Beuth to England in 1926. Ibid., p. 141.

20. For Heinrich Altcappenberg, they clearly hover above this fictional office, possibly sustained by an invisible buoying force, a motif that Schinkel might have known from aerobatic performances in theater. Heinrich Schulze Altcappenberg and Rolf H. Johansen, eds., *Karl Friedrich Schinkel: Geschichte und Poesie* (Munich: Hirmer, 2012), p. 246.

21. See Reinhart Strecke, *Pegasus oder Schinkel und Berlins erster Eisenbahnhof* (Berlin: Transit, 2008), p. 87. For Strecke, the soap bubbles evoke the clouds of smoke produced by a steam car, a connection underscored not only by the iconography, but also by the fact that one of the first six locomotives to run between Berlin and Potsdam was named Pegasus.

22. Rarely can it be said that we not just consume the atmosphere we inhabit, but also a particular building or piece of architecture. Such was the case with Diller Scofidio's Blur Building for the 2002 Swiss Expo, a tensegrity structure clouded in fine mist. In a 2013 interview with Anthony Vidler, Elizabeth Diller recalls her struggles with the respective building authorities, making explicit reference to the vulnerability of our lungs: "But we had a big epiphany when we realized that filtering the lake water before it was atomized was a matter of life and death. Unlike the intestines, the lungs are incapable of processing bacteria. If we did not succeed in purifying the water beyond drinking-water standards, we would have created the equivalent of the Legionnaires' disease, potentially killing off visitors." Elizabeth Diller and Anthony Vidler, "Architecture Is a Technology That Has Not yet Discovered Its Agency," *Log*, no. 28 (Summer 2013), p. 24.

Index

Zone Books series design by Bruce Mau
Image placement and production by Julie Fry
Typesetting by Meighan Gale
Printed and bound by Maple Press